Basic COBOL

Basic COBOL

Anju Bhati

CENTRUM PRESS
NEW DELHI-110002 (INDIA)

CENTRUM PRESS
H.O.: 4360/4, Ansari Road, Daryaganj,
New Delhi-110002 (India)
Tel: 23278000, 23261597, 23255577, 23286875

B.O.: No. 1015, Ist Main Road, BSK IIIrd Stage,
IIIrd Phase, IIIrd Block, Bangalore-560085 (INDIA)
Tel: 080-41723429

Email: centrumpress@gmail.com
Visit us at: www.centrumpress.com

Basic COBOL

First Edition, 2011

PRINTED IN INDIA

Printed at Tarun Offset Printers, Delhi-110053

Contents

Contents

Preface

The language continues to evolve today. In the early 1990s it was decided to add object-orientation in the next full revision of COBOL. The initial estimate was to have this revision completed by 1997 and an ISO CD introduced object-oriented syntax based on the 1997.

COBOL programs are in use globally in governmental and military agencies and in commercial enterprises, and are running on operating systems such as IBM's z/OS, the POSIX families and Microsoft's Windows as well as ICL's VME operating system and Unisys' OS 2200. In 1997, the Gartner Group reported that 80% of the world's business ran on COBOL with over 200 billion lines of code in existence and with an estimated 5 billion lines of new code annually.

Author

1

Introduction

BASIC

DEFINITION

COBOL is a high-level programming language first developed by the CODASYL Committee (Conference on Data Systems Languages) in 1960. Since then, responsibility for developing new COBOL standards has been assumed by the American National Standards Institute (ANSI).

Three ANSI standards for COBOL have been produced: in 1968, 1974 and 1985. A new COBOL standard introducing object-oriented programming to COBOL, is due within the next few years.

The word COBOL is an acronym that stands for COmmon Business OrientedLanguage. As the the expanded acronym indicates, COBOL is designed for developing business, typically file-oriented, applications. It is not designed for writing systems programmes. For instance you would not develop an operating system or a compiler using COBOL.

USES

For over four decades COBOL has been the dominant programming language in the business computing domain. In that time it it has seen off the challenges of a number of other languages such as PL1, Algol68, Pascal, Modula, Ada, C, C++. All these languages have found a niche but none has yet displaced COBOL. Two recent challengers though, Java and Visual Basic, are proving to be serious contenders.

COBOL's dominance in underlined by the reports from the Gartner group. In 1997 they estimated that there were about 300 billion lines of computer code in use in the world. Of that they estimated that about 80% (240 billion lines) were in COBOL and 20% (60 billion lines) were written in all the other computer languages combined.

In 1999 they reported that over 50% of all new mission-critical applications were still being done in COBOL and their recent estimates indicate that through 2004-2005 15% of all new applications (5 billion lines) will be developed in COBOL while 80% of all deployed applications will include extensions to existing legacy (usually COBOL) programmes. Gartner estimates for 2002 are that there are about two million COBOL programmers world-wide compared to about about one million Java programmers and one million C^{++} programmers.

SURPRISED BY COBOL'S SUCCESS

People are often surprised when presented with the evidence for COBOL's dominance in the market place. The hype that surrounds some computer languages would persuade you to believe that most of the production business applications in the world are written in Java, C, C++ or Visual Basic and that only a small percentage are written in COBOL. In fact, the reverse is actually the case. One reason for this misconception lies in the difference between the vertical and the horizontal software markets. In the vertical software market (sometimes called "bespoke" software) applications cost many millions of dollars to produce, are tailored to a specified company, encapsulate the business

DECLARING DATA IN COBOL

The aim of this unit is give you an understanding of the different categories of data used in a COBOL programme and to demonstrate how items of each category may be created and used.

By the end of this unit you should:

- Know how to use and create literals, variables and Figurative Constants.

- Understand how to declare numeric, alphabetic and alphanumeric data-items.
- Be able to create a record structure by assigning the appropriate level numbers to its data-items.
- Understand the difference between group and an elementary data-items.
- Be able to assign an initial value to a variable.

But more information on declaring data items in COBOL can be found in the units covering:

- Edited Pictures
- Sequential Files
- The USAGE clause

More information on declaring data items in COBOL can be found in the units covering:

- Edited Pictures
- Sequential Files
- The USAGE clause

CATEGORIES OF COBOL DATA

There are three categories of data item used in COBOL programmes:

Variables

A data-name or identifier is the name used to identify the area of memory reserved for a variable. A variable is a named location in memory into which a programme can put data, and from which it can retrieve data.

Every variable used in a COBOL programme must be described in the DATA DIVISION. In addition to the data-name, a variable declaration also defines the type of data to be stored in the variable. This is known as the variable's data type.

Literals

Some languages like Modula-2,Pascal or Ada are described as being *strongly typed*. In these languages there are a large number of different data types and the distinction between them is rigorously enforced by the compiler. For instance, the compiler will reject a statement that attempts to assign character value to an integer data item.

In COBOL, there are really only three data types:

1. Numeric
2. Alphanumeric (text/string)
3. Alphabetic

The distinction between these data types is a little blurred and only weakly enforced by the compiler. For instance, it is perfectly possible to assign a non-numeric value to a data item that has been declared to be numeric.

The problem with this lax approach to data typing is that, since COBOL programmes crash (halt unexpectedly) if they attempt to do computations on items that contain non-numeric data, it is up to the programmer to make sure this never happens.

COBOL programmers must make sure that non-numeric data is never assigned to numeric items intended for use in calculations. Programmers who use strongly typed languages don't need this level of discipline because the compiler ensures that a variable of a particular types can only be assigned appropriate values.

Figurative Constants

A literal is a data-item that consists only of the data-item value itself. It cannot be referred to by a name. By definition, literals are constant data-items.

HISTORY AND PURPOSES

HISTORY

The name of this programming language, COBOL, is an acronym that is derived from the statement "COmmon Business Oriented Language". The first proposal on this programming language was presented in april 1960, in a report made by CODASYL (Conference On Data System Languages). A lot of improvement was done during the sixties ending up with an ANSI-definition in 1974. For a decade thousands of programmers wrote millions (billions ?) of lines of source code in this language. In 1985 ANSI released a new definition of the language, called COBOL-85.

This new version of the language introduced improvement in at least two areas:

- Features that increase structured programming capability
- Features that facilitate code clarity and simplicity
- Miscellaneous features that provide additional functions

Because the language has such a long history, it is filled with obsolete constructs. The largest single reason for this, is the fact that many tasks have been automated by modern operating systems.

COBOL (Common Business Oriented Language) was one of the earliest high-level programming languages. It was developed in 1959 by a group of computer professionals called the Conference on Data Systems Languages (CODASYL). Since 1959 it has undergone several modifications and improvements. In an attempt to overcome the problem of incompatibility between different versions of COBOL, the American National Standards Institute (ANSI) developed a standard form of the language in 1968. This version was known as American National Standard (ANS) COBOL.

In 1974, ANSI published a revised version of (ANS) COBOL, containing a number of features that were not in the 1968 version. In 1985, ANSI published still another revised version that had new features not in the 1974 standard. The language continues to evolve today. Object-oriented COBOL is a subset of COBOL 97, which is the fourth edition in the continuing evolution of ANSI/ISO standard COBOL. COBOL 97 includes conventional improvements as well as object-oriented features. Like the C++ programming language, object-oriented COBOL compilers are available even as the language moves towards standardization.

SIGNIFICANT LANGUAGE FEATURES

- The language that automated business
- *Allows names to be truly connotative*: Permits both long

names (up to 30 characters) and word-connector characters (dashes)

- *Every variable is defined in detail*: This includes number of decimal digits and the location of the implied decimal point
- *File records are also described with great detail, as are lines to be output to a printer*: Ideal for printing accounting reports
- Offers object, visual programming environments
- Class Libraries
- Rapid Application Capabilities
- Integration with the World Wide Web

COBOL, long associated with green screens, core dumps, and traditional mainframe connections, may at first glance seem at odds with object technology, push-button graphical interfaces, and interactive development environments. This perceived incongruity, however, is more a reflection of the mainframe's ability to keep pace with the innovations of desktop and client-server computing than a flaw in the COBOL language

AREAS OF APPLICATION

COBOL is ideally suited for the solution of business problems. For example, if a company wanted to keep track of its employees' annual wages, COBOL would be ideal language for implementation. It is interesting to note that COBOL was the first programming language whose use was mandated by the Department of Defence (DoD).

STRENGTHS AND WEAKNESSES OF COBOL

If we compare COBOL with languages such as C++ or Pascal, the standard comment is that COBOL is hopelessly out of date and completely impossible to work with. However, closer study of the three programming languages results in a somewhat subtler answer. COBOL contains a great many more possibilities for editing output than the other languages. The same number can, of course, be achieved in, for example, in C++, but only by drawing up and using a series of library routines.

COBOL has three facilities that make it head and shoulders above C and Pascal Index sequential files:

- Report management (COBOL's Report Writer Control System)
- Conversion between data types.

COBOL has its weaknesses, of course:

- Handling text strings
- No pointer concept and no dynamic storage allocation
- Recursive call is not usually supported
- No support of OOP in the standard, most common COBOL

Programmes in the three languages are not equally easy to port between various platforms. Due to the supporting library modules Pascal and C++ are usually more difficult to port. But it is of cause possible to write programmes in Cobol, that are hard to port too.

COBOL'S SYNTAX

There are syntax rules for both the vertical and the horizontal structure of a COBOL-source code.

Format of Source Lines

A COBOL source programme is built up of lines in a rigid format that dates back to the time when the punched card was the normal (the only!) medium for inputting data. If syntax errors are to be avoided it is vital to adhere to this format strictly.

- *Positions* 1 - 6: Previously used for line numbers, but no longer serve any formal purpose. I have seen these positions used for simple version-dating, *i.e.* when inserting new lines into the programme, each new line had the date of insertion in these 6 positions. From the programmes maintenance log, it is possible to see how have made the change.
- *Position* 7: Position 7 is used for marking line types. There are five important options:
  - "*" The line is a comment line.

  - Any characters to the right of position 7 is ignored by the compiler. Exclusion of lines from a programme can be done by simply placing a "*" in position 7. In combination with a date of change in positions 1-6, all changes in the programme are documented.
  - "-" The line is a continuation of the previous line.
  - This is normally only used when a text between inverted commas continues beyond position 72.
  - "/" If a compiler listing is being used a slash in position 7 will give an obligatory page break.
  - "D" The line is to be used as part of a debug operation.
  - Modern compilers have tools that make visual code inspection possible. F.x. "animator" in MicroFocus compilers.
  - "$" Directive to the compiler.
- *Positions* 8 - 11: These positions are known collectively as Column A.

  All division, sections and paragraph names are to be defined starting in position 8, t hough they can of course continue as far as position 72.
- *Positions 12 - 72*: Known collectively as column B. Used for writing statements.
- *Position 73 end of line*:

  Texts written here are treated as comments.

MicroFocus compilers support a special kind of syntax for comments, called an inline comment. A space followed by the two characters "*>" tells the compiler that the remainder of the line is for commentary purpose only.

BASIC STRUCTURE OF A COBOL LSOURCE PROGRAMME

Every COBOL programme is vertically subdivided into four divisions:

- *The identification division*: Can be used to provide a brief description of the programme, but there is only one mandatory element:

  - PROGRAMME-ID.
  - PROGRAMME-ID is used to assign a name to the programme for links between different programmes.
- *The Environment Division*: Used to describe the programme environment – primarily the name and organization of the associated data files.
- *The Data Division*: Used to describe the data structures of data files, programme variables, and the interface used when calling other programmes.
- *The Procedure Division*: The procedure division is used to write the statements themselves, *i.e.* the programs' algorithm.

A source file contains one or more blocks with the structure described above, *i.e.* one for each module. Note too, that a procedure division can have a number of entry points.

CBL NOTATION

All COBOL statements are to be concluded with a full stop (a period).Even though COBOL is subject to ANSI, there are still many facilities that have been added on by the various compiler suppliers. It is therefore necessary to have access to the correct manuals in order to know the precise syntax required. However, some points are more obviously open to creativity than others.

Every COBOL manual starts with an explanation of how syntax definitions are to be read. Square brackets, vertical lines and ellipses are part of this notation. COBOL syntax is not recursive which means, among other things, that it is not possible to use function calls and arithmetic expressions in a parameter list.

This is an obvious weakness compared to languages such as C++, but that's just the way it is. There is, however, obvious advantages in this:- a COBOL programme is almost all ways better to read and understand, compared to a C++ programme. This also means less programming errors.

The limited amount of standard routines, is counterbalanced by the relatively large number of different implementations of instructions in COBOL. For example, for calculations, the compiler itself takes care of conversions between the various data formats. The programmer do not have do deal with these trivial necessities, there is however, the possibility that a programme will perform a vast number of conversions between data formats, that could have been avoided easy by moving a value to an appropriate field, just once. This is left for a thoroughly examination of the programme.

Detailed Structure of a COBOL Source Programme

Each division contains a number of standard sections, each with their own special purpose. Some of these are optional.

This review of these sections follows the order found in the general source programme structure:

```
IDENTIFICATION DIVISION.
PROGRAMME-ID. Programme name.
AUTHOR. Programmer's name added as a comment.
...
ENVIRONMENT DIVISION.
CONFIGURATION SECTION.
SPECIAL-NAMES.
  CONSOLE IS CRT
  DECIMAL-POINT IS COMMA.
INPUT-OUTPUT SECTION.
FILE-CONTROL.
SELECT file name......    File control entry.
...
DATA DIVISION.
FILE SECTION.
FD file-name....          Record description.
WORKING-STORAGE SECTION.
                       Declaration of variables.
REPORT SECTION.
                       Description of a report.
LINKAGE SECTION.
                       Definition of CALL
parameters.
```

```
PROCEDURE DIVISION
DECLARATIVES.
...                           Handling IO errors.
END DECLARATIVES.
                              Algorithm.
{section-name SECTION [segment-number].
{paragraph-name.
   Sentence.
}}
```

A Description of Programmer-Defined Sections and Paragraphs

A programmer-defined section should be viewed as an independent element of a COBOL programme. A section represents a partially closed area within a programme. By "partially" is meant that a section can function as a separate entity, but with full access to the programme variables.

A paragraph is a named part of a section. A paragraph can therefore function independently, but can only be called from the section to which it belongs.

Sections and paragraphs are not the equivalent of a function in C++ or Pascal. Neither sections nor paragraphs can have their own local variables, nor can they be called using parameters. They have to access the global variables of the programme of which they are a part.

A segment number is used to define whether a segment is to be resident or whether it is to be loaded as required (overlayable).

This example shows a programmer defined section (main) and two paragraphs (open-file, read-record):

```
* —— executable instructions.
   main section.
   perform open-file.
   perform read-record.
   perform process
     until eof.
  perform close-file.
  stop run.
```

```
*
*
open-file.
  open input isamfile,
     output rep-file.
  initiate report.
*
read-record.
  read isamfile next
     at end move 1 to eof-code.
```

COBOL AND SCREENS

COBOL has two instructions for managing input (ACCEPT) and output (DISPLAY) via the screen, and they are available in innumerable variations.

Normally, however, these instructions are not used at all, and these operations are instead controlled by library routines working with a screen generator. A more detailed description of these operations falls outside the scope of this textbook. This example shows some simple variations of accept and display.

The instructions begins by clearing the screen. After that the system date is copied into the variable "today". At the end the programme prompts twice for the user to enter a figure, which is then read from the keyboard.

```
000000* A sample programme showing the use of
ACCEPT and DISPLAY
       identification division.
      * ———      identifying the programme.
       programme-id.  accdisp.
       author. kik.
       environment division.
      * ——— programme environment
       configuration section.
       special-names.
          console is crt
          decimal-point is comma.
      * ——— Variables
       data division.
```

```
  working-storage section.
  77 ind-1   pic 9999.
  77 ind-2   pic 9999.
  01 todayis.
   05 filler1 pic x(10) value "Today is:".
   05 today pic x(8).
  procedure division.
* ——— The instructions
main section.
   display space.
   accept today from date.
   display todayis line 3 position 10.
   display "Enter 1st figure:" line 5
  position 10.
   accept ind-1 line 5 position 27.
   display "Enter 2nd figure:" line 6
  position 10.
       accept ind-2 line 6 position 27.
       exit programme.
```

Exercise

I have chosen this exercise to provide an example of how to enter and compile COBOL programmes. There is a tradition that an introduction to a new programming language should start with a programme example which merely prints the text "Hello world" on the screen.

Enter and compile this small COBOL programme.

Model answer for this exercise:

```
 identification division.
* —— programme identification.
 programme-id. hello.
 author. kik.
 environment division.
* ------ programme environment.
 configuration section.
 special-names.
       console is crt.
 data division.
```

```
procedure division.
* ------ executable instructions.
main section.
     display space.
     display "Hello world" line 5 column 30.
     stop run.
```

Notice that in the the line:

```
     display "Hello world" line 5 column 30.
```

you might have to substitute the word "column" by "position".

PERSONAL COBOL FOR WINDOWS

If you install Micro Focus Personal COBOL for Windows onto your PC the default folder location will be C:\PCOBWIN Remember that in DOS notation "C" is your system's hard drive and "A" is your floppy disk drive.

If you have other devices installed, such as CD-ROM or Zip drives, or are attached to a network these may be labeled as drives "D", "E", "F", etc.See Appendix B of your text book for detailed instructions for installing the software on your computer.

Once the software is installed you may access COBOL from your Start menu. Click the Start button, then point to Programmes. On the Programmes submenu point toPersonal COBOL.

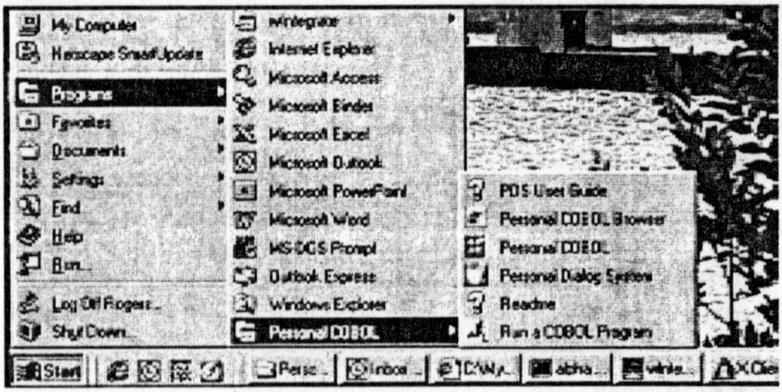

To put a "shortcut" to Cobol on your desktop click the Start button. Point to Programmes. On the Programmes submenu *right-click* on the Personal COBOL folder. Then click Open. This window should open:

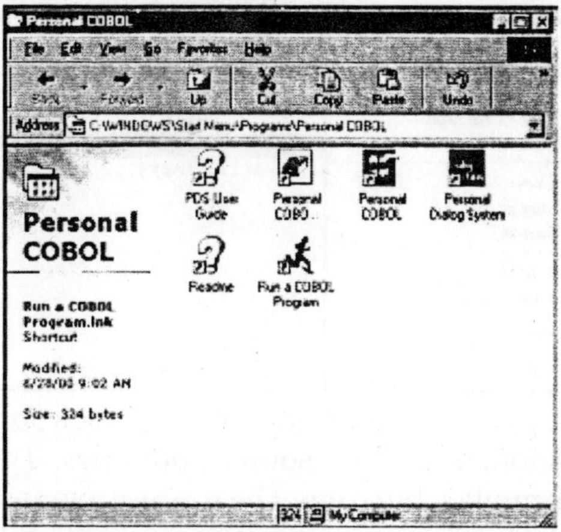

Right-drag the icon onto the desktop. On the pop-up menu select Create Shortcut Here.

The development environment is called "Animator". Click on Personal COBOL to begin an Animator session.When Animator opens take a look at the menu bar and toolbar buttons across the top of the window.

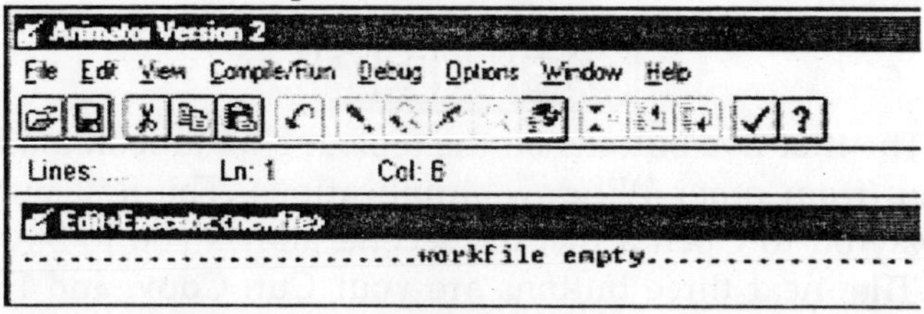

The pulldown File menu includes the New command which allows you to create a new file. Close allows you to close the current file without exiting from Animator. Notice that there are two commands to open existing files: Open for Edit and Open for Execution.

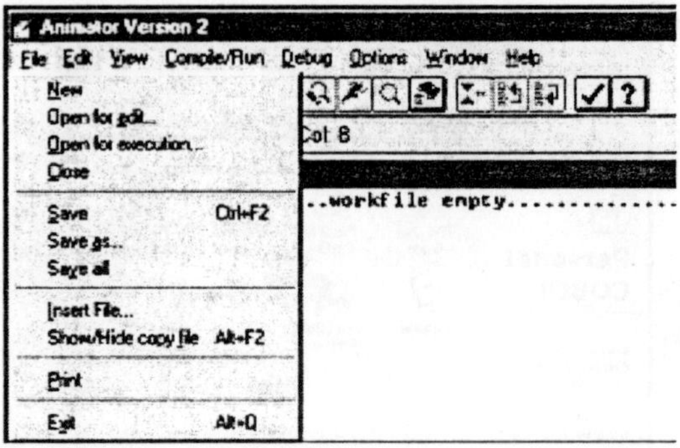

If you Open for Edit Animator will look for files with a.CBL extension. These are source code files. They may be edited and compiled, but cannot be run as programmes. When you are ready to run your programme you must be in Open for Execution mode which allows you to run a programme as well as edit it. When looking for files to execute Animator is looking for file names with the.INT extension.

The default mode when you open a new file in Animator is Edit and Execute. If you are in Edit mode and want to run your programme you must first compile it, then select Open for Execution from the File menu, open the corresponding.INT file, and then choose Run from the Compile/Run pulldown menu.As you type in the source code for your programme you will find the functions on the pulldown Edit menu useful. These include the familiar Cut, Copy, Paste, Undo, Find and Replace, etc. You may also notice some helpful old friends on the toolbar.

The first five buttons on the toolbar should look familiar to you from other Windows applications. The first button allows you to Open a file, the second allows you to Save to disk. The next three buttons are your Cut, Copy, and Paste functions. After you have typed in your programme you need to compile it. The compiler checks the syntax and creates an executable file. To compile your programme pull down theCompile/Run menu and select Compile Programme. Or, you can simply click on the ✓ button.

The compiler will highlight any syntax errors in your code. You can click on [toolbar buttons] buttons on the toolbar to move to the previous and next error.

The compiler can find syntax errors in your code. After you remove all the syntax errors and get a clean (no errors) compile you next have to test for logic errors by attempting to execute your programme. You do this by selecting Run from the Compile/Run menu. Or, you can click the [button] button on the toolbar.

When you run your programme the output appears in a separate window. If you wish to run your programme again you must select Restart Application from the Compile/Run menu.

When you are trying to debug (find the logic errors in) your programme you may want to step through your programme one instruction at a time. To do this select Stepfrom the Compile/Run menu or click the [button] button on the toolbar.

As you step through your programme you can examine the value of a particular data item by double-clicking the name of the data item anywhere it appears in your

FIRST PROGRAMME

Now, we shall write a very simple programme which performs some useless operations on useless data. Please note that the objective is to demonstrate how COBOL code is writen, which are the essesntial parts of a COBOL programme, how a COBOL is programme is compiled and run.

Our programme objective is to tell the user whether a number he/she enters is add or even.

Suppose we want the message,

"Enter ant integer:"

to appear in the middle of the screen; and when the user enters the number and hits the ENTER key, we want to display "Even" or "Odd" accordingly just next to the entered number.To key-in the source of our programme, we shall need a text editor. Actually, any editor will do. Even the Notepad utility of MS-Windows... I would recommend you to use the

MS-DOS standard text editor which you can invoke with the EDIT command. Before you start creating your source file, do not forget to create your own sub-directory at a convenient place on the PC disks and change your default directory to this working space.

```
MKDIR \CUAYFER
CD \CUAYFER
EDIT PROG1.CBL
```

Please note that the file extension for our source file is CBL. This is a convention of the RM-COBOL compiler that we shall be using and not necessarily same for all COBOL compilers.

Since every COBOL programme must have an identification division, you should start with something like this:

```
IDENTIFICATION DIVISION.
PROGRAMME-ID. MY-FIRST-COBOL-PROGRAMME.
```

Please note that these lines Should start on column 8. You can see the cursor position at the right bottom corner of the editor screen.

Please also note the "." characters, especially at the ends of the command lines. In very near future, you shall be hunting extra and/or missing "."s in your programmes.:)

The next division we should enter is the ENVIRONMENT division:

```
ENVIRONMENT DIVISION.
CONFIGURATION SECTION.
SOURCE-COMPUTER. ANY-MS-DOS-PC.
OBJECT-COMPUTER. ANY-MS-DOS-PC.
```

Please also note the dash "-" characters even in commentary fields (MY-FIRST-COBOL-PROGRAMME, ANY-MS-DOS-PC). Although some compilers will let you use blanks in these fields; RM-COBOL won't!

Since we shall not be using any disk/tape files and/or Printers in our programme, we do not need to have an INPUT-OUTPUT SECTION. Although we shall be using Input-Output statements, we do not need any special declarations for the CONSOLE CRT SCREEN I/O.

Next, the DATA DIVISON! Since we shall not use any disk/tape files or printers, we need not use a FILE SECTION.

Therefore we proceed right next to the WORKING-STORAGE SECTION. In the working-storage section, we have to declare all memory variables that we shall use in our programme. Normally, you wouldn't know all the variables and their types that you will use in the pgm. While you are writing your code, whenever you mention a new variable, you must come back to this section and declare it!

For our simple programme, we can decide NOW that we should use at least two emory variables; one for the number that user will enter and the other for the remainder when we divide this number by two.Lets choose the variable names NUMBER-ENTERED and REMNANT for the remainder. The variable name REMAINDER would not be a good choice,

BECAUSE IT IS A RESERVED WORD

Next, we should decide the types and length of thse variables. In this example they certainly will be numercial; the input value can be limited to 9 digits, and REMNANT can be be a single digit number.

The working-storage declarations for these SCALAR variables can be:

```
77 NUMBER-ENTERED PIC 9(9).
77 REMNANT PIC 9.
```

Note that the 77's start at column 8, the variable names start at column 12 or beyond col 12!Now are ready to proceed to PROCEDURE DIVISION. This is the part of the COBOL code where we shall do our actual work.All COBOL procedure divisions start with a *PARAGRAPH NAME* at column 8. Any name will do but it is customary to use the name MAIN for the first paragraph.

By the way, a COBOL paragraph is a group of procedure division statements that are collected under a common paragraph name and make some sense together with the other statements in the paragraph. The rules related to paragraphs are very loose except the first one.

An analogy to COBOL paragraphs are LABELS in other programming languages. With the use of various sequence control statements (like GO TO, PERFORM), you can branch the execution sequence to paragraphs, or in other words, to first statements of paragraphs.

Our Procedure Division can go like this:

```
PROCEDURE DIVISION.
 MAIN.
*
  DISPLAY "Enter an integer:" LINE 12 POSITION
20 ERASE.
  DISPLAY "Enter a zero to terminate the
programme" LINE 24
POSITION 20.
  ACCEPT NUMBER-ENTERED LINE 12 POSITION 40.
  IF NUMBER-ENTERED = ZERO THEN
    DISPLAY "Normal Termination!" LINE 1
    POSITION 1 ERASE STOP RUN.
*
  DIVIDE 2 INTO NUMBER-ENTERED GIVING USELESS-
RESULT REMAINDER REMNANT.
```

Ooops! We had to introduce a new variable "USELESS-RESULT" which will hold the quotient of division. We do need the value but the DIVIDE statement needs it. We have to go back to working-storage section and declare it too!

The modified declaration statement group would look like:

```
77 NUMBER-ENTERED PIC 9(9).
77 REMNANT PIC 9.
77 USELESS-RESULT PIC 9(9).
Now back to our procedure...
PROCEDURE DIVISION.
 MAIN.
*
   DISPLAY "Enter an integer:" LINE 12 POSITION
20 ERASE.
   DISPLAY "Enter a zero to terminate the
programme" LINE 24
POSITION 20.
   ACCEPT NUMBER-ENTERED LINE 12 POSITION 40.
   IF NUMBER-ENTERED = ZERO THEN
     DISPLAY "Normal Termination!" LINE 1
```

```
POSITION   1 ERASE
      STOP RUN.
 *
    DIVIDE 2 INTO NUMBER-ENTERED GIVING USELESS-
RESULT REMAINDER REMNANT.
 *
    IF REMNANT = 1 THEN
      DISPLAY "Odd" LINE 12 POSITION 52
      ELSE
    DISPLAY "Even" LINE 12 POSITION 52.
 *
    DISPLAY "Hit ENTER key to continue..." LINE
24  POSITION 20.
    ACCEPT XDUMMY.
    GO MAIN.
```

See? Another variable.... This time we shall add the statement

```
77 XDUMMY PIC X.
```

We shouldn't use PIC 9 for this variable because the user might enter a letter or a special character just before hitting the ENTER key and cause trouble. Obviously the letter "A" cannot be read into a numeric variable.

Now, the complete programme should look somewhat like:

```
ENVIRONMENT DIVISION.
CONFIGURATION SECTION.
SOURCE-COMPUTER. ANY-MS-DOS-PC.
OBJECT-COMPUTER. ANY-MS-DOS-PC.
DATA DIVISION.
WORKING-STORAGE SECTION.
77   NUMBER-ENTERED   PIC 9(9).
77   REMNANT        PIC 9.
 77    USELESS-RESULT      PIC 9(9).
 77    XDUMMY              PIC X.
*
 PROCEDURE DIVISION.
 MAIN.
 *
      DISPLAY "Enter an integer:" LINE 12
```

```
POSITION  20 ERASE.
        DISPLAY "Enter a zero to terminate the
programme" LINE 24
POSITION 20.
        ACCEPT NUMBER-ENTERED LINE 12 POSITION
40.
        IF NUMBER-ENTERED = ZERO THEN
          DISPLAY "Normal Termination!" LINE 1
POSITION   1ERASE
        STOP RUN.
*
       DIVIDE 2 INTO NUMBER-ENTERED GIVING
USELESS-   RESULT REMAINDER REMNANT.
*
      IF REMNANT = 1 THEN
        DISPLAY "Odd" LINE 12 POSITION 52
        ELSE
      DISPLAY "Even" LINE 12 POSITION 52.
*
    DISPLAY "Hit ENTER key to continue..." LINE
24  POSITION 20.
    ACCEPT XDUMMY.
    GO MAIN.
```

Now, let's compile our programme and run it!

The MS-DOS command to invoke an RM-COBOL compilation is:

```
RMCOBOL PROG1
```

You do not need to specify the extension of the source file as long as it is.CBL.

Now try it!

Too many error messages! Right?

You couldn't even follow the long list of messages... Try the MS-DOS command

```
RMCOBOL PROG1 | MORE
```

To get the long message list with a pause between screen pages. Can you guess why you had so manu errors even in a small programme like this? Let me tell you! You typed beyond column 72 and the compiler simply ignored all characters you typed at columns 73, 74 etc.. No problem! Go back to the editor and insert new line characters into statements so that the new source looks something like:

```
 ENVIRONMENT DIVISION.
 CONFIGURATION SECTION.
 SOURCE-COMPUTER. ANY-MS-DOS-PC.
 OBJECT-COMPUTER. ANY-MS-DOS-PC.
 DATA DIVISION.
 WORKING-STORAGE SECTION.
 77 NUMBER-ENTERED PIC 9(9).
 77 REMNANT        PIC 9.
 77 USELESS-RESULT PIC 9(9).
 77 XDUMMY         PIC X.
*
 PROCEDURE DIVISION.
 MAIN.
*
     DISPLAY "Enter an integer:" LINE 12
                                 POSITION 20 ERASE.
     DISPLAY "Enter a zero to terminate the
programme"
                                 LINE 24 POSITION 20.
 ACCEPT NUMBER-ENTERED LINE 12 POSITION 40.
 IF NUMBER-ENTERED = ZERO THEN
 DISPLAY "Normal Termination!" LINE 1 POSITION
 1 ERASE
 STOP RUN.
*
 DIVIDE 2 INTO NUMBER-ENTERED GIVING
        USELESS-RESULT REMAINDER REMNANT.
*
 IF REMNANT = 1 THEN
     DISPLAY "Odd" LINE 12 POSITION 52
     ELSE
     DISPLAY "Even" LINE 12 POSITION 52.
*
 DISPLAY "Hit ENTER key to continue..."
                           LINE 24 POSITION 20.
```

```
ACCEPT XDUMMY.
GO MAIN.
```

IMPORTANT

You should NOT divide verbs, variable names etc when you insert new lines into your source. Also you should not put any "." at the end of lines. "."s are used to indicate end of statements, not end of lines! Try to compile your programme again... It should report "0 Errors". If you can compile without any errors; you are ready to execute your programme.

Type

```
RUNCOBOL PROG1
```

What happens is this: The compiler produces a file called PROG1.COB into your working directory and this is the "executable" (or rather "runnable") version of your programme. With the help of RUNCOBOL utility (actually is called "COBOL RUNTIME") you "sort of execute" your programme.

I use these vague terms "sort of..", "rather runnable" because unlike most compilers, RM-COBOL does NOT translate your source into machine code! It translates your programme into an "intermediate code" and then INTERPRETS this code with the help of its runtime; namely RUNCOBOL...

Anyway, when you run your programme you should get a feeling that it is running correctly except that the screen is a mess...The reason is straightforward! We did not clear the screen before we started displaying messages on the screen. Try adding the statement

```
DISPLAY " " LINE 1 POSITION 1 ERASE EOS.
```

This statement will display a blank character on the first row, first column of the screen and then EOS (erase to end of screen).

Now, try running your programme again. It looks much better now, doesn't it? The only problem is; you cannot see the "Normal Termination..." message when you enter a zero... Can you guess the reason? Please try to correct this defect! It can be good quiz question!:) Now you can play around with this programme and put some fancy features in it. For example, try to disable "beep" signal that you hear everytime a new number is accepted. You can also try to make the "Hit ENTER key to continue..." message blinking so that it gets the user's attention.

PARSING TECHNIQUES IN COBOL

Where I work, many programmes do some sort of text parsing. In particular they parse service orders, which are written in a strange and barbarous tongue peculiar to the telephone industry.

In the great wide world, parsing programmes- such as compilers and interpreters — are typically written in languages such as C, C++, or Pascal. These languages are well suited for processing text streams in complex ways. In addition, code generators such as lex and yacc can do much of the gruntwork.

At my company, service orders are processed largely by COBOL programmes.

Parsing Presents Special Problems for COBOL:

- COBOL is designed for fixed-length fields in fixed positions, not for free-flowing text.
- The COBOL culture does not include any tradition in techniques of parsing, and most COBOL programmers have no background or training in the subject.

So programmers cobble together whatever seems to work. For simpler parsing problems, it may be enough to use UNSTRING, INSPECT, and whatever else comes in handy. Often, however, especially for more complex grammars, the result is an ugly mishmash of fragile, ad-hoc, hard-to-maintain code.(Similar problems may arise at a later stage of processing. The best way to represent the results of parsing may be to use some combination of various data structures— linked lists, trees, and the like. Neither the COBOL language nor the COBOL culture is well equipped to handle such data structures.) These pages describe some techniques which have proven useful in the JOCKEY application. Though some of the discussion is theoretical, most of it comes from the real world of service order processing.

ISOLATION FROM PHYSICAL FORMAT

The first step is to extract the text from the physical format in which it is made available. For typical compilers, this step is mostly fairly straightforward, because the source code is already close to the proper format. This phase may include some minor reformatting. For example, a C compiler must recognize trigraphs, and then splice continued lines together.

For service orders this step is more substantial. Every kind of file has its own format for representing individual lines, and thus requires a customised approach. JOCKEY uses the JKBLLOAD routine to load input lines into a standardized format. Other routines can then access them without regard to the original source of the text. We can reuse the parsing modules in multiple contexts.

ONE CHARACTER AT A TIME

Generally the next step is to break the text down into individual characters, and process them one at a time.For COBOL programmers this approach does not come naturally. We are used to moving whole blocks of characters in and out of fixed fields. For a very simple parsing task, this traditional approach can work just fine, and more powerful techniques are overkill. For more complex grammars, however, it is cumbersome and inefficient at best. After loading body lines with the JKBLLOAD routine, JOCKEY uses the JKBLREAD routine to read the stored input lines one character at a time.

NOW THE FUN BEGINS

At this point we have transformed the original input file into a stream of individual characters. But we haven't yet addressed the nub of the problem: how can a programme make sense of the text? Sometimes the simplest thing to do is to code a bunch of IF statements and PERFORM statements, in an ad hoc manner, to do whatever you need to do. That's a little vague, but there's not much more to say. The details of what you code depend on the details of what you need. It's more interesting to consider some more generic techniques which may be applied to any parsing problem.

LEXICAL AND SEMANTIC ANALYSIS

The usual textbook approach divides parsing into several phases:

- *Lexical analysis looks at successive characters to identify tokens*: Atomic units of syntax such as keywords, variable names, and elements of punctuation.
- Syntactical analysis looks at successive tokens to identify larger units of meaning, such as statements and expressions.
- Semantic analysis looks at these larger units to identify the meaning which they represent.

These pages mainly describe how JOCKEY performs lexical analysis. The higher levels of analysis are rudimentary, if not downright ugly.

FINITE STATE MACHINES

In non-trivial cases, JOCKEY relies on a finite state machine (or "FSM") to perform its lexical analysis. Each FSM is specialized for a specific task.We have one FSM to extract listing names, one to extract telephone numbers, another to extract addresses, and so forth.

Briefly, an FSM consists of a set of defined states which respond to a set of defined events. At any one time the FSM is in a single state.

When an event occurs, the FSM responds with the corresponding action, depending on its current state. Each state has a different mapping of events to actions. An action may include a transition to a different state.

In the context of parsing, an event is usually an input character from the text to be parsed. The significance of a given character depends on the surrounding characters. The rules for the various states reflect those dependencies. Eventually the FSM reaches a terminal state — which may be either an error state (signifying a syntax error in the input text) or an accepting state (signifying the recognition of a token).

HOW JOCKEY APPROACHES A SERVICE ORDER

JOCKEY does not attempt to parse an entire service order, mainly because big chunks of the order are irrelevant to JOCKEY. We ignore some sections entirely. In other sections we look for specific kinds of lines and ignore the rest.In any case, JOCKEY parses only a few lines at a time. Each set of lines begins with a USOC (Universal Service Order Code) or a FID (Field IDentifier) at the left side. Following the USOC or FID there is typically some additional data, which may overflow onto continuation lines.

The first step is to load the USOC or FID, together with all of its continuation lines, into memory via calls to JKBLLOAD.For a FID, the next step may be to extract the data we want by calling a specialized routine. For example, one routine extracts the listing name. Internally, these routines call JKBLREAD to fetch the stored text one character at a time.

The next step is to look for any relevant data tags. A tag consists of a slash ('/') followed by an identifier. The tag for a telephone number, for example, is '/TN'.Tags appear in free-form fashion, following the USOC or FID. We use a FINDTAG routine to paw through the text looking for useful tags.

When we find a tag, we may need to look for some additional data following it. For example, if we find/TN, we call a specialized routine to extract a telephone number. If we find/DZIP we call a different routine to extract a ZIP code.

DEVELOPING COBOL APPLICATIONS

Object COBOL for UNIX provides everything you need to develop COBOL applications to run on UNIX systems. It also provides for problem-free migration of COBOL applications from a large number of other systems and dialects, including IBM mainframe COBOL, and UNIX systems. Before reading this chapter you should have read your Getting Started, which tells you how to install the COBOL system and gives a brief overview of using it.

This chapter gives an overview of the steps required to create executable files from COBOL source code, and the tools available to help you develop applications. If you want to create object oriented COBOL programmes, you need additional information; refer to your *OO* Programming with Object COBOL for details.

THE DEVELOPMENT CYCLE

The basic steps in creating an application are shown in Figure below:

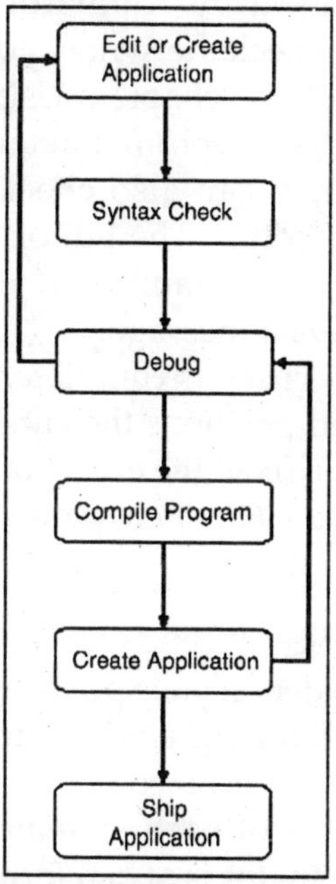

Fig. Application Development Cycle

Object COBOL provides tools and utilities to help you develop COBOL programmes and applications. These are described in the following sections.

CREATING AND EDITING PROGRAMMES

Creating and editing programmes is one of the most basic functions you need when writing applications. You can edit your programmes using the Editor. The Editor is described in detail in the chapter Editor in your Object COBOL Character Tools. Alternatively, you can edit programmes using system editors, such as vi.

Checking the Syntax of Your Programme

Before you can debug your programme, you must check its syntax. Syntax-checking is the first phase of compilation.

The Syntax-Check Creates:

- An intermediate code file
- An Animator dictionary file with the extension.idy

These files are used by Animator when debugging a programme. You can check the syntax your programme using the cob command. See the chapters Using the Compiler and COBOL System Interface (cob) for details on compiling and the cob command. You can also check the syntax of your programme from the Editor. The Editor calls the Compiler to check the syntax of a programme. If the Compiler finds a syntax error it displays a message.

When the syntax check is complete, the Editor returns to the editing screen and positions the cursor in the first error it found. When you have fixed the error you can move the cursor to the next error. See the *Editor* chapter in your Object COBOL Character Tools for details.

Debugging Your Programme

Use Animator to debug your programme. Animator offers a comprehensive debugging environment. Animator shows you both the source code of your programmes as they are running and the effect of each statement as it is executed. Debugging using Animator is also referred to as "animating".

When you debug a programme using Animator you can:

- Step through your program's execution
- Set breakpoints
- Run any part of the programme at full speed
- Alter the sequence of execution
- Enter COBOL statements for immediate execution
- View and monitor the contents of any data items

To learn how to use Animator, follow the sample session described in your *Getting Started.*

You can use Animator very effectively by knowing how to use the basic functions:

- Step

- Perform Step
- Perform Exit
- Breakpoint Set
- Zoom
- View
- Locate
- Query
- Monitor (on the Query menu)

When you are familiar with these and with using Animator, you should become familiar with the following additional functions:

- Breakpoint Do
- Do statement
- Reset Quit
- Split Text
- Breakpoint If
- Environment Threshold
- Backtrack

For detailed information on using Animator, see your *Object COBOL Character Tools.*

Compiling your Programme

When you have debugged your programme you need to compile it to create an an executable file format (the types of executable file are described in the sectionExecutable File Types in the chapter Packaging Applications). If you choose to create a system executable file you have to link the programme after it has been compiled. For more details on how to compile programmes, see the chapter Compiling Programmes.

PACKAGING APPLICATIONS

Object COBOL offers alternative methods for packaging applications; each method has its advantages and disadvantages. The methods used to package applications are described in detail in the chapter Packaging Applications.

You can package applications by:

- Using intermediate and generated code files
- Linking programmes

An overview of these methods is given in the sections below.

Using Intermediate and Generated Code Files

Object COBOL enables all subprograms and support modules required by an application to be kept in memory. This avoids the need for the link step usually required to create an application. To use Object COBOL in this way, your programmes must be compiled to intermediate code or generated code. You can simply ship the programmes in your application as intermediate or generated code files. Executable file formats are described in the chapter Packaging Applications.

Linking your Programme

You can link a programme, using cob, to create an executable file. Linking programmes is a two stage process. First, the source code is compiled to create a file in object code format. The object code file is then linked to create a system executable file or a dynamic link library file. Linking is described in detail in the chapter Linking Programmes. Usually you compile and link in one step using the cob command.

RUNNING YOUR APPLICATION

When you have packaged an application using one of the methods described earlier in this chapter, you can run the application. An application can be run by typing the name of the executable file at the command line. For example,

If you have linked your application to create an executable file myprog, this could be run by typing:

```
myprog
```

at the command line.

If your programme reads the command line using an ACCEPT... FROM COMMAND-LINE statement, enter the required command following the name. For example:

```
myprog in-file new-file
```

If your application is built using intermediate or generated code files, you might need to use the cobrun trigger.

For example:

```
cobrun myprog
```

Shipping Applications

When you have created and tested your application, you can, if necessary, ship it to your end-users. To ship an application, you need to ship all of the executable programmes that make up your application, along with any configuration files and data files. You also need to ship Application Server, which contains all of the Micro Focus Object COBOL system files required by the application.

More Information

For more information see the following chapters:

- *Packaging Applications*: Describes the types of executable file you can create using the Object COBOL system, and gives general information on the available methods for packaging applications
- *Compiling Programmes:* For more information on compiling
- *Linking Programmes:* For more information on linking
- *Running Applications:* For more information on running programmes

2

Programming Standards

STRUCTURE DESIGN

Nowadays it is common practice to use a particular method of Structured Design before producing the code that will fulfil a particular function. No matter what Design Methodology is used, the whole object of using structured programming techniques is lost if the actual code produced is badly written. Not only must the code fulfil its desired function, and perform it efficiently, it must also be maintainable by all those programmers who follow in your wake. In the life of any programme more time is spent on maintenance and enhancement than was ever spent on the original implementation.

COBOL is a flexible, free-format language that has very few internal constraints. It does not enforce any particular structural method, instead it allows the individual to adopt whatever structure their particular level of mentality can imagine.

The author of this document has over a decade's worth of experience in writing COBOL programmes, and has encountered many different standards, each with its own set of strong as well as weak points. Some are too rigid and unnecessarily restrictive, while others are too flexible and open to misinterpretation. Those which do not encourage or promote efficient, readable and maintainable code have been discarded, and the remainder have been reviewed and modified in the light of experience, common sense and logic. In those installations where programmers are allowed to adopt whatever style takes their fancy it is sometimes necessary to be familiar with an individual's style before it is possible to work on one of their programmes. If a programme has been worked on by several different programmers the mixture in styles can sometimes be very confusing. However, in those installations where proper standards and a common style of coding have been adopted it should be possible for any programmer to work on any programme without knowing the identity of the previous authors.

This is known as "ego-less programming", and is something which this document is intended to encourage and promote. These standards are meant to show how code can be written in such a way as to be more readable, easier to understand and therefore more maintainable. A well-written programme should read like a piece of prose, not a bunch of gobbledygook.

SOURCE CODE DOCUMENTATION

I am a great believer in having my source code liberally sprinkled with documentation in the form of comment lines (those with an asterisk in column seven). Any programme which does not contain comments is immediately suspect - it may actually work, but how easy is it to maintain or modify?

There may be separate written documentation, but there re distinct advantages in producing self- documenting code:

- Separate documentation (if it exists at all!) has a habit of becoming 'misplaced', whereas the program's source code is always available, either on magnetic disc or tape, or in a filed listing.
- Separate documentation has a habit of not being updated to reflect changes made to the source code. All too often documentation updates are left till last, or not done at all.
- It is sometimes quite difficult to identify which piece of code is responsible for performing a particular function outlined in the documentation.

How can self-documenting code be produced?

- Meaningful data names in the data division.

- Meaningful section/paragraph names in the procedure division.
- Plenty of comment lines to explain to the reader what is happening, and why.

It helps if all comments are in lower-case, to differentiate from actual commands which should always be in upper-case. Leave only one space between the asterisk in column seven and the start of the comment - more spaces are laborious to enter in the first place, and certainly don't make the comments easier to read.

There is one acid test to prove that your programme is adequately documented - can you reconstruct all the written documentation from your source code? If the answer is NO, then you have failed. There are some products available nowadays which will do the job for you - they read your source code and produce all the separate documentation that you require. It should be obvious, therefore, that products such as these cannot extract information which is not there to begin with.

PROGRAMME IDENTIFICATION

The Identifation Division of any COBOL programme must contain at least the programme name. This is also the best place in which to record other useful information which will serve as an introduction to the programme as a whole. *Such 'useful information' can be summarised as follows:*

a. *Programme Name:* This should follow the company's naming conventions, it should be unique for each programme, and should also be linked with the name of the source file.
b. *Author*: So we will know who to blame when things go wrong!
c. *Date-Written*: This gives us the age of the original version.
d. *Date-Compiled*: This is automatically inserted by the COBOL compiler, and shows the age of the current version of this programme.
e. *Programme Function*: What is its purpose? Is it a stand-

alone programme, or part of a suite of programmes? When is it run?

f. *Database Access*: What databases are used, and in what modes?
g. *Dataset Access*: What datasets are used, and how are they accessed (read, write, update or delete)?
h. *Non-Database File Access (MPE, KSAM)*: Identify which files are accessed, and how.
i. *Print Files:* What reports are produced, and what special stationery is required?
j. *VPLUS Processing*: What is the name of the forms file, and what are the names of the individual forms?
k. *Subroutine Usage*: Identify any subroutines called by this programme, giving the name and a brief description.
l. *Amendment History*: Each time a programme is changed you should insert a note giving the amendment date, a brief description of the amendment, plus your name.

Items (a) (b) (c) and (d) can be specified using the standard COBOL Identification Division statements. The remainder should be included as comment lines.

Even though all of the above information can be obtained by close examination of the code, it saves a lot of time (and time is money!) by having it laid out at the start of each programme listing.

PROGRAMME DATA

RECORD DEFINITIONS

The DATA DIVISION of any programme is a mixture of individual record names subdivided into numerous item names, which in turn can be subdivided into various sub-items. Items which are not subdivided are known as elementary items.

Items which are subdivided are known as group items, with the record name being equivalent to the highest level of group item.

In COBOL all data items are defined in the following manner:

<level-number> <data-name> <picture clause>

where:

<level-number>	Is a two-digit number which starts at 01 for record names and ascends up to 49 for all data items which are to be considered part of that record definition.
<data-name>	Is the name by which that particular data area can be referenced from within the programme.
<picture clause>	Describes the format of that particular data-name (alphabetic, numeric, etc.)

The picture clause is required only for elementary items - record names and group items assume a picture of PIC X(n) where 'n' is the combined length of all the subordinate items within that group definition.

It is therefore possible to construct a record definition as follows:

```
01 RECORD-NAME.
02 DATA-NAME-1-ALPHA PIC X(2).
02 DATA-NAME-2.
03 DATA-NAME-3-NUMERIC PIC 99.
03 DATA-NAME-4.
04 DATA-NAME-5-ALPHA PIC X(2).
04 DATA-NAME-6-NUMERIC PIC 9(5).
02 DATA-NAME-7-ALPHA PIC X(6).
```

This layout, however, is totally unacceptable in a structured programme because it is not easy to determine which elementary items go with which group items.

It would be easier to read if some sort of indentation was used to differentiate between the various level numbers, and if there was some space between the data name and the picture clause.

This example shows the effect of indenting the data names but not the level numbers:

```
01 RECORD-NAME.
05      DATA-NAME-1-ALPHA          PIC X(2).
05      DATA-NAME-2.
10          DATA-NAME-3-NUMERIC    PIC 99.
```

```
10        DATA-NAME-4.
15           DATA-NAME-5-ALPHA     PIC X(2).
15           DATA-NAME-6-NUMERIC   PIC 9(5).
05     DATA-NAME-7-ALPHA           PIC X(6).
```

This example shows the effect of indenting the level numbers, but not the data names:

```
01 RECORD-NAME.
 05       DATA-NAME-1-ALPHA    PIC X(2).
 05       DATA-NAME-2.
   10     DATA-NAME-3-NUMERIC PIC 99.
   10     DATA-NAME-4.
     15 DATA-NAME-5-ALPHA     PIC X(2).
     15 DATA-NAME-6-NUMERIC   PIC 9(5).
 05       DATA-NAME-7-ALPHA    PIC X(6).
```

The following example is the best because it indents both the level number and its associated dataname.

Note that each different level number is aligned in a separate column, making it easier to spot any mistakes.

```
01 RECORD-NAME.
  05         DATA-NAME-1-ALPHA     PIC X(2).
  05         DATA-NAME-2.
     10      DATA-NAME-3-NUMERIC   PIC 99.
     10      DATA-NAME-4.
        15 DATA-NAME-5-ALPHA       PIC X(2).
        15 DATA-NAME-6-NUMERIC     PIC 9(5).
  05 DATA-NAME-7-ALPHA             PIC X(6).
```

Note that all the picture clauses are aligned in the same place, usually at column 40. Where a data name flows into this column the most common practice is to put the picture clause on the following line, thus keeping the alignment consistent, eg:

```
  05 DATA-NAME-2.
     10 DATA-NAME-2A.
        15 THIS-IS-ANOTHER-LONG-DATANAME
                                   PIC X(2).
        15 THIS-IS-YET-ANOTHER-LONG-DATANAME
                                   PIC 9(5).
```

The guidelines for record layouts can be summarised as follows:

a. Level numbers should be incremented by more than

one in order to leave room for future additions of group items without having to renumber a whole section (increments of 01, 03, 05, etc are acceptable, but 01, 05, 10, etc is even better).

b. Level 01 should start in column 8, and all following numbers should be indented so that each different level number is aligned in a different column.

c. The indentation between one level number and the next should be 4 columns.

d. There should be 2 spaces between a level number and its associated data name.

The effect of items (c) and (d) is that the data names for one level are aligned in the same column as the level numbers for the next level. This may seem irrelevant, but I think that it looks better. When using the QEDIT text editor in full-screen mode it is possible to define the tab stops at columns 8,12,16,20,24,28 etc, therefore the same tab settings can be used for both level numbers and data names.

PRINT LINE DEFINITIONS

Now for some advice on how to describe headings for batch reports. Here are three ways of describing the same print line:

Example 1:

```
01 HEADING          PIC X(132) VALUE
   "ITEM DESCRIPTION     QUANTITY UNIT PRIC
-   "E TOTAL PRICE VAT".
```

Example 2:

```
01 HEADING.
   05 FILLER          PIC X(4) VALUE
                      "ITEM".
   05 FILLER          PIC X(6) VALUE
                      SPACES.
   05 FILLER          PIC X(11) VALUE
                      "DESCRIPTION".
   05 FILLER          PIC X(19) VALUE
                      SPACES.
  05 FILLER       PIC X(8) VALUE
```

```
              "QUANTITY".
  05 FILLER      PIC X(2) VALUE
              SPACES.
  05 FILLER      PIC X(10) VALUE
              "UNIT PRICE".
  05 FILLER      PIC X(2) VALUE
              SPACES.
  05 FILLER      PIC X(11) VALUE
              "TOTAL PRICE".
  05 FILLER      PIC X(1) VALUE
              SPACE.
  05 FILLER      PIC X(3) VALUE
               "VAT".
```

Example 3:

```
01 HEADING.
   05 FILLER           PIC X(10) VALUE "ITEM".
   05 FILLER           PIC X(30) VALUE "DESCRIPTION".
   05 FILLER           PIC X(10) VALUE "QUANTITY".
   05 FILLER           PIC X(12) VALUE "UNIT PRICE".
   05 FILLER           PIC X(12) VALUE "TOTAL PRICE".
   05 FILLER           PIC X(03) VALUE "VAT".
```

Of these three examples you should see that the third is more 'readable' and therefore easier to maintain.

RECORD MNEMONICS

Even though COBOL allows the same data-name to be used more than once in different record definitions (each occurrence can be uniquely addressed by the construct <data-name> OF <record-name>) it is common practice to make each occurrence unique by adding a record mnemonic as either a prefix or a suffix. Each record definition should be allocated its own mnemonic which should then be attached to all data items within that record. Please refer to the section on Naming Standards in the manual on Project Development Standards for more details on how to assign prefix values for IMAGE datasets and VPLUS screen buffers.

If a suffix is used it produces code which looks like the following:

```
01 ACCOUNT-RECORD.
```

```
    05 ACCOUNT-TYPE-ACC              PIC X(2).
    05 ACCOUNT-NUMBER-ACC.
       10 GROUP-ACC                  PIC 99.
       10 CLASSIFICATION-ACC.
          15 CLASS-CODE-ACC          PIC X(2).
          15 CLASS-NUMBER-ACC        PIC 9(5).
    05 CLIENT-NAME-ACC               PIC X(6).
```

However, I think a prefix produces better code, as follows:

```
 01 ACCOUNT-RECORD.
    05 ACC-ACCOUNT-TYPE              PIC X(2).
    05 ACC-ACCOUNT-NUMBER.
       10 ACC-GROUP                  PIC 99.
       10 ACC-CLASSIFICATION.
          15 ACC-CLASS-CODE          PIC X(2).
          15 ACC-CLASS-NUMBER        PIC 9(5).
    05 ACC-CLIENT-NAME               PIC X(6).
```

In the procedure division this would produce code similar to this:

```
   MOVE ACC-ACCOUNT-TYPE   TO PRT-ACCOUNT-TYPE.
   MOVE ACC-ACCOUNT-NUMBER TO PRT-ACCOUNT-NUMBER.
   MOVE ACC-GROUP          TO PRT-GROUP.
   MOVE ACC-<etc>          TO PRT-<etc>
```

The use of a prefix also makes it easier to search through your source code (with your particular text editor) to list all those places in a programme where a record is referenced:

```
 LIST "ACC-"
 LIST "MOVE ACC-"
 LIST "TO ACC-"
```

ITEM NAMES

COBOL allows data names to be up to 30 characters in length. However, most programmes which run on the HP3000 tend to have some sort of access to either IMAGE databases or VPLUS screens, where the length of data items is limited to 16 and 15 characters respectively.

Item names should convey some sort of description as to their content, and in order not to exceed this 15-character limit it is sometimes necessary to use abbreviated terms. Whatever abbreviation is chosen it is important that the same one is used throughout the system.

For example, the following combination of item names within the same system is very sloppy:

```
LINE-NUMBER
ACCOUNT-NBR
INVOICE-NUM
DOC-NO
```

Where the same item appears in more than one place within the system (eg: in an IMAGE dataset, or a VPLUS screen) it is a very good idea to keep to the same spelling.

Where the item is subsequently defined within a program's data division (eg: in the dataset buffer, the screen buffer, or a print buffer) it is also a very good idea to keep to the same spelling. The only difference should be in the prefix, which acts as an identifier for the particular buffer.

The only exception to this guideline is where an item occurs more than once on a VPLUS screen. As the OCCURS clause does not exist within FORMSPEC it is necessary to give each occurrence of the item a unique name. This is done by appending a 2 digit sequence number (starting at "01") to each occurrence of that item name. This suffix can be dropped within the COBOL definition as the OCCURS clause can be used instead. There should then be a direct relationship between the hard-coded number in the forms file and the occurrence number within the COBOL array, as demonstrated in the following example:

```
VPLUS:   ITEM-NAME01,ITEM-NAME02,,,,,,ITEM-
         NAME09,ITEM-NAME10
COBOL:   ITEM-NAME PIC X(?) OCCURS 10.
```

If it becomes necessary within your programme to identify one of these field names (eg: to pass to the SCVSETERROR routine after a failure in some validation) it can be constructed as ITEM-NAMEnn where nn is the occurrence number.

WORKING STORAGE DEFINITIONS

Data definitions within a program's WORKING-STORAGE section can be a mixture of dataset buffers, screen buffers, and general work areas. Each item name should be prefixed by a different mnemonic depending on the record definition in which it appears. IMAGE dataset buffers and VPLUS screen buffers should have been allocated their own unique mnemonics, but what of the general work areas?

Some standards say that all working Storage definitions must be prefixed with the letter 'W', but in very large sections it can be a long-winded process to find an individual definition.

Other standards say that the prefix should be two characters in order to denote the general usage, as in the following:

```
WA- accumulators
WC- constants
WI- indicators/flags/switches
WM- modifiers/subscripts
WT- tables/arrays
```

However, I much prefer to see groupings of items which are related logically, rather than functionally, as in the following:

```
01   T01-COMPONENT-TABLE.
 05  T01-MAX         PIC 99 VALUE 20.  <constant>
 05  T01-CURR        PIC S9(4) COMP.   <subscript>
 05  T01-LAST        PIC S9(4) COMP.   <subscript>
 05  T01-TABLE-ENTRY OCCURS 20.
     10 T01-CODE   PIC X(6).
     10 T01-DESCRIPTION PIC X(30).
     10 T01-VALUE  PIC S9(7)V99 COMP.
 05  T01-TOTAL-VALUE  PIC  S9(7)V99  COMP.
<accumulator>
```

Even though each item has a different function, they are all logically related, as they are concerned with that particular table and no other. It also makes it easier to search through the source code to find any reference to this data area simply by specifying a search string of "T01".

The following definition is also acceptable, but it has a distinct advantage when using the COBOL'85 compiler, which allows a group of data items to be reset to blanks or spaces with a single statement.

```
01 T01-MAX                     PIC S9(4)COMP VALUE 20.
01 T01-COMPONENT-TABLE.
   05 T01-CURR                 PIC S9(4) COMP.
   05 T01-LAST                 PIC S9(4) COMP.
   05 T01-TABLE-ENTRY          OCCURS 20.
      10 T01-CODE              PIC X(6).
      10 T01-DESCRIPTION       PIC X(30).
      10 T01-VALUE             PIC S9(7)V99 COMP.
   05 T01-TOTAL-VALUE          PIC S9(7)V99 COMP.
```

Although the item T01-MAX has been taken out of the original layout and changed from an 05 level to an 01 level it has still retained the T01- prefix to show that it is still related logically. As a general rule, then, the WORKING-STORAGE section should be laid out in logical groups with prefixes as follows:

```
Tnn- tables/arrays
Wnn- other
```

These should be defined in their proper sequence so that it is easy to locate any individual data item when searching through a programme listing. Any copy library members for dataset/file buffers should be correctly sequenced by their respective prefix values.

This avoids the need to produce a cross-reference listing which incurs a considerable overhead, both in compilation time and printing time.

SUBSCRIPTS AND INDICES

Some people like to define global subscripts/indices in the form SUB1, SUB2....SUBn (or INDX1, INDX2,,,INDXn). This is bad practice because there is no logical relationship with any particular table/array, and the names do not convey any sort of meaning.

It can take a long time to debug a programme if the same subscript is accidentally used to reference two different tables at the same time, or two different subscripts are accidentally used to reference the same table at the same time.

This is not a problem if the name of the subscript/index item is constructed in the format <prefix>-<usage> where:

<prefix>	Indicates the table to which it has been associated,
<usage>	Indicates how this particular item is used.

As can be seen in the previous section the subscript item used to access T01-TABLE-ENTRY is named T01-CURR. This cannot easily be confused with T01-MAX, which is used to indicate the maximum number of entries the table may contain, and T01-LAST which indicates the actual number of entries in the table at present.

CONDITION NAMES

Condition names are used to show an expected range of values for a particular data item. Once a condition-name has been defined, that particular name can be used instead of testing the data item for a specific value (or range of values).

Take the following definition in a program's working-storage section:

```
05   IMAGE-STATUS    PIC S9(4) COMP.
 88 IMAGE-OK         VALUE ZERO.
 88 IMAGE-ERROR           VALUE -9999 THRU -1,
                            +1 THRU +9999.
 88 IMAGE-BEG-OF-FILE     VALUE 10 12.
 88 IMAGE-END-OF-FILE     VALUE 11 13.
 88 IMAGE-BEG-OF-CHAIN    VALUE 14.
 88 IMAGE-END-OF-CHAIN    VALUE 15.
 88 IMAGE-DSET-FULL       VALUE 16.
 88 IMAGE-NO-ENTRY        VALUE 17.
 88 IMAGE-LOCK-FAILURE    VALUE 20 THRU 25
```

The contents of IMAGE-STATUS can be determined in two ways:

IF IMAGE-STATUS = ZERO	becomes	IF IMAGE-OK
IF IMAGE-STATUS NOT = ZERO	becomes or	IF NOT IMAGE OK
		IF IMAGE-ERROR

With COBOL'85 it is now possible to set a condition by referring to the name instead of the actual value, eg:

```
MOVE 0 TO IMAGE-STATUS
```

Is the same as

```
SET IMAGE-OK TO TRUE
```

There are only 2 simple guidelines to follow when defining condition-names:

1. Use a meaningful description for each condition;
2. Use a prefix which links the condition-name with the particular data item for which it is defined. This makes it easier to locate the reference in the working-storage section, and in most cases should make the condition being tested completely obvious (eg.IMAGE-OK, KSAM-OK or VPLUS-OK).

FLAGS/INDICATORS/SWITCHES

As a general rule any programme that uses its own set of switches or indicators is badly written. Most conditions can be handled by data areas that have already been defined (eg: the status areas for VPLUS, IMAGE and KSAM).

If it does become necessary to use a separate indicator then please follow these simple guidelines:

- Use meaningful data names (not SW1, SW2, SW3, etc).
- Do not use an indicator for more than one purpose.

Here are a few more observations regarding flags and switches:

- In an online programme it is not necessary to define a flag which shows the success or failure of a validation routine as the itemVIEW-NUMERRS is already available for this purpose. This has the condition names VEDIT-ERRORS and NO-VEDIT-ERRORS.
- Do not use a flag to test for a condition if that condition can be obtained from other means, as in the following example:

```
IF LINE-COUNT > LINE-MAX (ie: the current
  page is full)
MOVE 1 TO NEW-PAGE-REQUIRED.
  ........
 IF NEW-PAGE-REQUIRED = 1
     PERFORM XA-START-NEW-PAGE.
```

Can be replaced by:

```
IF LINE-COUNT > LINE-MAX
```

```
PERFORM XA-START-NEW-PAGE.
```

- When reading a serial file it is not necessary to define a flag to show when end-of-file has been encountered, as the same result can be achieved by setting the file's record area to HIGH-VALUES, as in the following example:

```
MOVE LOW-VALUES TO ABC-REC.
PERFORM UNTIL ABC-REC = HIGH-VALUES
 READ ABC
 AT END

 MOVE HIGH-VALUES TO ABC-REC
 NOT AT END
 PERFORM CA-PROCESS-ABC-REC
 END-READ
END-PERFORM.
```

PROGRAMME CODE

INTRODUCTION

Each SECTION contains one or more PARAGRAPHS; each PARAGRAPH contains one or more SENTENCES; and each SENTENCE contains one or more STATEMENTS.

- A SECTION is identified by having a unique name starting in column 8 followed by the reserved-word 'SECTION'. It ends with the start of the next section, and NOT when an 'EXIT' statement is encountered.
- A PARAGRAPH is identified by having a unique name starting in column 8 (the name must be unique within a section, but may be duplicated in other sections). It ends with the start of the next paragraph. There need be no relationship between a Section name and its associated PARAGRAPH name(s).
- A SENTENCE starts in column 12, can continue over several lines, and is terminated by a full stop.
- A STATEMENT contains a single COBOL verb, a subject name, and an optional object name (eg: MOVE A TO B, ADD C TO D, PERFORM E).

Control can be passed from one point in a programme to another by means of the following statements:

```
PERFORM <section>.
PERFORM <paragraph>.
PERFORM <paragraph1> THRU <paragraph2>.
GO TO <paragraph>.
```

These guidelines are extremely flexible, but without additional guidelines the resulting code can be as manageable as a plate of limp spaghetti - please read on for your elucidation and edification.

PROGRAMME STRUCTURE

Module Hierarchy

It is common practice in modern programming to split the code into logical sections or modules. Each section/module performs a particular function, and is invoked by the statement:

```
PERFORM <section-name>.
```

Each section/module can, in its turn, invoke other sections to perform lower level functions. This produces a modular hierarchy or structure, hence the term 'structured programming'. It is usual to plan the structure of a programme at the design stage before writing any code, in order to produce a structure similar to that shown in Figure 1:

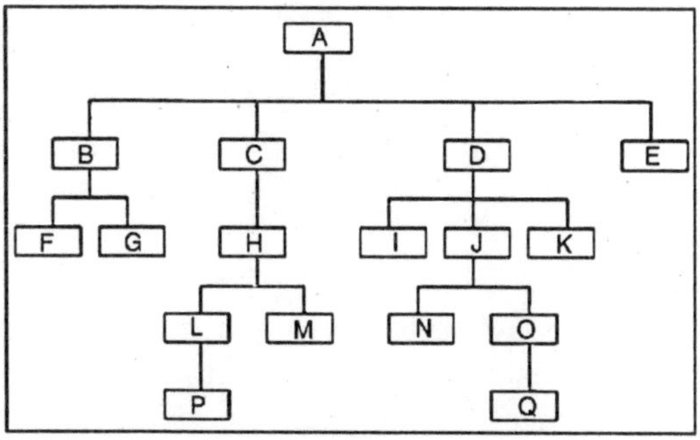

Fig. Module Hierarchy

Each box represents a separate module, and where two boxes are joined together it indicates that the box at the lower level is PERFORMed by the box at the higher level. In this particular example it shows that module Q can only be processed by passing control through modules A, D, J, O to Q. It is possible for any module to be called from more than one higher- level module, and this should be indicated on the chart.

If you have a low-level module which can be called from numerous places (eg: an error routine) it is permissible to leave it out of the chart completely, as it does nothing but complicate the overall picture. Routines such as this are called 'transparent'. It should be emphasised that only generalised routines which are common to ALL programmes should be regarded as transparent - those which perform a function peculiar to individual programmes must appear on the module hierarchy.

Some design methodologies like you to show on this chart how the various modules are invoked, using the terminology SEQUENCE, ITERATION, and SELECTION, denoted by a symbol in the top right-hand corner of each box.

- Is where modules are always PERFORMed, and in the indicated sequence. (symbol is '+').
- Is where a module is PERFORMed any number of times, from zero upwards. (symbol is '*').
- Is where a module is PERFORMed only if a condition is met. (symbol is 'O').

Where the initial design produces a box which is a combination of ITERATION/SEQUENCE or ITERATION/ SELECTION most methodologies insist that the structure be preserved by splitting the two and performing the ITERATION part at a lower level.

Module Naming

It is common practice to give each module some sort of mnemonic to denote its position in the module hierarchy, both horizontal and vertical. In the example given in section 5.2.1 each module is named from left-to-right and top-to-bottom, but there is no relationship between the mnemonics of modules which have some sort of logical association.

There are two other methods of arriving at mnemonic names, and these are discussed below:

Positional

The mnemonic has two alphabetic characters, the first denotes the LEVEL (top to bottom) while the second denotes the SEQUENCE (left to right). Using the same hierarchy as shown in Figure this is demonstrated in Figure.

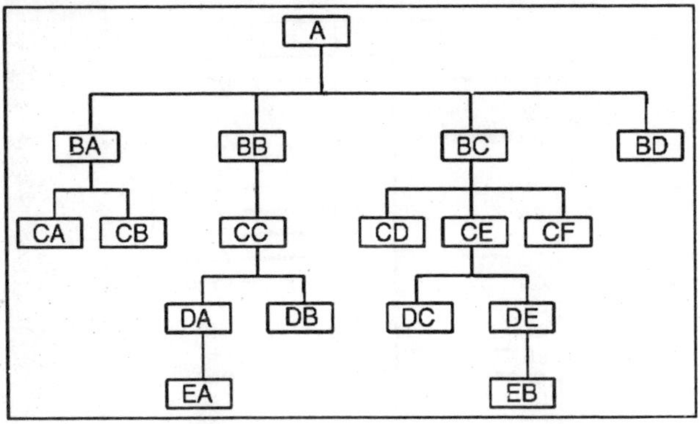

Fig. Module Hierarchy (Positional)

Functional

The first character denotes the sequence of the top-level function, while the second and subsequent characters denote a combination of level-within-function and sequence-within-level. This is demonstrated in Figure.

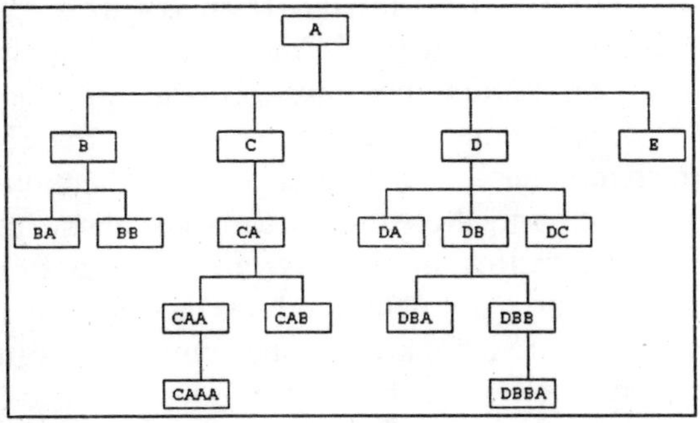

Fig. Module Hierarchy (Functional)

Now let us discuss the relative merits of both methods. It is common sense when coding the procedure division to place the sections in mnemonic sequence - this makes it easier to find your way through the listing. In method this means that each leg within the programme structure forms a contiguous block, whereas inmethod the same sections are spread out all over the place.

This is shown more clearly in Figure:

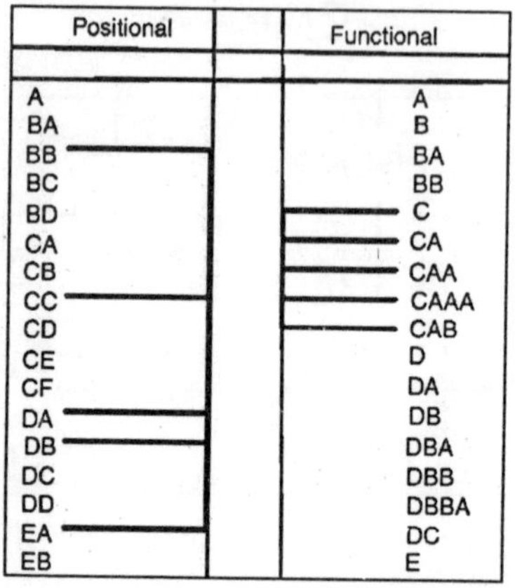

Fig. - Positional vs. Functional Naming

Using method it is possible to increase or decrease the number of sections in a particular processing leg without having to rename any other sections in order to maintain the naming sequence. See how easy it is in method to split section "DA" into "DAA" and "DAB", then try and make the corresponding change in method. Another advantage of method is that when a programme becomes too large for a single unit and needs to be segmented or split into subprograms it is easy to identify which modules are logically related and therefore eligible for separation. Compare those modules marked above in method with the corresponding modules from method. In a large, complex programme with many modules method may produce mnemonics which are large and cumbersome - how can this be overcome? Common sense to the rescue - identify a sub-function with a large number of modules and start naming them using a different letter from the alphabet, as shown in Figure:

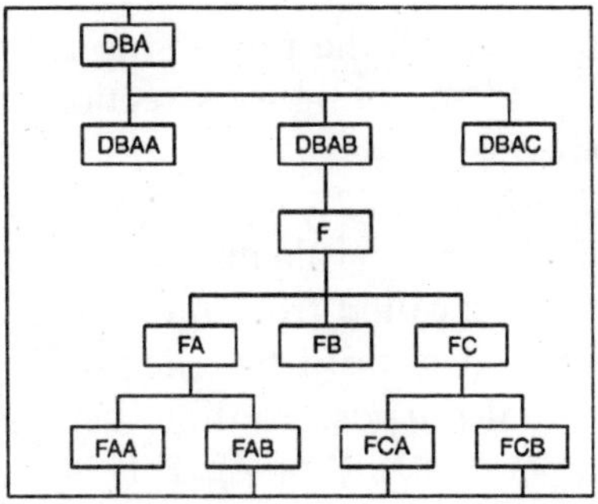

Fig. - Restarting the Prefix Character

For a sorted report which has a large number of control breaks it is acceptable to introduce a number into the mnemonic, and to increment this number for each lower level instead of increasing the length of the mnemonic by adding another character. This would produce a structure chart something like the one in Figure:

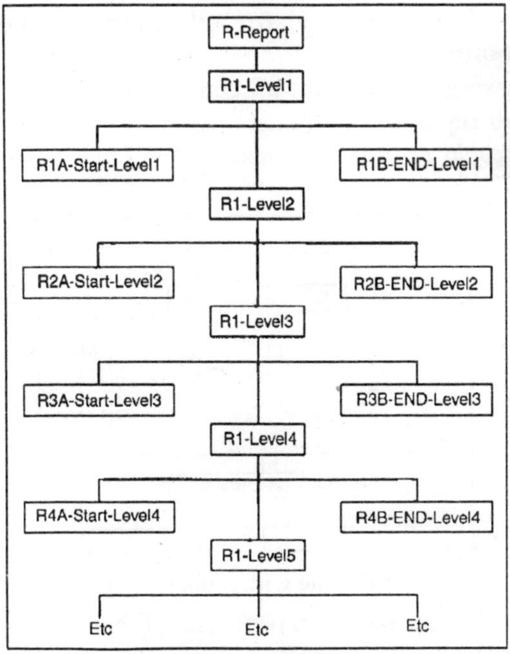

Fig. Numerical Sequencing

With this method all the processing for a particular sort level would be held in contiguous sections as the sequence would be as follows:-

R, R1, R1A, R1B, R2, R2A, R2B, R3, R3A, R3B, R4, R4A, R4B, R5

Some standards have a rule that if a section has more than one parent (ie: can be called from more than one section at a higher level) then it should be allocated a prefix which represents a general-purpose routine, usually at the bottom end of the alphabet (eg: X, Y or Z). This is fine if it is a small section with limited processing, but what if it is just the start of a significant piece of coding?

Take the following example - A database is comprised of customers who are grouped into countries, which in turn are grouped into regions.

A programme processes the details for customers at the end of each month, but the selection criteria can be one of the following:

- A single customer,
- A single country, for all customers within that country,
- A single region, for all countries within that region,
- All regions (ie: all customers).

This would produce a structure chart something like the one shown in Figure:

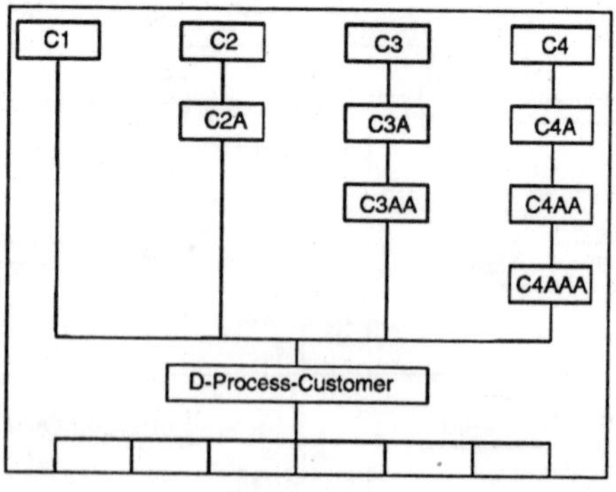

Fig. A Module with Multiple Parents

Notice that the selection processing is handled by modules which have the "C" prefix, while the actual customer processing (regardless of the selection method) has a separate prefix. This makes tracing your way through the source code a lot easier, which is more important than conforming to inflexible rules with their artificial restraints.

SECTIONS

The guidelines for sections can be summarised as follows:

- Each section should start on a new page.
- Each section name should be prefixed by a unique mnemonic containing one or more alphanumeric characters to denote that section's position in the program's hierarchy of sections.
- Each section name should be a short but meaningful description of the function of that section (eg: CA-Select-component, DEA-UPDATE- COMPONENT).
- The entire PROCEDURE DIVISION should be arranged in mnemonic sequence so that individual sections can be found more easily.
- Control should be passed from one section to another by means of the PERFORM <section> statement, and not the GO TO <paragraph> statement, nor the PERFORM <para1> THRU <para2> statement.
- Each section must have a single entry point (the first paragraph) and a single exit point (the last paragraph).
- Each section should be limited to perform one basic function, whether it be HIGH-LEVEL (eg: deciding which selection of lower level procedures to perform) or LOW-LEVEL (*e.g*: reading from or adding to a data file).
- Each section should be short enough to be contained on a single page of listing paper. Anything longer than this should be broken down into a series of sub-sections, each with its own separate function.
- Between the section-name and first paragraph-name there should be a brief comment as to the overall function of that particular section (leave more detailed comments until you get to the actual code). It helps to make this description more distinctive if

it is enclosed by a line of asterisks immediately before and after, producing a 'box' effect.

PARAGRAPHS

The guidelines for paragraphs can be summarised as follows:

- Each paragraph name should be a short but meaningful description of the function of that paragraph.
- Each paragraph name should be prefixed by the mnemonic that has been previously assigned to that section, plus an ascending sequence number, (eg: BA-10-READ-NEXT, BA-20-UPDATE).
- This sequence number should be in increments of ten, starting at ten for each new section. This leaves adequate room for future additions without having to renumber existing paragraphs.
- Two digits are adequate for the sequence number - if any more are required it means that you have already broken the guideline regarding the size of your section.
- The last paragraph should contain nothing but the EXIT statement, and need not have a sequence number (*e.g*: BA-99-EXIT orBA-EXIT).
- If you need to pass control to another point within the same section use the GO TO <paragraph-name> statement. Do NOT use the PERFORM <paragraph-name> statement.
- If you need to pass control to another section use the PERFORM <section-name> statement. Do NOT use the GO TO statement on anything other than a paragraph-name within the current section.
- If you feel it necessary to insert a comment (or two) about the paragraph, please put it AFTER the paragraph name and BEFORE the first line of code.

SENTENCES AND STATEMENTS

The guidelines for sentences and statements can be summarised as follows.

- Each sentence should start in column 12.
- Each statement within a sentence (if there is more than one) should start on a separate line. This means that statements can be added or deleted quite easily, without having to change other lines unnecessarily.
- If a statement is too long to fit on one line DO NOT split a data-name across two lines - instead move the whole name (along with the TO, FROM, BY or GIVING portion of the verb) onto the next line, indenting by four character positions.
- Do not use weird spacing between each word - one is enough! There is only one exception to this guideline that I find acceptable, and that is when there is a group of MOVE..... TO..... statements. In this case it makes the code more readable if all the TO portions are aligned under a common column, as in the following example:

```
MOVE "AA" TO ACC-ACCOUNT-TYPE.
 MOVE ABC-GROUPTO ACC-GROUP.
 MOVE ABC-CLASSIFICATION TO ACC- ____
 CLASSIFICATION.
 MOVE ABC-NAME TO ACC-NAME.
```

Guidelines (c) and (d) come in handy when searching a source file for a particular references to a data-name, as with:

```
LIST "MOVE ABC-GROUP"
LIST "TO ACC-GROUP"
```

This is not so easy to do if the data-name is split in two, or if more than one space is used between words.

- Do not put a space line between individual statements. It is permissible, however, to have a space line between groups of statements in order to show a logical separation.
- Even though it should be obvious what a piece of code does, it may not be obvious why it does it, or why it is necessary to do it at that particular point in the programme. To aid the maintenance programmer

some sort of comment may be worth its weight in gold. Don't worry if the comment stretches over several lines - a single- line comment is worthless if it is incomplete.

CONDITIONAL PROCESSING

This is where a lot of uneducated programmers come unstuck! Even though COBOL allows the following:

```
IF <condition> {THEN} <statement1>ELSE<statement-
2> {END-IF}.
```

There are some basic guidelines which can be applied in order to make the code more readable and easier to maintain.

These are:

- Each portion (condition, ELSE, statement-1, statement-2, END-IF) should be on a separate line. This allows for future additions or deletions without having to modify more lines than is necessary.
- The word ELSE should be aligned in exactly the same column as the IF to which it is associated. This makes the association more obvious in the listing, especially with multiple or nested IFs.
- COBOL'85 allows each condition to be terminated with an END-IF. Its use should be encouraged as it makes it absolutely clear where each condition is supposed to end, thus avoiding the possibility of confusion and mistakes. Like the ELSE, the END-IFshould be aligned in exactly the same column as IF with which it is associated.
- Statement-1 and statement-2 should be indented, usually by four character positions. This allows the IF, ELSE and END-IF to be more distinctive in the listing.

This now gives us the following construction:

```
IF <condition>
     <statement-1>
ELSE
      <statement-2>
END-IF.
```

Here are some extra guidelines for nested IFs:

- For each level of nested IF indent all associated lines by four characters.

  This gives the following:

```
IF <condition-1>
  IF <condition-2>
     <statement-1>
     <statement-2>
 END-IF
   ELSE
     <statement-3>
 END-IF.
```

- Don't ever use more than three levels of nested IF - they are extremely difficult to debug and maintain.
- Remember that each ELSE is paired with the IF that immediately precedes it in the code, not necessarily the one under which it is aligned. Take the following example:

```
IF <condition-1>
  IF <condition-2>
      <statement-2>
 ELSE
      <statement-1>.
```

According to the indentation <statement-1> is supposed to be executed if <condition-1> is false, but COBOL follows its own rules and executes <statement1> if <condition-1> is true and <condition-2> is false.

This type of error is more avoidable if theEND-IF is used, as in the following example:

```
IF <condition-1>
    IF <condition-2>
         <statement-2>
    END-IF
ELSE
    <statement-1>
END-IF.
```

or...

```
IF <condition1>
    IF <condition2>
         <statement-2>
    ELSE
         <statement-1>
    END-IF
END-IF.
```

- In the case where an ELSE is immediately followed by an IF without any intervening statements (ie: where only one out of a series of conditions will be TRUE) it is not necessary to indent at each new

IF otherwise you will quickly fall off the page. Consider the following example:

```
IF X-VALUE = 1
   <statememt-1>
ELSE
IF X-VALUE = 2
   <statement-2>
ELSE
IF X-VALUE = 3
   <statement-3>
ELSE
IF X-VALUE = 4
   <statement-4>
ELSE
IF X-VALUE = 5
   <statement-5>
etc.
IF X-VALUE = 1
      <statememt-1>
ELSE
    IF X-VALUE = 2
  <statement-2>
ELSE
   IF X-VALUE = 3
     <statement-3>
   ELSE
     IF X-VALUE = 4
```

```
          <statement-4>
        ELSE
          IF X-VALUE = 5
             <statement-5>
          etc.
```

With the arrival of COBOL'85 this should be written as follows:

```
EVALUATE X-VALUE
   WHEN 1 <statement-1>
   WHEN 2 <statement-2>
   WHEN 3 <statement-3>
   WHEN 4 <statement-4>
   WHEN 5 <statement-5>
   WHEN OTHER.....
 END-EVALUATE.
```

Here are even more guidelines for complex conditions:

- Enclose each individual condition in parentheses.
- If several conditions combine to form a group condition, (ie. all conditions have to be true in order to make the group condition true) then enclose the whole group in parentheses as well.
- By having each condition on a separate line, and by careful alignment of ANDs and ORs, it is possible to make absolutely clear that conditions are linked or are alternatives.

These guidelines should produce something like this:

```
IF ((A = 1 OR 2 OR 3)
        AND
    (B NOT = 4))
OR ((C = "A" OR "Z")
        OR
       (D < E))
   <statement>
ENDIF.
```

This example, however, is rapidly approaching the stage at which it becomes too unwieldy to be maintainable. Don't be afraid to split a complex condition into its component parts, even if it involves the use of the GO TO statement. Don't try to prove how clever you can be - keep it simple and straightforward.

HINTS, NOTES AND WARNINGS

Perform <section>

Even though COBOL allows the PERFORM command to be used on paragraphs as well as sections, its use should be limited to sections only. If necessary make the offending paragraph into a self-contained section, or an in-line PERFORM (if it is small enough).

This guideline then avoids the possibility that someone may split the paragraph in two, thereby causing the PERFORM to terminate at the new paragraph name.

Please note that if the word SECTION is missed out on a section name it will be treated as a paragraph. As there is usually nothing but comments between the section name and the next paragraph it means that no code will actually be executed by that PERFORMstatement. Unfortunately the code WILL be included in the PERFORM of the preceding section. This usually causes lots of confusion.

Perform... Through

Avoid the use of PERFORM <procedure-A> THROUGH <procedure-Z>. It is good practice to name each procedure (section) explicitly - this makes it easier to search a source file for all occurrences of PERFORM <sectionname>, and also avoids the possibility that someone may add a new section between existing sections without realising that it now falls within the bounds of the PERFORM <A> THROUGH <C> statement.

A programme can produce some very peculiar results if a section is 'accidentally' performed out of sequence, and is not easy to debug.

The EXIT Statement

The EXIT verb in COBOL does not produce an Exit instruction in the object programme - it is ignored, but is maintained for documentation purposes only. Whenever a section is Performed COBOL will generate its own (hidden) EXIT instruction when the next section-name is encountered

If a section-name in your source file has the word Section missing, COBOL will treat it as a continuation of the preceding section - this can cause some very peculiar results (refer to PERFORM <section>).

The GO TO Statement

Do not use the GO TO verb to transfer control to a point which is outside the current section as any implied EXIT points will be ignored. This means that the programme will go where it thinks it should go, which is probably NOT where it is supposed to go.

The ALTER Statement

DO NOT USE THE ALTER STATEMENT! If you need to change the processing sequence due to a certain condition, then use an alternative set of PERFORM or GO TO statements - trying to debug a programme where the instruction as it appears in the listing may not be the actual instruction encountered by the programme at run time is a very frustrating experience. If it makes the maintenance programmer's job more difficult then *DO NOT USE IT!*

Move Corresponding

This may seem to be an economical way of writing source code as this single statement will represent several actual MOVE's. However, in the event of an error caused by an illegal ASCII digit (or similar) the diagnostic trace will not be able to identify which elementary item within the group of items actually generated the fault, which means that it will take longer to identify and solve the problem.

The COMPUTE Statement

The COMPUTE verb should be used only for complex arithmetic operations, and not for simple additions or subtractions. For example, use ADD 1 TO VALUE instead of COMPUTE VALUE = VALUE + 1 as it is more efficient in machine resources. The data items within a COMPUTE statement should, if possible, all have the same data type. If there is a mixture of COMP, COMP-3 andDISPLAY fields they will be converted (for the duration of the COMPUTE operation) to a common type before the calculation can take place.

Be aware that the number of decimal places used in evaluating an arithmetic expression is determined by the maximum number of decimal places within the expression. This has implications when doing any divisions, especially when calculating percentages which have an implied division by 100.

For example, to apply a rate of 17.25% you have the choice of either:

- Including the division by 100 within the calculation by specifying * 17.25/ 100, or
- Performing the division by 100 separately and specifying * 0.1725 within the calculation.

If none of the items within the calculation has at least 4 decimal places then the intermediate result from (a) above will not be accurate, whereas method (b) avoids this problem by ensuring that the result of the division is stored in a field which has the correct number of decimal places.

AUTOREADS in VPLUS

It has always been the standard within Hewlett-Packard's block-mode screen processing that the user either presses the ENTER key to process the current screen of data, or presses one of the other function keys to do something else.

The AUTOREAD facility was provided to cater for those special circumstances where it is necessary to capture the current screen contents without the user being able to press the ENTER key - for example, when using the HELP subsystem. This facility was NOT provided so that the user could bypass the ENTER key altogether, and should not be used as such.

The SORT Statement

A SORT can be performed in one of the following ways:

- Internally, using the construct:

```
SORT.... INPUT PROCEDURE IS.....
          OUTPUT PROCEDURE IS....
```

- Internally, using the construct:

```
SORT.... USING <file> GIVING <file>
```

3

Compiling

COMPILING PROGRAMMES

INTRODUCTION

As you saw in the section Executable File Types in the chapter Packaging Applications,

you can create three types of executable files:

- System executable files
- Generated code files
- Intermediate code files

To create an executable file you need to compile your programme using the Compiler. If you want to create a system executable file, you will subsequently need to link the compiled file. Note that compiling and linking can be done in one step using cob.

The Compiler compiles a programme in two phases:

- The first phase checks the syntax of your COBOL source code. It is during this phase that intermediate code is created.
- The second phase generates either native object code or generated code. The type of code generated is specified by you.

If you compile a programme to object code, you must subsequently link the file using cob.

To compile, you use the cob command. The sections below give you general information on compiling programmes using the cob command. For detailed information on using cob, see the chapter *COBOL* System Interface (cob).

CREATING INTERMEDIATE CODE FILES

You can create an intermediate code file using the Compiler directly. There is no need to link the programme. However, you will need to run the programme using the cobrun programme, or create a system executable file that calls the programme. For more details see the chapter *Packaging Applications*.

You can compile the source code file myprog.cbl to intermediate code as follows:

```
cob -i myprog.cbl
```

This creates an intermediate code file called myprog.int.

The Command:

```
cob -a myprog.cbl
```

Also creates an intermediate code file, along with files for use by Animator.

CREATING GENERATED CODE FILES

You create a generated code file using the Compiler. There is no need to link the programme.

However, to run the programme you need to do one of the following:

- Run the programme using the cobrun programme
- Create a system executable file that calls the programme

For example, you can compile the source code file myprog.cbl to generated code as follows:

```
cob -u myprog.cbl
```

This creates a generated code file called myprog.gnt.

You can also create a.gnt file from an.int file using:

```
cob -u myprog.int
```

CREATING SYSTEM EXECUTABLE FILES

Creating a system executable file involves two steps:

1. Creating native object code
2. Linking the file containing the native object code file, to create an executable file

Both steps are done using the cob command. For example, if the file myprog.cbl contains the source programme, you can compile the programme to a system executable file in one step, as follows:

```
cob -x myprog.cbl
```

This creates a system executable file called myprog.

USING COMPILER DIRECTIVES

Many options are available for controlling the way your programme is compiled. These options are specified using directives when you invoke the Compiler. You can enter Compiler directives individually on the command line, or you can create default directives which are then invoked as a group either automatically, or from the command line, or from within the source code.

For normal operation you need to know about and use very few directives. In the majority of cases you will use the default values. If you do need to use other directives they are described in detail in the chapter Directives for Compiler.

Many directives direct the Compiler to create code which is compatible with other COBOL compilers. More details of these can be found in your Compatibility Guide. The directives you are most likely to use are those that define the output produced by the Compiler. For more information about setting directives, see the section Directives in the chapter Using the Compiler.

OBTAINING THE FASTEST COMPILATION TIME

This section shows you the best way to use the Compiler to keep your compilation time down.

Compiling Using.int Files

If you are creating a large application, you can cut down the amount of time taken to compile a programme by compiling using.int files. If you compile using the intermediate code file instead of the source file the Compiler will omit the check phase and go straight to the generate phase.

For example, to compile myprog.int to a.gnt file you would need to type:

```
cob -u myprog.int
```

This would create the generated code file myprog.gnt.

To create a system executable file from an.int file you would type:

```
cob -x myprog.int
```

Compiling to Generated Code

Compiling to generated code takes longer than compiling to intermediate code. You only need to create generated code when your programme is free of bugs and ready for production.

Using Directives for Fast Compilation

There are several Compiler directives that affect the speed of a compilation.

They are:

- ALTER
- COPYLIST
- LIST
- QUAL
- QUALPROC
- SEG

These directives are described briefly below. For more information on all directives, see the chapter Directives for Compiler.

ALTER	The ALTER directive enables the use of ALTER statements in your programme. If you know there are no ALTER statements in your source code, specifying NOALTER enables the Compiler to produce slightly more efficient code and produce it more quickly. The Compiler assumes ALTER as the default.
COPYLIST	COPYLIST tells the Compiler to list the contents of all copyfiles and include files. If you are creating a listing file, specifying NOCOPYLIST results in faster compilation time, as COBOL copyfiles are not expanded in the listing. The Compiler assumes COPYLIST as the default.
LIST	LIST specifies that you want a listing file to be created. If you do not need to create a listing file, specifying NOLIST (the default) speeds up the compilation process.

QUAL	QUAL is only required if you are using qualified data-names; for example: **`elementary-item-a of group-item-1`** The Compiler assumes QUAL as the default.
QUALPROC	If your programme uses qualified data-names, but not qualified paragraph-names, compilation can be accelerated by specifying NOQUALPROC. The Compiler assumes QUALPROC as the default.
SEG	The SEG directive enables the use of segments in your programme. If you know there are no segments in your source code, specifying NO enables the Compiler to produce slightly more efficient code and produce it more quickly. The Compiler assumes SEG as the default.

If you will always compile a programme with a particular directive set you could use the $SET command in your programme code to set the directive. For example, if your programme does not use ALTER statements, you could set the directive in your programme:

$SET noalter

See the section Directives in the chapter Using the Compiler for more information on setting directives.

FOR MORE INFORMATION

For more information on compiling and linking programmes, see the following chapters in this manual:

- *Using the Compiler*: Invoking the Compiler, and setting directives
- *Linking:* Linking programmes
- *COBOL System Interface (cob)*: The cob command

For information on Compiler directives, see the chapter *Directives for Compiler.*

USING THE COMPILER

INTRODUCTION

The Object COBOL Compiler compiles a programme in two phases:

- The first phase is the syntax-check phase. The Compiler checks the syntax of your Object COBOL source code for errors and creates an intermediate code file with the extension.int. During this phase the compiler also can also create files for use with Animator.

- The second phase is the generate phase. The Compiler generates either a native object code file with the extension.o, or a generated code file with the extension.gnt, depending on parameters you specify when you compile your programme.

You use the cob command to specify whether the Compiler is to perform its syntax-check or generate phase, or both phases.

Object code files contain no direct calls to the operating system, nor do they access the devices on your computer. Instead they contain calls to the run-time system, or to run-time support modules, that do the detailed work of calling the operating system to open and close files or to access the hardware devices on your computer. An object code file must be linked to create an executable file.

Callable shared object files.int files and.gnt files are executable files that can be run without linking into a system executable file.

Executable file types are described in detail in the chapter Packaging Applications. You can control the way your programme is compiled by specifying Compiler directives. For example, you use a Compiler directive to specify that you want the Compiler to send a full listing to the screen as well as the printer.

INVOKING THE COMPILER

Programmes are compiled using the cob command. The operation of the cob command is controlled by various flags. The cob command is described in the chapterCOBOL System Interface (cob). The cob flags are described in the chapter Descriptions of cob Flags. Compiler directives are specified on the cob command line.

Source code is usually held in files with the extension.cbl.CBL or.cob. You can specify the verbose option (using the -v cob flag) on the cob command line if you want to view any messages or errors issued during compiling or generating. If you do not specify the verbose option, then compilation or generation proceeds without displaying any messages unless an error is found.

If you specify the verbose option, each option is acknowledged by the Compiler on a separate line and is either accepted, rejected or ignored. Those options that are ignored are those that are not applicable to your environment, or to the compile or generate phase. After all the options have been acknowledged, the Compiler opens its files and starts the compilation process.

While compiling or generating your programme, the Compiler creates a number of temporary work files in the directory indicated by the environment variable TMPDIR, or in the directory/tmp or/usr/tmp if TMPDIR does not exist (see the appendix Micro Focus Environment Variables for details on TMPDIR). The size of the files depends on the end point specified to cob, the content of your programme and the directives used; in particular the number of data and procedure names. Before starting the compilation, you should ensure there is enough free space in the temporary area. Note that the most space is generally used while building executable files.

Temporary files are normally deleted by the Compiler before it terminates. If the Compiler is interrupted or is terminated by machine failure, it does not go through its clean-up routines; in this case, files can be left on your disk. These files have names of the form check.*vnn*. You can delete them, if cob is not running in any other session.

SYNTAX-CHECK PHASE

The Compiler, by default, compiles COBOL source code files into.int files, and also produces.idy files containing information for the Animator, unless some other end point is specified to the cob command.

If you compile a source file that contains multiple programmes, the resulting output file for the first programme in that sequence is named *source-file*.int (and source-file.idy); the output files for subsequent programmes in that source file is named programme-id.int (and programme-id.idy). For example, if you compile the source filefile1 that contains two programmes ab and *bc,* ab is output to file1.int, while *bc* is output to bc.int.

If the verbose option was specified, then when the syntax-check phase begins, the Compiler displays:

`* Compiling filename`

Followed by other Compiler messages.

If the Compiler cannot open your source file, it issues the message:

`Open fail: filename`

The compilation is aborted and control is returned to UNIX. The most likely causes of errors at this time are:

- You have not provided the correct filename
- Your source file extension is not.cbl.CBL or.cob, and you have not used the -k cob flag to identify a non-standard filename extension (see the chapter Descriptions of cob Flags for information on the -k cob flag).
- Your file is not in the directory you have specified, or it is not in the current directory if you did not specify a path-name
- You do not have read permission for a source or copyfile or write permission for the.int or.idy file, or the files are in use by another process.

If the Compiler finds syntax errors in your source code, it lists each line that contains an error, with an error message that briefly explains the problem. For further information on errors and error messages, see your Error Messages. If your source code contains no syntax errors, then the system prompt reappears when compilation is complete. If you set the -v cob flag, then the Compiler first provides statistics on data and code size.

Listing Format

When the compiling process is complete, a listing file

containing information on the compiled programme is displayed if the compilation listing option (-P cob flag) was set before compilation.

The listing below illustrates the information contained in a full listing:

```
* Micro Focus COBOL for UNIX VX.x revision xxx
15-Apr-96 16.49 Page 1
*          filename
Options: list-of-directives
   1     Statement 1
   :
   :
   n     Statement n
* Micro Focus COBOL for UNIX VX.x revision xxx
Compiler
* Copyright (c) 1984-1996 Micro Focus Ltd URN
xxxxx/xxn/nnnnnx
                  REF xxx-nnnnnnnnnxn-xxxnnn
* * Last message on page: nn
*
* Total messages: n
* Unrecoverable:  n Severe: n
* Errors: n Warnings: n
* Informational:  n Flags: n
* Data = nnnnnnnnn Code = nnnnnnnnn
```

The first line of the listing displays the product name and version number and notes the date and time the listing was produced. The filename of the compiled programme appears on the second line. If the FLAG Compiler directive was set, the second line also includes the setting of this directive. These two lines appear at the top of each page of the listing file. A list of the directives specified appears on the next line.

If you specify the REF directive during compilation, a hexadecimal value denoting the address of each data-name or procedure statement appears to the right of the page. Addresses of data names are relative to the start of the data area, while addresses of procedures (that is sections and paragraphs) are relative to the start of the code area. There is some overhead at the start of the data area, and some at the start of the procedure area, including a few bytes of initialization code for each SELECT statement. The body of the listing displays your source code, providing details on flags and syntax errors.

A flag is marked in the listing by a flagging line with the following format:

```
nn              flagged-feature
**—nnn—dialect————————(nnnn)—
** description
```

where the variables are:

nn	The sequence number of the flagged line.
flagged-feature	The coding that caused the flag to be raised.
nnn	The flag number.
dialect	Represents a language-level that does include the flagged syntax. For full details on the FLAG directive, see the chapter *Directives for Compiler*.
nnnn	Indicates the page of the listing the previous flag occurred. This enables you to trace back from one flag to the previous one.
Description	Indicates why the feature was flagged.

A programme in which flags are indicated can still be run. Further details can be found in your *Error Messages*. If the Compiler detects an error in a data declaration, it can skip some subsequent data declarations, so spurious error messages are produced when references are made to data items whose declarations have been skipped.

A syntax error is marked in the listing by an error line with the following format:

```
nn  illegal-statement
* nnn *A *** ******************* (nnnn**)
** description
```

Where the variables are:

nn	The sequence number of the erroneous line.
illegal-statement	The coding that caused the error
nnn	The Compiler error number.
A	A single alphabetic character representing

	the category of the severity of the error: U Unrecoverable S Severe E Error W Warning I Informational In some circumstances, the Compiler does not echo the erroneous line to the terminal. Check the previous line if there is any doubt. See the section *Compiler Error Messages* below for further details.
nnnn	The page of the listing on which the previous error occurred. This enables you to trace back from one error to the previous one.
description	Indicates why the syntax produced an error.

A summary appears at the end of the listing. The first line of the listing summary repeats the product name and version number and the component name. Copyright information, the user reference number and the Compiler reference number appear on the next two lines. If any errors or messages were issued, the Compiler displays the page-number of the listing on which the last message appeared, followed by the total number of messages, the number of messages in each severity and the total number of flags raised.

If no errors or messages were issued, then the following line appears instead:

```
* Total Messages: 0
```

The last line provides information on the data and code size in the following format:

```
Data=nnnnnnnnn Code=mmmmmmmmm
```

Where the variables are:

nnnnnnnnn	The size, in bytes, of the data division, including literals (if you have less than 64 Kilobytes of data)
mmmmmmmmm	The size of compiled intermediate code.

COMPILER ERROR MESSAGES

Error messages issued by the Compiler are classed according to their severity, as follows:

Severity	Description
Unrecoverable	Indicates a fatal error
Severe	Indicates an error that the Compiler was unable to correct. Compilation continues, but the statement at fault is not compiled
Error	Indicates an error that the Compiler has tried to correct
Warning	Flags a statement that although is syntactically correct can contain a possible error
Informational	Draws your attention to something in your source code you should be aware of

The Compiler returns a value to the operating system to show the most severe type of message it issued. The possible severity and the corresponding return values are shown in the following table:

Severity	Return Value
Unrecoverable	16
Severe	12
Error	8
Warning	4
Informational	See INFORETURN directive
No messages	0

U-level and S-level errors are always output by the Compiler. You can force the Compiler to output any of the remaining three levels of errors by setting the WARNING Compiler directive. See the chapter Directives for Compiler for details. An unrecoverable error always causes the Compiler to stop, outputting the relevant error message as it does so. By default, a severe error causes processing of the cob command to stop after an intermediate code file has been produced, but you can override this by using the -W flag on the cob command line. This flag controls the error-level that causes cob to stop processing. See the chapterDescriptions of cob Flags for full details on this flag.

If any S-, E-, W- or I-level errors are output by the Compiler, a message given at the end of its run indicates both the number of errors that occurred and the category these were in.

You can not run or generate intermediate code programmes that contain any U-level errors. You first have to correct these errors and resubmit your source-code to the Compiler via the cob command.

You can run programmes that contain S-level errors only if you set the E run-time switch on. See the chapter Descriptions of Run-time Switches for full details of how you can do this. If the E run-time switch is set off (-E), that is its default setting, trying to run intermediate code programmes that contain S-level errors, gives a run-time error, and the programme run terminates.

You can not produce generated or object code from intermediate code programmes that contain S-level errors. Trying to do so results in a Compiler error in the generate phase.

You can animate programmes with S-level errors regardless of the setting of the E run-time switch. If you animate such a programme with the -E switch setting, a run-time error is reported, but animation does not terminate.

You can animate, run, and produce object files from intermediate code files that contain E-, W- and I-level errors, regardless of the setting of the E run-time switch.

A full list of Compiler error messages together with recovery hints can be found in your Error Messages.

Redirection of Compiler Output

All output from the Compiler to the screen can be redirected to a file by use of the standard UNIX redirection facilities (> and >>). For example, to put all the Compiler output from two successive compilations, myprog and subprog, into a single file, compout.log, enter:

```
cob myprog.cbl -C ans85 > compout.log
```

To create the redirection file containing the output from myprog, and then:

```
cob subprog.cbl -C ans85 >> compout.log
```

To append the output from subprog to the redirection file.If you are compiling with the ERRQ directive, the prompts normally displayed by the Compiler is also redirected. Consequently.

The Compiler appears to hang when really it is waiting for your response. If you think this is the case, use the interrupt key to terminate the compilation, and restart it without the ERRQ directive set.

THE GENERATE PHASE

After acknowledging all the cob options, the Compiler opens its files and starts the generate phase.

At this point, if the verbose option is set, the Compiler displays the message:

```
* Generating filename
```

If the Compiler cannot open your source file, it issues the message:

```
* File open failure: filename
```

The generate phase is aborted and control is returned to UNIX. The most likely causes of errors are:

- You have not provided the correct filename
- You have not provided the file extension (the extension must be specified, even if it is.int). However,

If you are processing.cbl files to.gnt files in one step as follows:

```
cob -u filename.cbl
```

Then cob creates an.int, and then the.gnt file.

- Your file is not in the directory you have specified, it is not in the current directory if you did not specify a path-name, or you do not have the necessary access permission(s).

If no errors occur, then the system prompt reappears when the generating process is complete. If you set the -v cob flag, then the Compiler first provides statistics on data and code size.

Generating Segmented Programmes

When you generate native code for a segmented programme, you specify on the cob command line only the name of the root segment intermediate code file. The compiler uses this name and automatically generates the segments. The output files mirror the input files: a root generated code file with extension.gnt and overlays with extensions.g*nn*, where *nn* is in the range 50-99 corresponding to the COBOL segment numbers.

The exception to this is when a programme is generated for static linking. In this instance, all the overlays are contained in the root file, that has the extension.o. On some environments, a single.gnt file is produced for a segmented programme. On all environments, you can force a single.gnt to be created by specifying the NOSEG directive (see the chapter Directives for Compiler for details). This has no effect on the running of the programme.

Directives are used to specify options that affect the way the Compiler behaves, what output it produces, what code is actually compiled and how the compiled code behaves when run. All directives have a default built into the Compiler; however, you can override these defaults as described in the section Setting Directives.

The following sections describe how you can specify directives. Descriptions of the individual directives are contained in the chapter Directives for Compiler.

Directives Syntax

Compiler directives are specified using a cob flag. Directives that affect the syntax-check phase are set using the -C cob flag. Directives that affect the generate phase are set using the -N cob flag.

The format for setting directives is:

```
-flag [no]keyword["parameter"]
```

Where the parameters are:

Flag	The cob command line flag used to specify directives. *flag* is C for syntax-check phase directives, N for generate phase directives.

No	Turns *keyword* off. no must adjoin *keyword*. no applies only to certain directives where specified in their description in the chapter *Directives for Compiler*.
Keyword	One or more of the Compiler directives described in the chapter *Directives for Compiler*. If you do specify more than one directive, they must all be enclosed in quotation marks. This informs UNIX that all the directives in them are grouped together. If you omit the quotation marks, second and subsequent directives are ignored although no warning to this effect is given.
Parameter	A qualifier to *keyword* and applies only to certain directives where specified in their description in the chapter *Directives for Compiler*. It must appear in one of the following forms: *"parameter"* or *=parameter* or *(parameter)* and must adjoin *keyword*. You must not include any spaces in a Compiler option. This is because UNIX treats the space character as an option delimiter, so if you include any spaces in a Compiler option, UNIX regards the option as more than one option. If *parameter* is *filename*, then it can be a fully specified filename, including path, unless otherwise stated. If you specify a Compiler option in a $SET statement or in a DIRECTIVES file, *parameter* cannot be preceded by an equals sign (=). It must be enclosed either in double quotation marks (" ") or parentheses.

We recommend that where possible you use the format of the option that contains an equal sign before any parameter. cob maps the equals sign (that has no special meaning to UNIX) to the format that uses parentheses (as these do have a special meaning to UNIX). You are recommended to use this format because if you use either of the other possible formats, you must escape the quotation marks or parentheses with the backslash character (\ ) whenever they might be misinterpreted by the UNIX shell. As the equals sign has no special meaning, it does not need to be escaped.

Examples

The following examples illustrate two ways to specify the same Compiler directives using the equals sign before parameters as recommended:

```
cob -C assign=external -C flag=ans85 pi.cbl
or
cob -C "assign=external flag=ans85" pi.cbl
```

Both examples cause the Compiler to assume that all file assignments to data names are resolved externally and to flag features in your programme that are not in the ANSI'85 dialect of the COBOL language. In the first example, the -C cob flag is specified immediately before each Compiler directive. In the second, quotation marks are used to inform UNIX that all the directives in them are grouped behind the -C flag.

Setting Directives

Directives can be entered in a number of ways. The order in which the various options are passed to the Compiler determines their precedence. See the chapter*COBOL System Interface (cob)* for details. Regardless of where they are specified, Compiler directives that affect the syntax-check phase always follow the -C cob flag, while those that affect the generate phase always follow the -N flag.

Full details on the directives available are contained in the chapter Directives for Compiler. Some of the directives are environment dependent and might not apply to your particular environment (any such restrictions are noted in the directive's description). The Compiler accepts them but treats them as documentary only.

COPY LIBRARIES

The COBOL COPY statement, described in the Language *Reference,* can be used to include COBOL source code from files other than the source code file being compiled. This section defines how the names used in the COPY statement relate to the physical files containing the source code to be included.

The basic COPY statement has the following format:

where the parameters are:

Text-name	Either a true COBOL user-defined word or a COBOL user-defined word that also includes embedded non-COBOL characters. It is not enclosed in quotation marks. This COBOL system allows non-COBOL characters to be embedded in text-name for compatibility with other COBOL dialects, but Micro Focus recommends that you avoid using this non-standard COBOL facility as it can limit source portability. *text-name* is equivalent to an *external*-filename-literal in which text-name is converted to upper-case and enclosed in quotation marks.
External-Filename-Literal	The name of a file, in quotation marks. This COPY filename can have an extension and can incorporate a path-name if there is no*library-name* or *library-name-literal*. A simple COPY filename is one that includes just the basename of the file and an optional extension. A qualified COPY filename is one that includes additional path details, with any relative path being relative to the current directory. If the filename has a trailing period, the extension is assumed to be spaces. The name of the file can be folded to upper or lower case using the directive FOLDCOPYNAME.
Library-Name	A COBOL user-defined word. It is not enclosed in quotation marks. library-name is equivalent to a library-name-literal in which library-name is converted to upper-case and enclosed in quotation marks.
Library-Name-Literal	The name of a directory or library, in quotation marks. This COPY library-name can incorporate a path-name with any relative path being relative to

the current directory. The name of the file can be folded to upper or lower case using the directive FOLDCOPYNAME.

The COPY statement must be terminated with a period (.). The Compiler treats a COPY library-name as the name of a directory, unless you use the COPYLBR directive. See the chapter *Directives for Compiler* for details. If the optional phrases of the COPY statement are not specified, then the Compiler acts as if the directory containing the main source file had been specified as a library-name.

Portability

COBOL allows great flexibility in naming copyfiles. However, if you include any operating system dependent detail in the name then your COBOL source code might not readily compile if you move the source file to another operating system. Micro Focus recommends that you provide the name of the copyfile as a literal, in lower case, with the extension.cpy, and with no path. If you need to include a path, do not use the colon (:). You can retain the forward slash (/) in your pathnames, rather than use the backslash (\).

Search Sequence

A COPY statement must identify a file that contains the text to be copied or the compiler either gives an error or prompts for the file interactively depending on the setting of the QUERY directive (see the chapter *Directives for Compiler* for details). The COPY statement can identify a specific file, by using a qualified COPY filename with an extension, otherwise it identifies an incomplete filename.

A filename can be incomplete either because it lacks a filename extension or because it lacks a filename path; in both cases the Compiler conducts a search as described below. The Compiler stops the search as soon as it finds a matching file and uses the contents of that file as the COPY text.

If the Compiler encounters a COPY filename that has an extension, then it only looks for files that have that extension. If the COPY filename has no extension, then, for any particular directory, the Compiler looks for files in that directory with extensions given by the directives OSEXT and COPYEXT. The default values for these directives differ between products for the UNIX operating system and products for other environments. However, the default values can be readily changed by setting the OSEXT and COPYEXT directives. See the chapter Directives for Compiler for details.

The Compiler searches, by default, for files with the following extensions in the sequence:

- No extension
- The extension.cbl
- The extension.cpy

If the Compiler encounters a qualified COPY filename, then it only looks for the file in the directory specified in the COPY filename. If it encounters a simple COPY filename, then it looks for the file in the following directories in the sequence:

- The directory given by the COPY library-name or, if no library-name is given, in the directory containing the main source programme being compiled.
- Any directories that can be listed in the COBCPY environment variable.

The references to.cbl in table 9.1 of examples assume the UNIX default values for OSEXT and COPYEXT and that the main source file is in the current directory.

COBCPY Environment Variable

The COBCPY environment variable directs the Compiler to look in additional directories for simple COPY filenames if they cannot be located in the given or default library. COBCPY has no affect for qualified COPY filenames.

The required format for values for COBCPY are shown in the following:

```
COBCPY=path-name[:path-name]...
```

where *path-name* is a directory that the Compiler and Animator are to search when looking for copyfiles.

For example, if you specify the command line:

```
COBCPY="/usr/group/sharedcopy:.:/usr/mydir/mcpy"
export COBCPY
```

The Compiler searches for a copyfile in/usr/group/sharedcopy, then in the current directory and finally in/usr/mydir/mcpy until either the copyfile is found or it can be considered not found.

Table. Examples of Compiler Search Sequence

COPY Statement	Contents of $COBCPY (includes path)	Files Searched For
COPY f1	f1.cbl f1.cpy	
COPY "f1.cop"		f1.cop
COPY "f1.cop"	dir1	f1.cop dir1/f1.cop
COPY "dir/f1"	dir1	dir1/f1 dir1/f1.cbl dir1/f1.cpy
COPY f1 OF dir1		dir1/f1 dir1/f1.cbl dir1/f1.cpy
COPY f1	dir1/	f1 f1.cbl f1.cpy dir1/f1 dir1/f1.cbl dir1/f1.cpy
COPY f1 IN dir1	/dir2	dir1/f1 dir1/f1.cbl dir1/f1.cpy /dir2/f1 /dir2/f1.cbl /dir2/f1.cpy

Note: Before the system searches $COBCPY according to the rules given above, it searches for a dd_ environment variable in accordance with the rules given in the chapter *File Naming* in your *Programmer's Guide to File Handling*. Additional searches for the required copyfile are made according to the mapping in such a dd_ variable.

4

Linking

INTRODUCTION

The Micro Focus COBOL system enables you to execute dynamically linked, statically linked or unlinked programmes, all of which can be output by the cob command depending on the options specified to it.

The UNIX system provides basic functionality to build and execute programmes. Your COBOL system exploits this and provides additional COBOL-specific functionality. Normally, for simple applications, you do not need to know much detail about how COBOL builds and executes programmes as the cob utility provides generally useful defaults. In this case, you can skip this section and simply read the initial discussions on the cob command and default linking at the beginning of the section *Operation*. However, if you want to optimize the way UNIX handles your built application or if you want to include non-COBOL routines in your application, then you need to understand more of the functionality available and how the COBOL system uses it. In this case, you should read this section.

This section describes:

- The UNIX system linker and loader
- The COBOL link and load options

UNIX SYSTEM LINKER AND LOADER

Programming language compilers generally output a programme as an individual, unlinked object (.o) file. This type of file is incomplete and cannot be directly executed. It lacks the various system or language support routines and possibly called subroutines that are needed at run time. It can be used to build an executable object file using the system linker to link all the required run time procedure references to an instance of the required code.

A programme executable object file, which usually does not have a filename extension, can be run by simply entering the name of the file at the UNIX system prompt. UNIX invokes the system loader to load the programme file together with any linked procedures and to "bind" all procedure references to a loaded copy of the procedure.

The system's linker and loader supports one or two of the following types of linking and binding:

1. Dynamic linking and binding
2. Static linking

All UNIX systems support static linking but they do not all support dynamic linking and binding. Dynamic linking involves shared object files (.so files) that on some systems are known as shared library files (.sl files) and on others as.a files. Wherever this section refers to an.so file, you can take this to mean an.sl or an.a file if this is what your system uses. If dynamic linking is supported by your system, then it is generally the default type of linking. See your operating system documentation to find out whether and how your system supports dynamic linking and binding.

Dynamic Linking and Binding

Dynamic binding of a programme or sub-programme is carried out by the system loader at run time. The executable file contains a reference to an external procedure (sub-programme or even a main programme) in a shared object file and the system loader ensures that the procedure is made available for execution. The system loader ensures that, however many concurrent users or applications are dynamically bound to that procedure, they all share a single copy in memory of the dynamically-bound procedure.

Dynamic linking of a procedure is carried out by the system linker at link time. The linker does not include the code for a dynamically linked procedure in the executable file, but does include a reference to the shared object (.so) file that contains the procedure's object code.

Static Linking

Static linking of a programme or sub-programme is carried out by the linker at link time. The linker includes the object code for all statically linked procedures in the executable object file and resolves all procedure references to them. The linker can be considered to have statically bound these procedures as the system loader does not have to take any special action at run-time.

COBOL Link and Load Options

The Micro Focus COBOL system provides COBOL applications with the standard UNIX functionality for linking and loading as well as a separate COBOL loading facility. Three options are available, for each programme and sub-programme in a COBOL application, via the cob command that provides:

Dynamic Linking

A dynamically linked programme is a subprogram that is held in object form in a shared object or.so file and is referenced from within one or more executable object files.

Dynamic linking is only available if your Operating and COBOL systems support it.

Static Linking

A statically linked programme is a programme or subprogram that is held in object form in an executable object file. It cannot be referenced from other executable files.

Dynamic Loading (No Linking)

The COBOL Run-time system (RTS) enables you to run a dynamically loadable programme without needing to link it first. The run-time system provides a dynamic loader routine that, when linked in an executable object file, can load a dynamically loadable COBOL programme or sub-programme and execute it.

A dynamically loadable programme is either a COBOL intermediate code file or a COBOL generated code file. Dynamic linking enables.so files to be shared between users and applications and can result in reduced disk space for holding application executable files compared with static linking.

Dynamic linking enables shared objects to be shared between users and applications and can result in reduced memory use for multiple concurrent users of multiple applications at run time compared with static linking. Static linking lets multiple users share the same application's object code when running and can result in reduced memory use for multiple concurrent users of that one application at run time compared with dynamic loading.

Dynamic loading does not require any linking and can be invoked directly via the cobrun command (see the chapter Running for details). The dynamically loaded files cannot share memory between users at run time, unlike any linked portions of the application. For relatively small applications, relatively numerous applications and relatively small numbers of concurrent users, dynamic loading can result in reduced disk use for holding the applications as well as reduced memory use.

The most significant advantage of dynamic loading over dynamic and static linking is that it removes the need for a link process and so it speeds the compile to run process and gives increased run-time flexibility.

The following sections describe how to build an application, describing the three options available and providing guidance on when you might choose one over the other.

BUILDING AN APPLICATION

To run a COBOL application, you must first invoke a standard UNIX system executable file. This is loaded by the system loader and control is passed to the first programme or entry point. The application starts to run and control passes explicitly to called subroutines or implicitly to run-time support routines.

The default entry point is the start of the first programme file specified to the cob utility when building the application executable file. The first programme, if specified, can be a COBOL programme or a non-COBOL programme.

The default entry point can be overridden by the -e flag to cob, to specify an alternative first entry point or to specify that the name of the first entry point is provided at run time as the first parameter on the command line that invokes the executable file. See the chapter*COBOL* System Interface (cob) for details on the cob command.

An executable file that requires the first entry point to be specified at run time is generally known as an executable run-time system (RTS). The file $COBDIR/rts32is the default executable RTS. An executable file that has the first entry point built in at link time is generally known as an executable application.

Any programme, sub-programme or support routine can be dynamically linked or statically linked in the executable file.

Only COBOL programmes or sub-programmes can be dynamically loaded. If anything implies that dynamic loading might be required, then the dynamic loader support routine is linked in the executable file otherwise it is not. If an executable file is not linked with the dynamic loader, it is referred to as a "fully linked" executable.

The dynamic loader can be required if:

- The first entry point is specified at run time
- The Call data-name statement is used
- The on EXCEPTION clause to the call statement is used
- The flag -d is specified to cob.

Only the statement CALL literal with no On Exception clause, when used in a fully linked programme, does not imply dynamic loading but implies direct reference that is vastly superior to dynamic loading in terms of performance.

DYNAMIC LINKING

Dynamic linking is available only if it is supported by your system. (You can check by seeing if there is no 'B' in the version number on the first line of$COBDIR/cobver) Dynamically linkable code is held in shared object (.so) files. These files are left on disk until required at run time. A shared object is an executable file format produced by the system linker that, unlike a runnable object, lacks an initial entry point. Shared object modules can be used as a library that saves disk space and enables one copy of each sub-programme to be shared between several different processes.

If the appropriate shared object library cannot be found at link time, the equivalent archive library (.a) is used instead. In this case, the library is statically linked (see the section *Static Linking*). The startup code of any executable module that uses dynamic linking is always statically linked.

To execute a dynamically linked programme, you enter the programme-name and any parameters at the UNIX prompt, having previously set up the dynamic library path.

The path is typically set as the value of an environment variable:

- LD_LIBRARY_PATH on most UNIX systems
- LIBPATH on AIX systems
- SHLIB_PATH on HP/UX systems

See the appendix *Micro Focus Environment Variables* for details. Dynamic linking provides a number of advantages over static linking. Because the executable module contains only the name of the shared library rather than its contents, the size of the executable module can be greatly reduced. Similarly, since the linker is not actually linking with the library at link time, the link process is much faster. The memory used by a shared library at run time is shared between one or more concurrent run time systems or applications that use it.

STATIC LINKING

Statically linked code is held in the form of a standard system executable object module that has its code permanently linked in the executable object file. Any required run-time support libraries or object modules are linked in the executable object file, possibly with none, one or more programmes and sub-programmes for your application.

To execute a statically linked programme, you enter the programme-name and any parameters at the UNIX prompt.

A statically linked programme is more self-contained than a dynamically linked programme and can sometimes be more convenient when packaging an application for distribution.

DYNAMIC LOADING

UNIX normally requires the names of all called programmes to be provided at link time and requires that all called programmes themselves to be provided at link time. The COBOL system removes these requirements for COBOL programmes by providing dynamic loading of.int and.gnt files.

The COBOL system lets each call to a programme to either be linked directly to the programme, if it is available at link time, or to be linked to the dynamic loader. At run time, when the dynamic loader is provided with the programme name, it searches for the named programme and, if necessary, dynamically loads it.The programme name can be provided to the dynamic loader as either a literal or as the value of a data item.

The dynamic loader searches for the named programme in the following places:

- The list of dynamically or statically linked programmes, sub-programmes and routines in memory.

  The list also records the states of the programmes, sub-programmes and routines. The states are:

  - *Active*: The programme or routine (which must be recursive) is still on the call-stack
  - *Inactive*: The programme or routine has been called, control has returned to the calling programme, but the called programme or routine has not been cancelled
  - *Initialized:* The programme or routine is static-linked, but has yet to be called

  - *Logically Cancelled:* The programme or routine has been called and cancelled, but not yet purged from memory (see the -l (lower case "L" run-time switch).
- The file system for a dynamically loadable file for the programme.

See the chapter The COBOL Interfacing Environment in your Programmer's Guide to Writing Programmes for details on how the file is located.

You can use flags to the cob command to explicitly name the programmes that you want to be linked and directly referenced and those that you want to be dynamically loaded. Without explicit instructions, cob takes default actions that depend on how the COBOL source calls the programme.

Default Behavior

The statement CALL data-name enables the name of the called sub-programme to be specified dynamically at run time and implies dynamic loading. In a CALL statement, an ON EXCEPTION clause specifies the action to take if the sub-programme cannot be loaded. Linked programmes are not considered able to give an exception, unlike dynamically loaded programmes and so the ON EXCEPTION clause implies dynamic loading.

Only the statement CALL literal with no ON EXCEPTION clause, when used in a linked programme, does not imply dynamic loading.

If a programme is invoked in a way that implies dynamic loading, then it is invoked by the run-time system dynamic loader. The dynamic loader first searches the list of loaded programmes, sub-programmes and support routines before trying to load the programme dynamically from disk. If the programme is already loaded, by virtue of being linked or previously dynamically loaded without any intervening CANCEL, then the dynamic loader simply passes control to it. If the programme is not already loaded, then the dynamic loader searches for a suitable dynamically loadable file. The search order is affected by the environment variable

COBPATH and the run-time tunable program_search_order. See the appendix Micro Focus Environment Variables, for details on environment variables, and the the chapter Run-time Configuration for details on trun-time tunables. See also the chapter The COBOL Interfacing Environment in your Programmer's Guide to Writing Programsfor details of the search order used for dynamically loadable programmes.

Dynamically Loadable Files

There are two types of dynamically loadable programme: COBOL intermediate code (.int) files and COBOL generated code (.gnt) files. If a programme needs to be loaded, then the dynamic loader loads a.gnt file in preference to an.int file for any given programme. Although you can reference the name, extension and path of a programme file in a CALL statement, we recommend that you omit any path or extension and ensure that the basename of any dynamically loadable file corresponds to the programme name.

Programme Names and Entry Points

The COBOL system recognizes various forms of file for a programme and assumes all files for a given programme have filenames that share the same basename. This basename is taken to be the programme name. The COBOL system uses the programme name to identify a programme and the dynamic loader also uses it to locate a programme. Each programme has a main entry point identified with the programme name.

The main entry point into a programme is the default point where execution of the programme starts. This is the first non-declarative statement after the Procedure Division header. The COBOL language lets you to specify a programme-name in the PROGRAMME-ID paragraph.

If specified, the programme-name represents the name of the main entry point. The ENTRY statement (see your Language Reference for details) allows additional entry points to be named which represent alternative places for the programme to start.

The programme is identified by the programme name, but once a programme is loaded, by linking or dynamic loading, the names of the entry points become available for use by the CALL statement.

The CANCEL statement must only reference a programme name and when executed causes the programme to be unloaded, unless the programme is linked in the executable file. Also see the -l run-time switch.We suggest that, for your convenience, if the PROGRAMME-ID paragraph is specified, you make the programme-name and the basename of a programme source file the same.

Flexibility and Performance

Accessing a programme via the dynamic loader is much less efficient than accessing it directly via direct reference, even if the programme has been statically or dynamically linked. If the programme needs to be dynamically loaded, then performance drops still further. However, the dynamic loader does give great build and run time flexibility.

Dynamic loading of programmes is especially suitable in a development environment. This is because it requires no link process, speeding the edit, compile and run cycle. It also gives more flexibility; you can even, while debugging, reload a changed version of a sub-programme while the rest of the application remains running.

In environments where the application generally runs with a single user, you might need to use dynamically loaded programmes if the amount of memory available is limited. Dynamic loading allows you full use of the memory management options provided by the Micro Focus COBOL dynamic loader enabling you to control the amount of memory required by your application.

In environments where the application generally runs with multiple users, both memory efficiency and performance generally favour a fully linked application, unless the sub-programmes are very large or very numerous. See the chapter Writing Programmes in your Programmer's Guide to Writing Programmes for further details on performance.

OPERATION

The following sections summarize the operation of the cob command and explain how to create executable files that are dynamically or statically linked or provide dynamic loading.

THE COB COMMAND

The cob processing involved in creating a COBOL executable file is fully described in the chapter COBOL System Interface (cob). This section simply highlights and summarizes the most significant aspects of using cob for linking.

The cob processing for a source file, named myfile.cbl, that is input to the cob command with the -x flag specified, can be shown as:

```
myfile.cbl-> myfile.int-> myfile.o->myfile
```

where the final myfile is an executable module.

The cob command assumes that all files and options specified on the command line are required if the -x flag is included. The cob command recognizes many files by their filename extension and recognizes many flags and options. It acts upon recognized flags and convert recognized files to their end point. It then invokes the system linker (ld), passing programme files and options to it in the same order (except the +l, +L and +B flags; see the chapter Descriptions of cob Flags) that they were specified on the cob command line. The system linker then carries out the required type of linking to create the final executable file.

Take care when specifying files and flags to cob, as it passes them on to the linker unchanged if it does not recognize them. It cannot check unrecognized ones itself and so cannot flag any error. You should not specify.gnt files if the -x flag is specified. The default entry point for the final executable is the base-name of the first input file.

Simple, Default Linking

You can create an executable application file simply by specifying the -x flag to the cob utility together with a list of the application files that you want included in the executable file. The application files can include COBOL or C source files,

COBOL.int files or any type of.o object files. The name of the executable file is the basename of the first application file in the list unless you specify another name by using the -o flag. For example, the command line:

```
cob -x myprog.cbl
```

Compiles the programme myprog.cbl to native code and links it with the run-time support routines to produce an executable myprog. The programme can then be run by simply entering the name of the executable at the command line. If the current directory is not set in your PATH environment variable, you can run the programme with a command line:

```
./myprog
```

If your application contains several programmes, then all the programmes can be linked together.

For example, the command line:

```
cob -xv myprog.cbl mysub.int csub.c -o myapp
```

Converts myprog.cbl and mysub.int to native code, compiles the C sourcefile csub.c to an object file, links them together with the COBOL run-time support routines and creates an executable file myapp. The -v flag causes cob to give informational messages on its progress.

If your application needs to include routines that are held in dynamic (.so) libraries or archive (.a) libraries, then you should read the following sections.

Creating Executables that Use Dynamic Libraries

You can create an executable application file that is dynamically linked to a dynamic library using the -x flag together with the -B dynamic or +B dynamic flags on the cob command line. Full details on the -x, -B and +B flags are contained in the chapter Descriptions of cob Flags.

The command line should have the following form:

```
cob -x filenames [-B dynamic]
```

Where *filenames* is a list of the files input to the cob command. This links all the application programmes, sub-programmes, COBOL run-time system libraries and operating system support libraries, dynamically where shared libraries are available, otherwise statically. The result is an executable file that, when run, uses the necessary run-time system and other shared libraries.

On environments where dynamic linking is supported, -B dynamic is the default, so it need not be specified on the command line.

When creating an executable file that is dynamically linked, the code for any referenced modules that are held in shared libraries or shared objects are not included in your executable file. Instead, if such a module is referenced at run time, then the shared object is loaded into memory from the shared object file before control is passed to it.

The cob command uses a shared object (.so) library instead of an archive (.a) library of the same basename. If a cob flag names a library then cob assumes it is a shared object library, but if no such library exists then it uses an archive library of the same name.

For example, if you specify two libraries abc and xyz on the cob command line as follows:

```
cob -x prog.cbl -labc -lxyz
```

Where the libraries libxyz.so, libxyz.a and libabc.a exist, then only libxyz.so and libabc.a are scanned to resolve references and libxyz.a is ignored.

Bear in mind that a reference to a sub-programme held in a dynamic library creates a dynamic link to the whole library, whereas a reference to a sub-programme held in an archive library only statically links to that sub-programme. Unreferenced sub-programmes in a dynamic library can be available to the dynamic loader; unreferenced sub-programmes in the archive library are not available to the dynamic loader.

Creating Shared Object Libraries

The most significant benefits of dynamic linking over static linking apply when many concurrently running, yet different, applications share a significant amount of code. The COBOL run-time support routines represent just such a significant amount of code. For this reason, if dynamic linking is supported by your COBOL system, then the run-time support routines are provided as shared object libraries in $COBDIR/coblib. You do not need to build a shared object library to gain the benefits of dynamic linking.

If you want to build your own shared object libraries, then for non-COBOL programmes you normally have to build them using the linker. For information on how to create shared objects or archives, see your operating system documentation.

The COBOL system enables COBOL programmes to be included in shared libraries but only in certain environments. See your Release Notes for details on whether and how you can do this for your environment.

CREATING EXECUTABLES THAT ARE STATICALLY LINKED

You can create an executable application file that is statically linked using the -x flag together with the -B static or +B static flags on the cob command line. Full details on the -x, -B and +B flags are contained in the chapter Descriptions of cob Flags. The command line should have the following form:

```
cob -x filenames [-B static]
```

where filenames is a list of the files input to the cob command.This statically links all the application programmes and sub-programmes, as well as any required run-time system support routines from the COBOL system archive libraries, to create an executable file that has no dynamic links.

On environments where dynamic linking is not supported, static linking is the default and you should not specify the -B flag on the command line.

When creating a statically linked executable file, any programmes that are held in archives are only extracted and linked into your executable module if they are referenced by an object that has already been statically linked into the executable. The statement CALL data-name implies dynamic loading and so does any CALL statement with an ON EXCEPTION clause. By default, neither case causes any sub-programme to be linked at link time.

Only the CALL literal statement with no ON EXCEPTION clause, by default, causes the sub-programme named in literal to be linked at link time. The sub-programme named in literal must conform to any system linker rules for forming names and so cannot be a filename.

Default actions can generally be overridden by using the appropriate cob flag. Use the cob flag -d to specify dynamic loading for a named sub-programme so it does not get linked at link time. Use the -I cob flag to link the named sub-programme at link time. See the chapter Descriptions of cob Flags for a list and details of the available cob flags.

A fully linked executable is one that has no dynamic loading specified or implied. With no dynamic loading required at run time, the dynamic loader support module is not needed and is not included in the executable file. As a result, a fully linked executable file is slightly smaller and executes faster than an equivalent executable that is not fully linked.

If you are linking a large number of routines or large object modules, you should be aware of the following:

- If you are trying to link a large number of user routines to the run-time system, you can exceed the system linker limits. To overcome this, you can partially link modules with the system linker (ld -r) command. You can then link these partially linked modules to the run-time system in the usual way by specifying the -x cob flag.
- In some environments it might be necessary to increase the operating system parameter ulimit to enable linking of large object modules. This is necessary if your system linker cannot automatically override the ulimit on your machine. You should set ulimit to the size of the largest executable module you expect to produce.
- The programme name is used as the initial entry point name. On file systems that support long filenames, if the programme name is longer than the entry point name limit, then the programme name is truncated to this limit. Therefore, you are strongly recommended to keep the length of programme source filename below

the entry point name limit. See also the chapter System Limits and Programming Restrictions.

CREATING AN EXECUTABLE RTS

An executable RTS is an executable file that requires the first entry point to be be specified at run-time.

You can use cob to create an executable RTS using the cob command, for example:

```
cob -xo rts.new
```

You might also need to specify the -I symb flag for any additional support you require for your RTS. For example, you need to include -I COBWIN2 in the cob command if you want to create a new RTS that includes windowing support.

You can also create an executable RTS using the mkrts script file (supplied in $COBDIR/src/rts). If you use mkrts, your executable RTS will contain the same level of functionality as the default run-time system ($COBDIR/rts32).

For example, the command:

```
sh $COBDIR/src/rts/mkrts subprogs.c
```

creates an executable RTS, called rts32, that is equivalent to the default rts32 but which also includes the C subroutines held in the file subprogs.c.

CREATING EXECUTABLES THAT USE THE DYNAMIC LOADER

Any executable that is not fully linked potentially provides dynamic loading. See the section Creating Executables That are Statically Linked earlier in this chapter for a description of a fully linked executable. In most cases, the decision on whether the dynamic loader is required is automatic and depends on the form of the CALL statements used in the programme.

The dynamic loader can also be selected by cob flags used to build an executable with:

- Explicit dynamic loading requested for a named programme
- Implicit dynamic loading for run-time selection of entry point.

Specifying the cob option -d symb causes the executable to be built so if the programme named symb is called at run time, it is loaded dynamically; cob gives an error if the programme is presented to cob for static linking.

Specifying the cob option -e "" causes the executable to be built so the executable file entry point must be specified at run time. You specify the entry point at run time by including the name of the entry point on the command line. The dynamic loader is used to locate the named programme, first checking if the programme is dynamically or statically linked and, if not, trying to load the programme dynamically.

Full details on the -d and -e flags are contained in the chapter Descriptions of cob Flags.

The statement call data-name and any call statement that includes an ON EXCEPTION clause implies use of the dynamic loader. However, you might not want dynamic loading, for example if the sub-programme to be called is a C routine. If the sub-programme is called using the dynamic loader, then if the sub-programme is dynamically or statically linked in the executable file, the linked version is used and no attempt is made at run time to dynamically load it.

If you do not want a sub-programme to be dynamically loaded you can ensure that it is linked in one of two ways:

- Use the -I *symb* cob option where symb is the name of the sub-programme. For example:

  ```
  cob -x -llib prog.cbl -I rtnl -I rtn2
  ```

- Use a call literal with no ON EXCEPTION clause in one of the programmes linked in the executable file. For example, create a dummy COBOL source file of the following form containing calls to the modules:

```
procedure division.
 call "rtnl".
 call "rtn2".
  ...
 call "rtnn".
```

Then link this dummy file with the remaining modules, as follows:

```
cob -x -llib prog.cbl dummy.cbl
```

If the number of routines that you want to link is small, the -I option is ideal; if the number of routines is large, the creation of a dummy COBOL sub-programme is a more convenient method.

In the two examples above, the routines rtn1, rtn2...,rtn*n* are assumed to be included in the library lib. An archive library can also be specified directly as an input file, but the routines still need to be selected for linking in the same way.

Creating Dynamically Loadable Files

You can create a dynamically loadable file as either intermediate (.int) code or as generated (.gnt) code files from any COBOL source file. You cannot create a dynamically loadable file for non-COBOL programmes. Generated code files are machine code files that are tailored for a particular processor. They run much faster than the equivalent intermediate code file but are not portable between processors.

The cob command creates.int files by default, for example:

```
cob filenames
```

You can create.gnt files by using the -u flag, as follows:

```
cob -u filenames
```

Where *filenames* is list of the COBOL files input to the cob command.

To run dynamically loadable files, they must be called by an executable RTS or application. A convenient way is to use the cobrun command (see the chapter Running for details).

On file systems that support long filenames, filenames for programmes that are to be dynamically loadable must be unique in the first 30 characters. This is because filenames longer than the entry point name limit are truncated to that limit when statically linked or dynamically loaded. Therefore, you are recommended to keep programme source filenames below 30 characters long. See also the chapter System Limits and Programming Restrictions in your Programmer's Guide to Writing Programmes.

Examples

The following example illustrates the use of the -d cob

option to build an executable file that has the main programme prog statically linked and dynamically loads the sub-programsubprog at run time:

```
cob -x prog.cbl -d subprog
```

A typical command line for creating a dynamically loadable file for subprog as high performance machine code is:

```
cob -u subprog.cbl
```

At run time, the programme prog can be run by invoking the executable file:

```
prog
```

The dynamic loader loads the sub-programme when it is called. If the sub-programme cannot be found and loaded, then if an ON EXCEPTION clause for the CALL exists it is executed, otherwise the run-time system gives an error.

Note: To run an executable file by just giving its filename on the command line, the file must be held in a directory that appears in your PATH environment variable. Alternatively you can specify the full pathname, which for the above example would be./prog.

The following example illustrates how to build an executable RTS and statically link in the selection of C subroutines that are held in the file subprogs.c (see the section Creating an Executable *RTS* for further details). The cob option -e "" specifies that the entry point, or the main programme is given at run time and the -ooption specifies the name of the executable file as myrts.

The command line to build the executable file is:

```
cob -xe "" subprogs.c -o myrts
```

At run time, the dynamically loadable programme prog can be run with the following command line

```
myrts prog
```

The following example illustrates how to build an executable file that contains two programmes such that the programme to be run is selected at run time. If neither programme calls any sub-routines and the -e "" option is not used, the executable file is fully linked.

A typical command line to build the executable is:

```
cob -xe "" prog1.cbl prog2.cbl -o runprog
```

This creates an executable file runprog that has both programmes statically linked in. To run the first programme, enter the command line:

```
runprog prog1
```

And in order to run the second programme, enter the command line:

```
runprog prog2
```

AIX DYNAMIC LINKING AND SHARED LIBRARIES

This section is specific to IBM AIX systems, and describes how to create applications that use dynamic linking and shared libraries.

THE LIBPATH ENVIRONMENT VARIABLE

LIBPATH specifies where to look for shared libraries. This variable should be set to (or should include) $COBDIR/coblib. *For example:*

```
LIBPATH=$LIBPATH:$COBDIR/coblib
export LIBPATH
```

For more information on LIBPATH, see the appendix *Micro Focus Environment Variables.*

MIXED LANGUAGE PROGRAMMING

If your programme runs a mixture of non-COBOL and COBOL code and the main programme is not written in COBOL.

You must call the routine cobinit() from your non-COBOL code before you call your COBOL code. cobinit() should be called with no parameters. The call to cobinit() is required to initialize the COBOL environment. If cobinit() is not called, you will receive an initialization error when you enter your COBOL code.

COB FLAGS

You use the following cob flags to create dynamically linked programmes and shared libraries. For a full description of the cob flags see the chapter Descriptions of cob Flags in your Object COBOL User Guide.

Select System Linker's Binding Mode (–B static | dynamic)

Selects the file binding mode. Valid options are static for the production of a fully statically linked executable, and dynamic for production of an executable which uses dynamic linking. The default is dynamic.

The static binding mode applies to all libraries to which the application binds. It is not possible to set the binding mode for specific libraries. Specifying -B static creates a statically linked RTS by binding to a private copy of all libraries to which it binds. Specifying -B dynamic creates a dynamically linked RTS which takes advantage of any shared libraries.

Note: For AIX the +B flag has the same behavior and functionality as the -B flag.

Dynamically Load Symbol (-d *symb*)

In a dynamic linked executable, this option does not work on modules which are already linked into the run time system shared objects. To use this option on symbols already defined in the run time you need to build a statically linked executable by also specifying the "-B static" cob option.

Exclude Symbol from the Executable Output File (X symb)

In a dynamic linked executable this option will not work on modules which are already linked in to the run time system shared objects. To use this option on symbols already defined in the run time, you need to build a statically linked executable by also specifying the -B static cob option.

BUILDING USER COBOL SHARED LIBRARIES

COBOL object modules can be generated using the cob -xc flag. You can link COBOL object modules to shared objects using the system link editor (ld). See your AIX System Reference manuals for details on linking AIX shared objects.

Example: This example shows the commands required to create an AIX shared object from two COBOL programmes user.cbl and user1.cbl.

Refer to your AIX system documentation for more details on creating and using AIX shared objects.

- Generate the object files user.o and user1.o:
  ```
  cob -xc user.cbl user1.cbl
  ```
- Archive the objects into a temporary archive library:
  ```
  ar qv scratch.a user.o user1.o
  ```
- Create the shared object shr.o with the -bM:SRE option:
  ```
  ld -D0 -H512 -T512 -o shr.o scratch.a -
  bM:SRE -bE:shr.exp
  -L$COBDIR/coblib -lcobol.1.0 -lcrtn.1.0-lc
  ```
  The -bE:shr.exp option is used to export any external symbols specified in the shr.exp export file. The -L option is used to specify the library search path and the -l option to include any libraries needed to resolve all external references.
- Archive the shared object shr.o into the user library libuser.a:
  ```
  ar rv libuser.a shr.o
  ```

5

System Interface

INTRODUCTION

The cob command enables you to handle all the phases involved in the production of an executable programme by providing the interface between your COBOL source programme and the following COBOL system components:

- *The Compiler*: To syntax check and compile your COBOL source files into intermediate code files, and to generate the intermediate code files into generated code files or object code files
- *The system Linker*: To link object code with the COBOL libraries

It also provides an interface to cc (the C compiler) and as (the assembler).

USING COB

The cob command causes the named files to be processed with the aim of producing modules that can be linked or run.

There are three basic types of executable COBOL programme; the cob command provides a straightforward means of creating a mixture of any of these types of programme.

The executable files types are:

- Intermediate code files
- Generated code files
- System executable files

Intermediate code files (.int files) and generated code files (.gnt files) are dynamically loadable, and do not have to be linked to be executed. System executable files are files created from object code files by the Linker.

System executable files can be:

- *Dynamically linked*: For example, a standard UNIX System V Release 4 ELF executable object module that uses shared object files (.so files) (available only if your system supports dynamic linking)
- *Statically linked:* For example, a standard UNIX system executable object module

The type of file output by cob depends on the type of file you input to it and the options you specify to the cob command.

The file types recognized by cob are identified by their extensions as follows:

Extension	File Type
.cbl or.CBL or.cob	COBOL source file
.int	COBOL intermediate code file
.gnt	Dynamically loadable generated code file
.s	Assembler source file
.c	C source file
.a	Archive of object module files
.so	Shared object module file
.o	Object module file

Cob assumes that any unrecognized options are either input files or valid linker options to be saved and used at link time. In this way, any archive files you supply to the cob command are passed to the linker, which pulls out only the referenced files from the archive. You can use COBOL source files with extensions other than those listed above. To do so, you must specify the -k cob flag to identify them to cob (see the chapter Descriptions of cob Flags for details) or use the Cobextn facility.

INVOKING THE COB COMMAND

To invoke the cob command, enter the following at the UNIX system prompt:

```
cob [options|file-name]...
```

Where the parameters are:

Options	Either one cob option or a group of cob options comprising one or more cob flags. See the section Specifying cob Options for details on the format of cob options.
File-name	The name of an input file. These files can be any mixture of COBOL source code (.cbl.CBL or.cob), intermediate code (.int), linkable object code (.o or.so), C source (.c), Assembler source (.s), or archive (.a) files. On some sytems, cob rejects any filenames that contain more than one period (.). If you try to specify multiple periods in a file-name, you receive the following error: cob: "." is not a valid character in file-name stem

SPECIFYING COB OPTIONS

A cob option takes the form:

`flag-intro flag-letter [parameter]`

A group of cob options is equivalent to a separate option for each *flag-letter* with all options having the same *intro*. The *parameter*, if present, only apply to the last option.

It takes the form:

`flag-intro flag-letter[flag-letter]... [parameter]`

Where the parameters are:

Flag-intro	The hyphen (-) or the plus (+) character
Flag-letter	A letter (or occasionally letters) selected from those listed in the section *cob Flags* later in this chapter, that flags the required option.
Parameter	An optional string of characters that details exactly how the flagged option is to behave. The parameter cannot contain a space or tab character unless that character is contained in single (') or double (") quotation marks.

There must be no spaces between *flag-intro* and flag-letter or between two adjacent flag-letters but there can be one space between the last flag-letter and theparameter if it is present. (For example -xve "" in which "" represents a null parameter). The flag-intro must always be preceded by a space character.

Option Configuration

You can specify cob options in a number of ways, and the method used determines the order in which cob processes them. The cob command processes options from left to right for each method of specifying them. If an option appears more than once, cob uses the setting that it processed last for that option.

At startup, the cob command searches for options in the following sequence of locations:

- System default options in the file $COBDIR/cobopt
- User default options in the environment variable COBOPT
- Execution-time options on the cob command line

You might need to set options as a system or user default and then to unset them again in specific instances. By specifying a hyphen after the flag letter with no intervening space, you can unset the following options: -F, -c, -P and -U.

Options specified on the cob command line pass through the UNIX shell that carries out special processing on certain characters such as space, asterisk (*), parentheses (), single (') and double (") quotation marks before passing them to cob. If you need to pass these characters unchanged as part of an option, you must escape the shell processing. Under the UNIX shell this can be done by preceding the character with a backslash (\) or enclosing it in a pair of single or double quotation marks (see your UNIX system documentation for details of shell processing).

However, for your convenience cob enables you to use the syntax mode=setting in place of either "mode(setting)" or *mode\(setting\)* so enabling you to avoid these characters. The cob command converts any syntax using the equals sign (=) into the form "mode(*setting*)". To pass an actual equals sign (=) to the COBOL components, you must use two equals signs together (==).

The cob command treats the special characters single and double quotation marks in exactly the same way when used in an option, regardless of whether the option was specified on the command line or in one of the other locations. A parameter enclosed in a pair of quotation marks must not exceed 128 characters.

Example

Assuming the following line in $COBDIR/cobopt:

```
-U -P -C "ans85 noalter warning=1"
```

Specifying the cob command line:

```
cob -xU -C alter -C warning=2 prog.cbl
```

or the exact equivalent:

```
cob -xU -C "alter warning=2" prog.cbl
```

passes the COBOL source file prog.cbl to the Compiler with the final directive settings of ANS85 ALTER LIST(prog.lst) WARNING(2). An executable programme prog is built, with any unresolved symbcls not being dynamically loaded at run time but flagged as missing at link time.

The $COBDIR/Cobopt File

System-wide default options are defined in the file $COBDIR/cobopt. This is the file the cob command reads when first invoked.

Each line of this text file should correspond to one of the following formats:

```
[set environment-variable=value]
[options]...
[cobextn:.ext [.ext]...]
```

Where the parameters are:

Environment-variable	Any one of the environment variables supported by the COBOL System (see the appendix *Micro Focus Environment Variables* for details).
Value	The value to which you want to set the specified environment variable.
Options	Either one cob option or a group of cob options comprising one or more cob flags. See the start of

	section *Specifying cob Options* for details on the format of cob options.
.ext	A file-name extension that, in addition to the standard ones of.cob.cbl, or.CBL, denotes a file that cob should treat as a COBOL source file. The extension must begin with a period, and if more than one is specified on one line they must be separated by a space or tab character. You can use more than one cobextn line.

If a line does not begin with one of the identifiers set or cobextn:, it is taken as an options line.The contents of the file $COBDIR/cobopt affects the operation of COBOL for all users using the same $COBDIR; you should alter the file only after careful consideration of the implications.

Example

Assuming the following two lines in $COBDIR/cobopt:

```
cobextn:.AD.FD
-N "nobound" -C ans85
```

Specifying the cob command line:

```
cob -u a.FD b.AD
```

passes the COBOL source files a.FD and b.AD to the syntax-check phase of the Compiler to be translated, under the ANS85 directive, into intermediate code. The intermediate code is then passed in turn to the Compiler's generate phase to be translated, under the NOBOUND directive, into generated code.

The COBOPT Environment Variable

User default options are defined using the COBOPT environment variable. COBOPT can either contain options that supplement or override the system default options defined in $COBDIR/cobopt, or it can specify the path of a file that contains such options.

The options can extend over more than one line and each line must have the same format as described for the file $COBDIR/cobopt (*see the section* The $COBDIR/cobopt File*)*. The COBOPT environment variable can be set to a value that includes several lines by enclosing the entire value in single (') or double (") quotation marks that tells the UNIX shell to process each line as part of the one value. Under the Bourne shell, the Enter key can be typed to indicate the line-break. However, other types of shell might need a different way of showing the line-break. If you want to include a double quotation mark in the value, then remember to escape shell processing, for example by preceding it with a backslash (\) character.

UNIX system documentation for details of setting environment variables and shell processing.

You can include any valid cob command line in the COBOPT environment variable. If the line includes the -v cob flag, the whole line is echoed to the screen when it is passed to cob (see the chapter Descriptions of cob Flags for details on -v).

Examples

Specifying COBOPT as follows:

```
COBOPT="set COBCPY=/usr/lib/cblcpy:$COBDIR/
srclib:$HOME/mylib::
-N nobound -C \"ans85 noalter list\"
cobextn:.AD.FD"
export COBOPT
```

Causes cob to set the environment variable COBCPY for the duration of the cob command, it passes the directives ANS85 NOALTER LIST to the Compiler's syntax-check phase and passes the directive NOBOUND to the Compiler's generate phase. Note that $COBDIR and $HOME get expanded by the shell if the double quotation marks are used but not if single quotation marks are used.

Specifying COBOPT as follows:

```
COBOPT='-C "copyext=CPY,cpy nooptional-file" -N
"nobound"'
```

Causes cob to pass the directives COPYEXT(CPY,cpy) and NOOPTIONAL-FILE to the Compiler's syntax-check phase and the NOBOUND directive to the Compiler's generate phase.

The cob Command Line

Execution-time options (that is when cob executes, not when the application runs) are specified on the cob command line as described in the section Invoking the cob Command. Options given on the cob command line supplement or override any already specified in the $COBDIR/cobopt file or COBOPT environment variable.

You can specify on the command line any cob options listed in the section cob Flags later in this chapter and described in more detail in the chapter Descriptions of cob Flags.

Example

Assuming neither $COBDIR/cobopt nor $COBOPT exist, specifying the following on the cob command line:

```
cob -xve "" -o my_rts -C xopen prog.cbl prog2.c
```

Passes the XOPEN directive to the Compiler and instructs cob to compile the COBOL source file prog.cbl and the C source file prog2.c and to link the result into an executable file named my_rts that, when run, expects the name of the programme to run to be given on its own command line. The cob utility also gives verbose notification of its progress.

COB FILE PROCESSING

While creating an executable module, the cob command passes each input programme through a series of steps, each of which transforms the programme from one file type into another file type. Thus, an output file from one step can serve as an input file for a subsequent step.

These types are characterized by the file extensions as follows:

Input File Extension	Cob Processing	Output File Extension
.cbl, .CBL, .cob	Compile COBOL source code file into intermediate code file	.int
.int	Code generate for dynamic loading	.gnt
	Code generate for static linking	.o

.s	Pass to system assembler	.o
.c	Pass C source text file to C Compiler	.o
.a, .so, .o	Pass to system linker (ld)	No extension (also known as an a.out file)

By default, cob processing ends when all COBOL source files have been compiled for animation; that is, a dynamically loadable intermediate code file (with extension.int) and an Animator file (with extension.idy) have been created. Other end points can be specified by using cob options (see the section cob Flags later in this chapter).

If any of the input files are beyond the desired end point, cob statically links them with the dynamic loader. This produces an executable run time system, that can be used to load and run any dynamically loadable files.Any temporary files produced at any of the intermediate stages of processing are removed once used, with the exception of any.int and.o files, that are left in the same directory as their input file.

A dynamically linked, statically linked or dynamically loadable COBOL programme, can access (using the COBOL CALL verb) any other statically linked module in the same statically linked COBOL module or any other dynamically loadable module. Assembler, C, or any other language modules must conform to the C calling conventions and must be statically linked into the COBOL executable. For details on creating these types of modules, see the chapter Linking.

On file systems that support long filenames, you are recommended to keep the length of programme source filenames below the entry point name limit. See the chapter Linking for further details.

ACCESSING THE COBOL SYSTEM COMPONENTS

To access COBOL system components, the cob command must know where they are located. They must all be located in a directory in which a COBOL system has been installed and the directory is represented in this chapter as $COBDIR. The cob command assumes a default $COBDIR directory of/

opt/lib/cobol on UNIX System V Release 4, or/usr/lib/cobol otherwise. If your COBOL system has been installed here then you do not need to specify the COBDIR environment variable.

If you put the Micro Focus COBOL system software elsewhere, then you must set the COBDIR environment variable to tell cob in which directory to search for the system components. You can choose to install different versions of the COBOL system on your machine, in which case you select which one to use by simply setting its location in COBDIR. For example:

```
COBDIR=/usr/cob41u1
export COBDIR
```

Specifies that the system components are located in the directory/usr/cob41u1. If the cob command is not on the UNIX search path then you must change the value of PATH. For example:

```
PATH=$PATH:/usr/mfcobol/utils
export PATH
```

where/usr/mfcobol/utils is the directory where you installed the driver utilities.

On platforms that support dynamic linking, you should ensure that LD_LIBRARY_PATH (on UNIX SVR4-based systems), LIBPATH (on AIX), or SHLIB_PATH (on HP/UX systems) is set to $COBDIR/coblib.

By default, files output by the cob command are put in the current directory. By default, any temporary files created are put in the system temporary directory; however, you can put them elsewhere by setting the TMPDIR environment variable and specifying a valid path-name. See the appendix Micro Focus Environment Variables for details on using TMPDIR.

COB FLAGS

The following flags can be used with the cob command to specify any action the system components should take while creating an executable module and to determine the type of file output. For full details on the effect of these flags, see the chapter *Descriptions of cob Flags*.

Cob Flag	Function
-A *as_option*	Pass *as_option* to assembler (as)
-a	Compile for animation. This is the default
-B *mode[=lib]*	Select the system linker binding mode
+B *mode[=lib]*	Select the system linker binding mode and pass to system linker after COBOL libraries
-b *format*	Specify the object module format of any object produced (SCO Open Desktop 5 only).
-C *directive*	Pass syntax-check phase *directive* to the Compiler
-CC *cc_option*	Pass *cc_option* to C compiler (cc)
-c	Compile no further than statically linkable object module (.o)
-d *symb*	Dynamically load *symb*
-e *epsym*	Set initial entry point
-F	Create an RTS quickly
+F *symb*	Create an RTS quickly and add *symb* to a linked data table. (Not available on Linux)
-f	Reserved for future use by Micro Focus
-G	Generate for animation
-g	Create information for symbolic debugger
-I *symb*	Include *symb* in executable file
-i	Compile to.int code for unlinked environment
-k *cobol-file*	Recognize COBOL source file with non-standard file-name extension
-L *dir*	Pass option to system linker, changing search algorithm and maintaining relative ordering
+L *dir*	Pass option to system linker after all other options, changing search algorithm
-l *lib*	Pass option to system linker, maintaining relative ordering
+l *lib*	Pass option to system linker after all other options
-m *symb=newsym*	Map text *symb* onto *newsym*
-N *directive*	Pass generate phase *directive* to the Compiler
-O	Enable optimization
-o *file-name*	Specify output file-name
-P	Produce COBOL compilation listing file
-p	Pass flag to C compiler to use profiling routines. (Not available on Linux)

-Q *ld_option* or	Pass *ld_option* to system linker (ld) -Q,1 *ld_option* or -Q,2 *ld_option*
-q	Reserved for future use by Micro Focus
-U	Dynamically load unresolved symbols. (Not available on Linux)
-u	Compile to.gnt code for unlinked environment.
-V	Report version number
-v	Set verbose mode
-W *err-level*	Control error level for cob termination
-X *symb*	Exclude text *symb* from the executable output file
-x	Process to statically or dynamically linked executable module
-z	Reserved for future use by Micro Focus

Any options that are not recognized are passed to the system linker (ld). However, you are encouraged to use the -Q flag to explicitly pass options to the linker. Any linker flags that take parameters must be passed using the -Q flag. cob flags -c, -F, -P and -U are binary global options (that is, they select features that can potentially affect several of the input files).

Any of these options can be turned off once selected by appending a hyphen (–) to the option letter. This enables any global binary options selected in the system $COBDIR/cobopt file to be overridden.

Command Line Examples

These examples show several uses of the cob command to compile, code generate and link programmes:

- To compile the programme in pi.cbl into a file called pi.int suitable for animation, specify:
  ```
  cob pi.cbl
  ```
  As this is the default case, the -a flag does not need to be specified.
- To compile, code generate and then link the COBOL source file pi.cbl to the run-time support libraries to form a statically linked a.out file named pi, enter:
  ```
  cob -x pi.cbl
  ```

On systems that support dynamic linking, you also need to specify -B static to produce a static linked executable. Otherwise, a dynamically linked executable is produced by default. See the chapter *Linking*.

- To compile the COBOL source file pi.cbl for the unlinked environment to produce an intermediate code file, pi.int, enter:

  ```
  cob -i pi.cbl
  ```

  This differs from the default case, shown in the first example, because an end-point has been specified. In this case pi.int is not suitable for animation.
- To compile and code generate the programme in pi.cbl into a dynamically loadable native code file called pi.gnt, enter:

  ```
  cob -u pi.cbl
  ```

- To compile, code generate and link the programme contained in pi.cbl to form a dynamically linked or a statically linked executable file named pi, enter:

  ```
  cob -x -e "" pi.cbl
  ```

  Specifying the -e flag with a null parameter (that is, "") ensures that the entry point is read from the command line at run time. In effect, pi is linked to a full RTS as a callable subprogram, so to invoke pi you would use the command:

  ```
  pi pi
  ```

- To build just a run-time system than can dynamically run any.int or.gnt files, enter:

  ```
  cob -xo newrts
  ```

- To build a run-time system that has linked in C routines, enter:

  ```
  cob -o newrts routines.c
  ```

- To build a run-time system that supports windowing syntax, enter:

  ```
  cob -xI COBWIN2 -o newrts
  ```

See your Programmer's Guide to User Interfaces for full details on windowing syntax. For details on how to execute the files produced using the cob command, see the chapter

Running. See also the chapters Compiling, Generating and Linking for additional details.

INTERFACE TO COMPILER

The cob command is used to interface to the COBOL compilation system. Compiler directives can be specified in a variety of ways, including via cob and via the programme source files. The following sections describe all the ways that compiler directives can be specified.

Programme Source Conventions

The Micro Focus COBOL Compiler accepts source from a standard UNIX text file (as created by a UNIX editor such as vi). The format of this is the same as for standard COBOL, described in your Language Reference. Each line of your COBOL source programmes, including the last line, must be terminated by a new line character. Your COBOL source programmes must not contain any control characters except the tab character, unless they are embedded in literal strings. Tab is expanded with spaces to the next character position that is a multiple of eight.

Specifying Compiler Directives

You can specify compiler directives in a number of ways, and the method used determines the order in which the compiler processes them. The Compiler processes directives from left to right for each method of specifying them. If a directive appears more than once, the Compiler uses the setting that it processed last for that directive.

The compiler searches for directives in the following sequence of locations:

1. COBOL system default directives in the file cobol.dir
2. System default directives contained in cob options in the file $COBDIR/cobopt
3. User default directives contained in cob options in the environment variable COBOPT
4. Compile-time directives contained in cob options on the cob command line

5. Programme-specific directives in the initial $SET statements in the source code file of each programme

These methods are listed in the order in which the compiler processes directives for each COBOL source file. This order of precedence means that a directive set on the command line would override another setting for that directive set in cobol.dir. For example, specifying the NOANS85 Compiler directive on the command line overrides ANS85 in cobol.dir.

You can further customise the Compiler's behavior by creating your own directives file; that is, an ASCII text file in which is defined an entire set of directives to be passed to the Compiler at one time. You can use either the DIRECTIVES or USE directive to pass this user directives file to the Compiler. You can determine the precedence for processing your directives file by specifying the DIRECTIVES or USE directive by any of the methods described above. See the section The DIRECTIVES *and* USE Directives later in the chapter.

Parameters to directives given in a $SET statement are converted to upper case; parameters to directives given on the cob command line or in a directives file retain their case.The methods of specifying cob options and of specifying compiler directives in cob options are given earlier in the section *Invoking the cob Command*. The additional methods of specifying Compiler directives are described in the following sections.

The cobol.dir Directives File

Cobol.dir is a directives file that is processed automatically by the Compiler, as if the directive:

```
directives"cobol.dir"
```

were encountered by the compiler as the very first directive after startup. Consequently, Compiler directives contained in cobol.dir override the defaults built into the Compiler but can be overridden in turn by directives specified in the ways listed above. Generate phase directives cannot be specified in the cobol.dir directives file. The Compiler looks for a cobol.dir file first in the current directory. If it finds one there, it uses it. Otherwise, it looks in the COBOL system directory $COBDIR.

If the Compiler rejects a directive contained in the cobol.dir file, compilation continues. However, if the Compiler rejects directives from either the command line or a directives file specified on the command line, compilation terminates. Therefore, if you create or change a cobol.dir file, you should do a trial compilation and watch for "rejected" messages at the beginning when the directives are being processed. If any occur, correct the cobol.dir file and retry until no errors are reported.

The $SET Statement

Many Compiler directives can be specified in the programme source code in $ SET statements. Compiler directives specified in this way supplement or override options specified in $COBDIR/cobopt or in COBOPT. Generate phase directives cannot be specified using $SET statements.

You specify the $SET statement in the following format with the $ character in column 7:

```
$SET directive["parameter"]...
```

Where the parameters are:

Directive	One of the Compiler directives described in the chapter *Directives for Compiler* whose phase is identified as "syntax check". It cannot be a generate phase directive (that is, one whose phase is identified as "generate").
Parameter	A qualifier to *directive.* It must appear in one of the following forms: *"parameter"* or *(parameter)* You cannot precede a parameter with an equals sign (=) in a $SET statement. *parameter* can contain spaces if enclosed in quotation marks (""), but not if enclosed in parentheses ().
...	Indicates that further Compiler directives can be specified following the same format.

The $ character must be in column 7; if it is not, the Compiler does not recognize it and can produce spurious errors. The same is true for any character at the start of a source file that the Compiler does not recognize. Additionally, the $SET statement must not be terminated with a period (.).

If more than one directive is specified they must be separated by spaces. A $SET statement cannot be continued onto a new line, but it can be followed by additional$SET statements.

You can specify any number of $SET statements in your source code, and these can appear anywhere in the code. If you want to specify a dialect-controlling Compiler option, for example ANS85, this must be an "initial" $SET statement; that is, one that is not preceded in the source file by any source statements except other $SET statements. Once you have set a dialect-controlling option at the beginning of your source code, you cannot unset it later in the programme. When a directive is specified on a $SET other than an initial $SET, it affects compilation from the point the $SET is encountered onwards.

The chapter Directives for Compiler indicates that Compiler directives are allowed on $SET statements, distinguishing those only allowed on initial $SET statements.

Examples

Both of the following examples have the same effect; they cause the Compiler to assume all file assignments to data names are resolved externally and to flag features in your programme that are not in the ANSI'85 dialect of the COBOL language:

```
$SET assign(external) flag(ans85)
$SET assign "external" flag"ans85"
```

The DIRECTIVES and USE Directives

The DIRECTIVES and USE Compiler directives enable you to pass to the Compiler a user file containing a predefined set of directives. You can specify the DIRECTIVES or USE directive on the command line, in a $SET statement, in the cobol.dir file or in the $COBDIR/cobopt file. Generate phase directives cannot be specified using DIRECTIVES or USE directives. The format for these directives is:

directives "file-name"

or

use "file-name"

where file-name is the name of the user file containing the set of directives you want to pass to the Compiler. It can be any valid file-name except cobol.dir or$COBDIR/cobopt.

A directives file is a standard ASCII text file containing any number of lines. Each line can contain one or more directives or comments. Directives in the directives file must be separated by a space and cannot be broken across two lines. Comment lines are indicated by an ampersand character (&) in column 1.

The Compiler reads the directives from the file until the end of file (EOF) is reached or another DIRECTIVES or USE Compiler directive is encountered.

If you specify the DIRECTIVES directive in another directives file, the Compiler switches to the new directives file for processing and then returns to the original directives file. When the Compiler completes processing the directives file, it then processes subsequent directives on the command line or in $SET statements.

Directives in a directives file are processed as if they were coded in place of the DIRECTIVES directive. Consequently, restrictions applying to any directive at that time also apply to all the directives in a directives file read at that time. See also the chapter Directives for Compile

DESCRIPTIONS OF COB FLAGS

Describes the flags that can be used with the cob command to specify any action the system components should take to determine the type of file output. As noted in the chapter *COBOL* System Interface (cob), the type of module output (for example.int.gnt and.o as well as executable modules) depends upon the type of file input and the options specified to the cob command. cob output files by default are placed in the source directory; if you want to put executable files created using cob in another directory, you can specify the -o flag (see the description later in this chapter).

The descriptions of flags appear alphabetically, with upper-case flags listed before lower-case flags. Each entry shows the function, flag and setting and any options required.

PASS OPTION TO ASSEMBLER (-A AS_OPTION)

Passes the specified option to the UNIX system assembler (as).

COMPILE FOR ANIMATION (-A)

Compiles the COBOL source files (with extension.cbl.CBL or.cob) input to the cob command into an intermediate code file (with the extension.int) and Animator files (with extension.idy), both of which are used by Animator (see the chapter Animator, in your Object COBOL Character Tools for details on using Animator.)

Any object module files (with extension.o), C source files, or assembler source files input to the cob command are linked with the COBOL libraries to form a single executable file, which also can be used by Animator. This enables you to animate programmes that call, or are called by, programmes that are written in languages other than COBOL.

The -a flag does not specify an end point for cob processing, only the type of intermediate code file produced by the COBOL Compiler.

Because this is the default action for the cob command, you do not actually have to specify the -a flag on the cob command line. However, you might find it useful to do so for clarity in your coding.

For example, if you use the command:

```
cob -a myfile.cbl c.o
```

The files myfile.int, myfile.idy and c are created. The file c contains the run-time system and the file c.o. The command:

```
cob myfile.cbl c.o
```

has the same effect. To animate myfile.int, use the commands:

```
COBSW=+A
export COBSW
c myfile.int
```

SELECT SYSTEM LINKER'S BINDING MODE (-B MODE[=LIB])

Selects the file binding mode used by the system linker and passes the -B*mode* option to the linker command line. Valid options are static for production of a fully statically linked executable, and dynamic for production of an executable which uses dynamic linking. The default is dynamic.

The -B flag is supported only on UNIX operating systems that support dynamic linking. If your operating system does support it (that is, the librarylibcobol.so exists in $COBDIR/coblib), see your operating system manual for more details on static and dynamic linking.

-B *mode* is added to the linker command line before the COBOL libraries. Any user-defined libraries specified with the -l flag inherit the current binding mode. If more than one -B flag is used, the binding mode for any subsequent user-defined libraries are set, but the user-defined libraries already defined are unaffected. The last -B flag sets the binding mode for the COBOL libraries.

If the binding mode is dynamic, then the shared object (.so) version of the library, if it exists, it is used. Otherwise, the archive (.a) version of the library is used. If the binding mode is static, then the choice of archive (.a) is forced, even if a shared object (.so) version also exists.

For example, entering the following on the cob command line:

```
cob -x prog.cbl -B static -lxyz -B dynamic
```

Specifies that the.a version of libxyz is to be used, but all other libraries (for example, the COBOL library libcobol, or the operating system library libc) are to use the.so version (where available).

Using the optional syntax =*lib* sets *mode* for the specified library only, where *lib* is any library that appears on the linker line, whether it is from the command line or a COBOL library defined in the file $COBDIR/coblib/liblist or as specified in the environment variable LIBLIST. If *mode* is dynamic and no.so version of the library specified exists, then the.a version (if one exists) is used.

When specifying libraries in this way, you should be aware of the following:

- A library specified more than once on the linker line has the same binding mode on each occasion.
- If *lib* is specified with both binding modes, then the last mode defined on the command line is used.

For example, entering the following on the cob command line:

```
cob -x prog.cbl -B dynamic -B static=screen
```

specifies that all the libraries are to be dynamic, except the COBOL library libscreen, which is to be statically linked. Thus, the shared object (.so) versions of libraries are chosen over corresponding archive (.a) versions, except library libscreen, where the archive version is chosen even if there is a shared object version.

SELECT SYSTEM LINKER'S BINDING MODE AND PASS TO SYSTEM LINKER AFTER COBOL LIBRARIES (+B MODE[=LIB])

Has the same effect as -B except that relative ordering is not preserved. +B *mode* is converted to -B *mode* and is passed to the system linker after the COBOL libraries and before the system libraries (specified in liblist).

The +B flag is supported only on UNIX operating systems that support dynamic linking. If your operating system does support it (that is, the librarylibcobol.so exists in $COBDIR/coblib), see your operating system manual for more details on static and dynamic linking.

Because -B *mode* is added to the linker command line after the COBOL libraries and before the system libraries, it defines the binding mode of only the system libraries and any user-defined libraries specified with the +l flag.

Using the optional syntax *=lib* sets *mode* for the specified library only.

For example, entering the following cob command line:

```
cob -x prog.cbl -lxyz -B static +B dynamic +labc
+B static
```

Creates a statically linked RTS with the user-specified libraries dynamically linked. Note that the default mode, -B dynamic, is implied before the -lxyz. Hence, the.so version of libxyz and libabc (if they exist) are used, while the.a versions of the COBOL and system libraries are forced by the -Bstatic and +Bstatic flags respectively.

The same result also could be produced by entering the cob command line:

```
cob -x prog.cbl -lxyz -B static +labc +B dynamic=abc
```

Note that -B dynamic is again implied before -lxyz.

SPECIFY THE OBJECT MODULE FORMAT OF ANY OBJECT PRODUCED (-B *FORMAT*)

SCO OpenServer Release 5:

This flag is only supported on SCO OpenServer Release 5, and specifies the object module format of any object produced, regardless of the source language (that is, COBOL, C, or assembler). This option behaves exactly the same as the cc -b option.

Format can have the value:

- Coff
- Ibcs2
- Elf

ibcs2 is an alias for coff. The values for *format* can take any case.

PASS SYNTAX-CHECK PHASE DIRECTIVE TO THE COMPILER (-C DIRECTIVE)

Passes directive to the Compiler's syntax-check phase, where directive is one or more of the Compiler directives listed in the chapter Directives for Compiler.

PASS OPTION TO THE C COMPILER (-CC CC_OPTION)

Passes *cc_option* to the C compiler via cc. If you specify the -CC cob flag, you must ensure that the only options you enter are options used by the C compiler itself. This is because the system assumes that if you are using the cob command rather than cc to compile a C programme, you want to link the C programme to COBOL programmes before it is run. To do this, cob needs the.o file output by the C compiler once it has compiled the C programme. cob can then take the resulting.o file and link it with other object modules to create a COBOL executable file. Therefore, you should not try to use the -CC flag to pass options that the Compiler normally would try to pass to the system linker.

COMPILE NO FURTHER THAN STATICALLY LINKABLE OBJECT MODULE (-C)

Suppresses the link editing of any static linked executable, so the object modules can subsequently be statically linked. This option does not specify an end point and has an effect only if the specified end point would cause link editing; for example, if the -x cob flag had been specified.

DYNAMICALLY LOAD SYMBOL (-D SYMB)

Causes the symbol *symb* to be dynamically loaded if it is called. *symb* is any valid COBOL name. This option can be used when producing a static or dynamic linked executable file, to specify any missing modules that are to be loaded dynamically at run time. Thus, you can use this flag to allow certain run-time support modules to be loaded as necessary rather than to be permanently loaded. For example, if in your programme there are Adis operations, the Adis module by default is linked to your programme. If, however, you want Adis to be dynamically loaded, you should specify the symbol ADIS behind the -d flag on the cob command line (for details on the Adis module, see the chapter *Adis*).

SET INITIAL ENTRY POINT (-E EPSYM)

Overrides the default entry point symbol, using instead the symbol identified by *epsym*, which must already have been defined in a COBOL module. By default, the entry point address for a statically or dynamically linked module is the base-name of the first file input to the cob command. If you want the entry point address to be read from the command line at run-time, you can define the value of *epsym* as null, that is -e "".

CREATE AN RTS QUICKLY (-F)

Allows the fast creation of a statically or dynamically linked executable module with dynamic load support by making all the entry points and external data (from both COBOL and C modules) available to dynamically loaded programmes.

This is achieved by cob creating an entry for each entry point and all external data in a loaded table (ldtab), when it produces a statically linked executable module.

Entries are created in ldtab only for modules named on the command line and in a default list found in $COBDIR/coblib/cobfsym. Any symbols for objects in archive (.a) or shared object (.so) files are not included in ldtab, thus reducing the time taken to create a statically linked executable module. If a reference from a dynamically loaded module is made to any name that is not in ldtab (even if it is included in the linked executable), then you receive RTS error 173:

`Called programme file not found in drive/directory`

See the +F flag for details of how to add symbols to ldtab. Note that you cannot specify this flag if you set the -U flag.

CREATE AN RTS QUICKLY AND ADD LIST OF SYMBOLS TO A LINKED DATA TABLE (-F,FNAME)

Provides the same behavior as the -F flag, except that the default list is taken from *fname* rather than from$COBDIR/coblib/cobfsym. There must be no spaces in-F,*fname*.

CREATE AN RTS QUICKLY AND ADD SYMBOL TO A LINKED DATA TABLE (+F SYMB)

Enables the fast creation of a statically or dynamically linked executable module with dynamic load support, as with the -F flag, and adds the specified symbol to the loaded table (ldtab). Once *symb* has been added to ldtab, any call to a module of that name causes control to be passed to the function identified by *symb*.

At link time, the error "undefined symbol(s)" occurs if *symb* is not part of the static linked executable being produced. You cannot specify this flag if you set the -U flag.

Linux:
You cannot use this option on Linux.

GENERATE FOR ANIMATION (-F)

Generates the files input to the cob command into a.gnt file and Animator information files (with the file extension.gdy), both of which are used by Animator (see the chapter *Animator* in your *Object COBOL Character Tools*).

CREATE INFORMATION FOR SYMBOLIC DEBUGGER (-G)

Creates additional information needed for the use of a symbolic debugger such as sdb. With this flag set, no symbols are stripped from the output file. This flag is passed through to the C compiler if any.c files are being processed, so it is useful if your programme contains some C functions that you want to debug. It also passes the ANIM directive to the Compiler.

INCLUDE SYMBOL IN EXECUTABLE FILE (-I *SYMB*)

Marks symb for inclusion in the executable output file. When symb is pulled in by the system linker, the entire object, as well as any other objects that are referenced, is pulled in. For example, you need to include -I COBWIN2 in the cob command if you want to create a new RTS that includes windowing support.

The -I flag is particularly useful with a static RTS, as certain modules not referenced by default can be included if required. This flag is not necessary with dynamic linking as anything referenced at run time is included automatically.

The following list shows the symbols that are automatically included in a build of a new RTS:

Symbol	Module
ANIM	Animator
COBCOMMS	ANSI communications support
DYNLOAD	Dynamic loader
INTERPRET	COBOL interpreter for.int code
PROFILE	COBOL Profiler

SORT	Sort module
USERCALL	Usercall support

The following list shows the symbols that are not automatically included in a build of a new RTS but can be included using the -I flag.

Some are only applicable if you are using a relevant add-on product.

Symbol	Module
CCINAMPU	CCI modules for named pipe support
CCITCP	CCI modules for TCP support
CICS	Pointer conversion utilities for OS/VS COBOL
COBWIN2	Windowing support
DSRTNS	Dialog System RTS support
FHREDIR	Fhredir file handling redirector
fhutil	File handler
OOPS	OO RTS support
SESSION	Session handling

Note: You can create an executable RTS using the mkrts script. mkrts includes in an executable RTS all of the functionality of rts32 (the default run-time system). See *Creating a Run-time Executable* in the chapter *Linking* for deatils.

COMPILE TO INTERMEDIATE CODE FOR UNLINKED ENVIRONMENT (-I)

Compiles the COBOL source code (.cbl.CBL or.cob) files input to the cob command into dynamically loadable intermediate code files (with the file extension.int). These files can then be run without any further processing.

RECOGNIZE COBOL SOURCE FILE WITH NON-STANDARD FILE-NAME EXTENSIONS (-K COBOL-FILE)

Identifies to cob COBOL source files either with no extensions or with extensions other than the default extensions.cbl.CBL or.cob. This allows COBOL files without the recognized extension to be compiled without having to alter their filename.

PASS OPTION TO SYSTEM LINKER CHANGING SEARCH ALGORITHM AND MAINTAINING RELATIVE ORDERING (-L DIR)

Changes the order in which the system linker searches for libraries that were specified with the -l cob flag. -L options affect only those -l options that they precede on the cob command line.

The -L cob flag is effectively the same as the -L option for the system linker, ld (see your operating system documentation for further details on this linker option). By default, the directories/lib (or/usr/ccs/lib) and/usr/lib are searched first for these libraries. However, specifying the -L flag causes the system linker instead to search the specified directory first for such libraries. The order in which -L options are specified is significant as directories are searched in that order.

On systems that support dynamic linking, paths in the environment variable LD_LIBRARY_PATH, or LIBPATH (on AIX systems) or SHLIB_PATH (on HP/UX systems) are searched before -L, +L and the default paths.

Example

The following example illustrates the use of the +L and -L flags in determining the order in which directories are searched for libraries:

```
cob +L/usr/mylib +llib1 object.o -L/usr/grouplib
-llib2 +llib3
```

The relative ordering of the options passed to the system linker (assuming the complete search path for every library needed to be searched) would be:

- Object.o
- -L $LD_LIBRARY_PATH -llib2
- -L/usr/grouplib -llib2
- -L/lib (or/usr/ccs/lib) -llib2 -L/usr/lib -llib2
- -L $LD_LIBRARY_PATH -llib1
- -L/user/grouplib -llib1 -L/usr/mylib -llib1
- -L/lib -llib1 -L/usr/lib -llib1
- -L $LD_LIBRARY_PATH -llib3

- -L/user/grouplib -llib3 -L/user/mylib -llib3
- -L/lib -llib3 -L/usr/lib -llib3

Note that LD_LIBRARY_PATH in the above example might be LIBPATH or SHLIB_PATH, depending on your UNIX system.

The complete search path for every library would be searched only if a status of "file not Found" is returned on earlier paths.

Pass Option to System Linker After all Other Options Changing the Search Algorithm (+L *dir*)

Has the same effect as -L except that relative ordering is not preserved. +L options are passed (as -L options) to the system linker after all other objects and linker options. The ordering of +L and +l options relative to each other is preserved. See the description of -L for an example of the search order.

PASS OPTION TO SYSTEM LINKER MAINTAINING RELATIVE ORDERING (-L LIB)

Causes the system linker to search the specified library for any external routines. For statically linked executables created using the -B static flag, *lib* takes the form lib*lib*.a. For dynamically linked executables created using -B dynamic, it takes the form lib*lib*.so. The -l cob flag is effectively the same as the -l option for the system linker, ld (see your operating system documentation for further details on this linker option). The order in which -l options are specified is significant as directories are searched in that order.

If you specify the -l flag with the -B static flag, the.a version of the library is searched for and loaded into the executable at link time. If you specify the -l flag with the -B dynamic flag, the.so version of the library is searched for and, if found, is used at run time. If no.so version exists, the.a version is then searched for and loaded. Thus, if you specifically want the archive library rather than a shared object library, you should use the -B static flag. A library is searched when its name is encountered, so the placement of the -l flag is significant. By default, libraries are located in the directories/lib (or/usr/ccs/lib) and/usr/lib. However, you can use the -L flag to specify an alternative search path.

Example

The following example illustrates the use of the +l and -l flags in determining the order in which libraries are searched for symbols:

```
cob -llib1 +llib2 obj1.o -llib3 obj2.o
```

The relative ordering of the options passed to the system linker would be:

- -llib1 obj1.o
- -llib3 obj2.o
- -llib2

The system linker accepts options delimited with a hyphen (-), so once the relative ordering has been determined, the +l flag options are converted to -l before being passed to the linker.

PASS OPTION TO SYSTEM LINKER AFTER ALL OTHER OPTIONS (+L LIB)

Has the same effect as -l *lib* except that relative ordering is not preserved. +l options are passed (as -l options) to the system linker after all other options and files. Thus libraries specified with +l are searched after the COBOL libraries. The ordering of the +L and +l options relative to each other is preserved. See the description of -L for an example of the search order.

MAP SYMBOL TO NEW SYMBOL (-M SYMB=NEWSYM)

Maps unresolved symbol *symb* to *newsym,* which must already have been defined in a COBOL module. This creates a stub routine to satisfy any references to *symb,* so if this new routine is called, control is passed to the routine that has the entry name *newsym.* This flag enables you to "dummy out" unwritten optimized routines into one general purpose routine, if the calling sequence is the same. For example:

```
cob -x -m s1=x1 -m s2=x2 myprog.cbl mylib.a
```

Maps the unwritten routines s1() and s2() to the functionally similar x1() and x2() routines, which must already have been coded. You also can use this flag to map parts of static or dynamic linked executables produced by cob onto user-supplied routines or tailored modules.

Possible RTS symbols that can be mapped are:

Symbol	Description
Sqfile	Sequential fixed length record file handler
Ixfile	Indexed fixed length record file handler
Rlfile	Relative fixed length record file handler
Lsfilev	Line sequential variable length record file handler
Sqfilev	Sequential variable length record file handler
Ixfilev	Indexed variable length record file handler
Rlfilev	Relative variable length record file handler

When mapping symbols from any of the COBOL libraries, such as the file handler symbols above, if *newsym* has unresolved references to a user library, use the +L and +l flags to specify the library search path and name to ensure references from the COBOL libraries to the new symbols are correctly located.

If you do use this option to substitute the file handler supplied by Micro Focus with your own file handler, your file handler must conform to the Micro Focus Callable File Handler interface standard (see the chapter *Callable File Handler* in your *Programmer's Guide to File Handling* for details). Additionally, you can use the -m flag to link with the RTS a version of C-ISAM other than the version supplied with your Micro Focus COBOL system.

PASS GENERATE PHASE DIRECTIVE (-N *DIRECTIVE*)

Passes the specified option to the Compiler's generate phase. *directive* is one or more of the generate phase directives listed in the chapter Directives for Compiler.

ENABLE OPTIMIZATION (-O)

Enables maximum performance at run time by carrying

out the minimum run-time checks. This option is for use after all debugging has taken place and maximum performance with minimum run-time checks is required. The exact operation of this flag is environment dependent, but at a minimum it passes the NOCHECK directive to the Compiler. If any.c files are being processed, this flag also is passed through to cc.

SPECIFY OUTPUT FILE-NAME (-O *FILENAME*)

Changes the default name of the static linked executable module created using the -x option to the filename specified. The default filename is the basename of the first file entered to the cob command.

PRODUCE LISTING FILE (-P)

Produces a listing file (with the extension.lst) for each COBOL source file input to the cob command. Any errors detected by the Compiler are also reported both on standard error and in the listing file (at the point at which the error was located).

PASS FLAG TO C COMPILER TO USE PROFILING ROUTINES (-P)

Passes the option -p to the C compiler. If linking to produce a statically or dynamically linked executable module, it causes cob to use profiling startup and termination routines that call monitor (3) and causes the monitor information to be written to the file mon.out on normal termination of the executable module. See your system manual for more details on the -p flag. Some operating systems do not support profiling for dynamically linkable executables, so if profiling is required, the executable should be compiled using the -B static flag.

Linux:

You cannot use this option on Linux.

PASS OPTION TO SYSTEM LINKER (-Q LD_OPTION OR -Q,1 LD_OPTION OR -Q,2 LD_OPTION)

Passes the specified cob option(s) to the system linker. The

Micro Focus COBOL system uses a two-pass link process to build a static or dynamic executable to support dynamic loading and reference to C external data. Specifying -Q *ld_option* passes the options to both linker passes (that is, calls of the command ld). Specifying -Q,1 *ld_option* passes the options to only the first linker pass. Specifying -Q,2 *ld_option* passes the options to only the second linker pass.

The -Q,2 *ld_option* flag cannot be used with the -F and +F flags. You must use a separate -Q flag for each option, and any options that begin with hyphens must be enclosed in quotation marks. Use the format -Q *"flag value"* only where *flag* and *value* are not separate arguments, but represent one argument containing an embedded space.

DYNAMICALLY LOAD UNRESOLVED REFERENCE (-U)

Causes any unresolved reference to be treated as a COBOL programme to be dynamically loaded. Normally, such references would cause a fatal error at link time.

This option cannot be used with the -F and +F flags.

Linux:

You cannot use this option on Linux.

COMPILE TO GENERATED CODE FOR UNLINKED ENVIRONMENT (-U)

Compiles the COBOL source code files (.cbl.CBL or.cob) into intermediate code and then generates them to dynamically loadable native code (generated code) files. These files have the file extension.gnt.

You can supply intermediate code files to the cob command instead of COBOL source code files; these are just code generated. You can also input any object module files (.o) to the cob command; these are statically linked to the dynamic loader to produce the static run-time library for dynamically loadable files. Dynamically loaded programmes can call any of the modules in the statically linked run-time library as well as any other valid dynamically loadable programme.

Examples

The following examples illustrate the types of processing available using the -u flag:

cob Command line	Output Files
cob -u tmp/a.cbl	a.int, a.gnt
cob -u b.cbl	b.int, b.gnt
cob -u a.int	a.gnt
cob -u tmp/b.int	b.gnt

REPORT VERSION NUMBER (-V)

Sends to the screen the version number of any of the COBOL system components that have been invoked. This option is passed to the system programming utilities (for example, cc and ld).

SET VERBOSE MODULE (-V)

Sends to the screen messages output by the Compiler concerning accepted directives, the size of the code and data areas, and the entry points of each module. This flag also outputs to the screen warning messages concerning non-error conditions (for example if a flag you have specified overrides one you have already set), which by default are suppressed. Additionally, it echoes to the screen the entire command line when it is passed to cob.

CONTROL ERROR LEVEL FOR COB TERMINATION (-W ERR-LEVEL)

Causes cob processing to terminate after the COBOL Compiler *err-level* has been exceeded. By default, the cob command terminates if your code contains reported errors in the category severe or above.

err-level is a single alphabetic character representing the possible levels of error:

Character	Level
u	Unrecoverable
s	Severe

e	Error
w	Warning
i	Information

The cob process (not the compile process) is terminated if your code contains an error at the specified level or higher, provided such errors are reported to the cob command by the Compiler.

This depends on the setting of the WARNING Compiler directive, which controls the level of error reported by the Compiler (see the chapter Directives for Compiler for details of this directive).

Thus, for example, if you set the WARNING directive to force the Compiler to report only unrecoverable, severe and error level errors, but also set the -W flag to abort the cob command if any errors at the information level (or above) are reported, errors only in the categories unrecoverable, severe or error actually causes the cob command to terminate, as warning and information errors are not reported.

EXCLUDE SYMBOL FROM THE EXECUTABLE OUTPUT FILE (-X SYMB)

Excludes the unresolved text symbol *symb* from the executable output file. It creates a stub routine to satisfy any reference to *symb*, which if called produces RTS error 107:

```
Operation not implemented in this Run-Time System
```

It can be used to satisfy undefined symbols to modules that you know are not required (but are referenced), thereby still allowing an executable file to be produced. The resulting file might not actually be any smaller than it would have been if you had not specified this flag. However, setting this flag does ensure that should you try to call any excluded module, you receive a meaningful error message.

See the description of the -I flag earlier in this section for descriptions of valid symbols.

PROCESS TO STATICALLY OR DYNAMICALLY LINKED EXECUTABLE MODULE (-X[,CC])

Creates a single statically or dynamically linked

executable module from the files input to the cob command. The input file can be any file type except a.gnt file. By default, the name of this module is the base-name of the first object being statically linked.

It has no extension. You also can use this option to produce a full RTS, for example,

```
cob -xo rts.new
```

You also might need to specify the -I *symb* flag for any additional support you require for your RTS. For example, you need to include -I COBWIN2 in the cob command if you want to create a new RTS that includes windowing support.

You can also create an executable RTS using the mkrts script. See the section *Creating an Executable RTS* in the chapter *Linking*.

The CC option to the -x flag enables you to link Cobol and C++ objects into an executable file. Note that this option does not enable you to compile C++ objects; you must use the C++ compiler to do that.

For example, if the local C++ compiler is CC, and you want to link the C++ programme cprg and the COBOL programme cobprg.cbl, use the following commands:

```
CC cprg.C
cob -x,CC
cobprg.cbl cprg.o
```

FLAGS RESERVED FOR FUTURE USE

The following cob flags are reserved for future use by Micro Focus:

```
-f
-q
-z
```

DESCRIPTIONS OF COB ERROR MESSAGES

Any of the Micro Focus COBOL components invoked by the cob command may return their own error messages.

These are documented in full in your *Error Messages*. However, in addition to these messages the cob command may output its own error messages.

Most of these messages are self-explanatory, but the following are worthy of special note:

- *Options clash*: Option-names
  - The options that you have specified to the cob command are not valid.
- *Argument expected*: option-name
  - The specified option requires an argument.
- *Entry defined*: entryname-1 conflicting "main" found in entrypoint-2
  - You have defined the symbol "main" in a module other than the specified entry point module. Note that if the first programme specified to cob when building an executable is a COBOL module, the COBOL system "main" routine is linked in from the COBOL libraries.
- *Entry*: entryname does not have "main" defined
  - The specified entry point module (which is a non-COBOL module) does not define the symbol "main". This is the compulsory entry point for any non-COBOL modules that are specified as the first programme on the cob command line when building an executable file.
- *Invalid entry point name*: *Entryname*
  - The specified entry point symbol is not a valid symbol name. Valid symbol names can consist of any of the characters a through z, A through Z, 0 through 9 or the underscore (_). A name cannot begin with a digit.
- *Cobol version number invalid* - Call Technical Support
  - The contents of the cobver file are incorrect.
- I see no use for *file-name*
  - cob is unable to process the files you have specified as they have already been progressed beyond the specified end-point, or the specified options are not recognized.

- I see no work
  - You have specified inappropriate parameters that do not match the options you have used.
- COBOL compiler argument exceeds 128 byte limit
  - You must amend the offending argument to ensure it does not exceed this limit.

6

Runnzing

INTRODUCTION

You can create runnable programmes in two ways:

- You can compile your source code to create an.int file or a.gnt file. These types of file are dynamically loadable and can be run without having to link them.
- You can also create a linked programme, which can be run directly from the command line.

See the chapter *Packaging Applications* for an introduction to executable file types.

When you run your programme, you can specify:

- Switches that control the behavior
- Command-line parameters that your programme can read.

RUNNING PROGRAMMES

The syntax for invoking a linked module varies slightly from that for invoking a dynamically loadable module. The command line for running each type of programme is described below.

Linked Programmes

To run a statically or dynamically linked programme, enter the following command line at the system prompt:

```
module-name [programme-params]
```

where the parameters are:

Module-name	The name of a system executable file output by the cob command. See the chapter *COBOL*

	System Interface (cob) for details on creating this type of file.
Programme-params	One or more parameters that are required by the programme. Each parameter is a string, separated from adjoining parameters by one or more spaces. These parameters can be read by the programme in a number of ways. See the chapter*Writing Programmes* in your *Programmer's Guide to Writing Programmes* for further details.

Dynamically linked modules are run in the same way as statically linked modules.

However, you must first set the environment variable:

- LD_LIBRARY_PATH on most UNIX systems
- LIBPATH on AIX
- SHLIB_PATH on HP/UX

See the appendix *Micro Focus Environment Variables* for details.

Dynamically Loadable Programmes

To run dynamically loadable programmes (that is.gnt files or.int files) enter the following command line at the system prompt:

`cobrun [switch-param] programme-name [programme-param]`

where the parameters are:

Switch-Param	One or more programmable and run-time switches that control events in a programme at run time (see the section *Switch Parameters* in this chapter).
Programme-Name	The name of a dynamically loadable programme, which is either an.int file or a.gnt file. See the chapter *COBOL System Interface (cob)* for details on creating these types of files. If both.int and.gnt versions of the programme exist, and you do not specify an explicit file extension in the cobrun command, then by default, the.gnt version is run.

Programme-param	One or more parameters that are required by the programme. Each parameter is a string, separated from adjoining parameters by one or more spaces. If any of the parameters contain an equal sign, the equal sign is mapped to parentheses as these have a special meaning to UNIX, whereas the equal sign does not. These parameters can be read by the programme in a number of ways. See the chapter *Writing Programmes* in your *Programmer's Guide to Writing Programmes* for further details.

Switch Parameters

A switch is a parameter you pass to the run-time system to control the behavior of your programme at run time. These switches fall into two categories: programmable switches and run-time switches. A full listing and description of the switches available are contained in the chapter *Descriptions of Run-time Switches.*

Programmable Switches

Programmable switches consist of a digit in the range 0 through . These switches correspond to the COBOL switches that you define in the Special-Names paragraph of your programme, enabling you to set these switches on or off when your programme begins executing.

Any changes made to the settings of these switches using the COBOL statement SET mnemonic-name TO ON or OFF is not effective once the application has terminated. For details of how to use the SET statement with COBOL switches, see your Language Reference.

Run-time Switches

Run-time switches are acted on by the run-time system itself. Each consists of an upper-case or lower-case letter. These switches affect optional aspects of the behavior of certain COBOL features at run time.

Setting Switches

Switches, that you specify before running your programme, can be set using the COBSW environment variable. Alternatively, if you are running a dynamically loadable programme, you can set them on the cobrun command line; however, we recommend that you use COBSW instead. To set a programmable switch or run-time switch on, precede it with a plus sign (+); to set it off, precede it with a minus sign (–). If you do not explicitly set any switches either in the COBSW environment variable or on the cobrun command line, then their default values, as shown in the section*Switches Available*, apply. The above rules are summarized in the following two diagrams.

The format for setting switches in COBSW is:

The format for setting switches on the command line is:

where the parameters are:

- A programmable or run-time switch. The plus sign (+) sets the switch *s* on, while the minus sign (–) sets it off.
- Either a programmable switch with a digit in the range 0-8, or a run-time switch with an upper-case or lower-case letter.

Notes:

You should note the following when setting switches:

- Switches can be separated by spaces (but this is not required); however, there must not be a space between the sign ("+" or "-") and its associated switch
- Switches can be specified in any order, but each programmable or alphabetic switch must be preceded by a sign
- Individual switches can be set more than once, but the last setting of any particular switch is the one accepted by the system
- Switches remain set when COBOL subprograms are called
- Switches set on the command line take precedence over those defined in the COBSW environment variable
- Switches are case sensitive.

Examples

Setting COBSW to:

```
COBSW=+1+4
```

Sets the programmable switches as follows:

0	Off
1	On
2	Off
3	Off
4	On
5	Off
6	Off
7	Off
8	Off

The Command

```
cobrun -2+5-7+7 myprog
```

loads the programme myprog from the current directory with programmable switches 5 and 7 on and switch 2 off. Note that since the last setting of switch 7 (that is +7) is the one used, that switch is turned on. Switches 0, 1, 3, 4, 6 and 8, which are not specified, are off by default.

SWITCHES AVAILABLE

The switch parameter *s* can be any of the programmable or run-time switches listed in the following table. The Function column describes the effect of the switch when it is set on, and the Default Setting column indicates the setting that applies if you do not explicitly set the switch. Full details on the function of each of these switches are provided in the chapter *Descriptions of Run-time Switches.*

Table. AvZailable Switches

Switch	Title	Function	Default Setting
0-8	Programmable	Enable or disable COBOL switches that you define in the Special-Names paragraph of your programme	Off

A	Animator	Invokes Animator debugger	Off
A1	Base Animator	Invokes the base Animator	Off
B, B1	Skip Locked Record	Enables you to skip locked records when equentially accessings a shared file	Off
D	ANSI COBOL Debug	Invokes the ANSI COBOL Debug module	Off
D	Dynamic Paging Buffer	Enables you to specify the amount of memory in bytes to be used for the RTS dynamic paging buffers	240 Kbytes
E	Error switch	Executes intermediate code output by cob which contains S-level compiler errors	Off
E	COBOL Symbol	Causes RTS to search for C programmes and symbols to satisfy CALL operations or EXTERNAL data items	On
F	Numeric Field Check	Enables various numeric data checks at run-time	On
I1	Programme-file Search Order	Changes the programme search order	On
I	Keyboard Interrupt switch	Enables keyboard interrupts (including the suspend key for systems that support Job Control)	On
K	Indexed Files Sequence Check	Enables sequence checking of indexed keys in ISAM files	Off
L2	Record Terminator	Determines the character to be treated as the record terminator (x"0D0A" or x"0A")	Off
L	Memory (lower-case L)	Enables you to set the size of available memory available	Maximum bytes to RTS
N	Null switch	Enables null insertion for line sequential files	On
O	Divide-by-Zero	Produces a run-time system error	On

		for a programme compiled using the CHECKDIV directivesmwith parameters "OSVS", "VSC2" or "COBOL370" if it attempts to divide by zero.	
P	Dynamic Linkage Fixup (lower-case P)	Causes the RTS to set up the addressability for all the Linkage Section items in a programme when it is called	On
Q	File Status Error	Causes an internal RTS table to map your code to a status which conforms with statuses returned in the COBOL dialect of your choice	Off
S	Sort	Causes duplicates in all SORT operations to be ordered. This switch has the same effect on MERGE operations, although the WITH DUPLICATES IN ORDER phrase is valid syntax only for SORT statements.	Off
S	Sort Memory	Specifies the amount of memory used as internal workspace when performing a SORT operation	3072 Kbytes
T	Tab	Enables tab insertion upon output for line sequential files	Off
Z	DBCS Space Conversion	Converts DBCS spaces to ASCII spaces when reading a line sequential file or console input.	Off

TMPDIR ENVIRONMENT VARIABLE

The TMPDIR environment variable enables you to specify a different path in which to store temporary files. This can be necessary if the run-time system needs to page data to disk when creating heaps or sorting. For details of setting the TMPDIR environment variable, see the appendix Micro Focus Environment Variables.

Accessing Command Line Parameters

You can access programme parameters in a number of ways. For example, you can use one of the following formats of the ACCEPT statement:

```
accept data-name from command-line
or
accept data-name from mnemonic-name
```

Where the parameters are:

data-name	The data item to receive the command line parameters.
mnemonic-name	Defined in the Special-Names paragraph as: command-line is *mnemonic-name*

Full details on the available methods of accessing command line parameters are contained in the chapter *Writing Programmes* in your *Programmer's Guide to Writing Programmes.*

Example

Running programme myprog with the command line:

```
COBSW=+1+7
export COBSW
myprog in-file.dat clear
```

Causes the statement:

```
accept cmd-line from command-line
```

in the programme to place

```
in-file.dat clear
```

into the data-item cmd-line.

RUN-TIME SYSTEM ERROR MESSAGES

A run-time system error message is returned on a programme that is syntactically correct but that encounters problems during the actual running of the programme. For example, you could receive such an error if you try to access a file in the wrong mode or if you use a corrupt file. Refer to your Error Messages for a description of the format and all the possible run-time system errors.

If you try to run a programme, but the run is not successful, you should be aware that the programme counter (pc) values for native code generated files and executable files are undefined.

RUN-TIME CONFIGURATION

INTRODUCTION

When your run-time system or statically linked executable starts up, it attempts to read the run-time configuration file. The run-time configuration file specifies values for the run-time configurables. It is shared by all users of the Object COBOL system.

Run-time Configuration File

The run-time configuration file is a text file, which you can edit with your standard text editor. It is an optional file (no error will be issued if it does not exist) with the default name $COBDIR/cobconfig. You can specify a filename for the configuration file by setting the environment variable COBCONFIG; for example:

```
COBCONFIG=$HOME/myconfig
export COBCONFIG
```

Each run-time configurable appears on a new line. Blank lines are ignored. A comment line starts with a #; however, as the configuration file is processed at run-time, we advise that you limit your comments, in order to keep to a minimum the time it takes to process it.

The maximum number of characters permitted in a comment line is 80, including any new-line or carriage return characters that may be placed at the end of the line by some editors.

You can use the configuration file to:

- Set environment variables, such as dd_ filename mappings, or other environment variables significant to Micro Focus Object COBOL. Environment variables set in this way override values already set in the environment.
- Set run-time tunables. These control the behavior of certain aspects of the COBOL run-time system.

FORMAT OF A RUN-TIME CONFIGURABLE

Each run-time configurable is specifed on one line in the run-time configuration file. The format for run-time tunables is:

```
set configurable_name=value
```

while for for environment variables, the format is:

```
configurable_name=value
export configurable_name
```

The parameters are:

Configurable_name	The name of the run-time configurable. This will be the name a run-time tunable described in this chapter, or an environment variable described in the appendix Micro Focus Environment Variables. For details on dd_ filename mappings see your *Programmer's Guide to File Handling*.
Value	The value to be assigned to the run-time configurable. The values that can be assigned to a run-time tunable are described in this chapter. For a run-time tunable, value is validated according to the type and values allowed for that tunable, and the value ofcobconfig_error_report. Where value is numeric, a leading zero indicates that the value should be treated as octal (that is, base 8). For example, 07 (octal) is 7 (decimal), while 010 (octal) is 8 (decimal); however, 08 (octal) and 09 (octal) are invalid octal values. Hexidecimal values can also be set by using numeric values that begin with with 0x.

Note that each space in the definition can be replaced with tabs or more than one space.

Example

```
dd_MYFILE/usr/mydir/myfile
export/usr/mydir/myfile
```

```
SOMESHORTNAMES="JOE FRED JACK MARY"
export SOMESHORTNAMES
```

RUN-TIME TUNABLES

The following sections describe the run-time tunables available.

animator_interrupt_char

Syntax:

```
set animator_interrupt_char=integer
```

Value:

integer

Where integer specifies the decimal value, in the range 0 - 255, of the key to be used as the interrupt in Animator.

When you are executing your programme using Animator's Zoom command, your application might not recognize the function or cursor keys. This is because on some keyboards the function and cursor keys send sequences beginning with the Escape character, that by default the Zoom command takes as the interrupt character.

To prevent this, you can set animator_interrupt_char to a more suitable value. The value represents the code generated by the keyboard for the key to use to interrupt Animator's Zoom and Go operations. You should use a value that is not already being used on your system, perhaps 2, that corresponds to Ctrl/B. The key must generate a single character.

The range allowed for integer means that you can assign a normal text key as the interrupt character; however, if you do, you can no longer use that key to enter its normal character.

Default:

27. This represents the Escape key.

bll_cell_address_check

Syntax:

```
set bll_cell_address_check={TRUE|FALSE}
```

Value:

TRUE or FALSE

If TRUE, a test is run to determine if the top bit of the address of any BLL cell is set. If this bit is set, run-time system error 181 "Invalid parameter error" might be returned when testing the address of shared memory.

If FALSE, the test is suppressed. This is the recommended setting if BLL-cells are being allocated in shared memory.

DEFAULT

TRUE

`cobconfig_error_report`

Syntax:

```
set cobconfig_error_report={TRUE|FALSE}
```

Value:

TRUE or FALSE

If FALSE, do not report any errors during processing of the configuration file.

Default:

TRUE. Any errors detected are reported and the run-time system terminates. Unknown or misspelt run-time tunables names are not reported.

`command_line_accept`

Syntax:

```
set command_line_accept={TRUE|FALSE}
```

Value:

TRUE or FALSE

If TRUE, the first ACCEPT takes the input from the command line.

Default:

FALSE. The first ACCEPT takes the input from the user. This provides direct ANSI conformance. You should set this if you want to execute a programme that has been generated from convert3 or convert5.

`command_line_linkage`

Syntax:

```
set command_line_linkage={TRUE|FALSE}
```

Value:

TRUE or FALSE.

If TRUE, enables you to call a programme and pass the command line to the main programme as a parameter to be accessed via the Linkage Section. See the chapterWriting

Programmes in your Programmer's Guide to Writing Programmes for information on passing the command line to a main programme.

Default:

TRUE

core_on_error

Syntax:

```
set core_on_error=integer
```

Value:

integer

where integer specifies in what circumstances a core file is produced. You can look at core files with the utility rtscore, if it available on your system.

Integer can be:

0	The run-time system never produces a core file on any signal or run-time system error. This is the default behavior of the run-time system and prevents use of rtscore.
1	The run-time system produces a core file when any system signal is received that would normally produce a core file on the host system; for example, SIGILL, SIGSEGV (which would usually produce an run-time system error 114), and so on.
2	Behaves in the same way as 1, with the addition that the run-time system produces a core file when any other error condition is diagnosed; for example, run-time system error 12 ("Attempt to open a file which is already open"). The error is reported first, before the core file is produced.

Note: When a core file is produced, the run-time system itself cannot clean up COBOL file buffers or free system resources. This could lead to data file corruption that might not have occurred if no core file was produced.

Default:

0

See Also:

signal_regime

detect_alt_ctrl

Syntax:

```
set detect_alt_ctrl={TRUE|FALSE}
```

Value:

TRUE or FALSE.

Most UNIX environments do not detect input when the Ctrl, Alt, or Shift keys are available on a keyboard and are pressed by themselves. In these cases, detect_alt_ctrl must be set to FALSE. The operating system SCO Open Desktop from version 2 onwards does detect these keys individually and detect_alt_ctrl can be set to TRUE.

If detect_alt_ctrl is set to TRUE, then the run-time system detects the Ctrl, Alt, and Shift keys. These keys can then be used for COBOL utilities that would otherwise use the alternate key sequences of/c for Ctrl or/a for Alt. For example, Toolbox is easier to use if detect_alt_ctrl can be set to TRUE.

Default:

FALSE

dynamic_dictionary_limit

Syntax:

```
set dynamic_dictionary_limit=integer
```

Value:

integer

where *integer* is the maximum size of memory to be allocated dynamically at run time for use by virtual heaps.

The Compiler uses virtual heaps when processing your programmes, and this size is operating system dependent. If the memory limit is exceeded, the memory allocated to virtual heaps is paged by the Micro Focus COBOL system onto disk. If the amount of memory allocated to virtual heaps is not large enough to process your programmes, then the compilation and generation times can be increased due to the overheads of paging the virtual heap accesses to disk.

This run-time tunable is equivalent to the -d run-time switch. The value of -d is used if the values are different.

Default:

30 buffers of 8K.

dynamic_memory_limit

Syntax:

```
set dynamic_memory_limit=integer
```

Value:

integer

where integer is the maximum size of memory to be allocated dynamically at run time, and is operating system dependent. Any CANCELs performed before this memory limit is reached do not release the memory occupied by the programme being CANCELed.

The programme is available to be reused and hence CALL/ CANCEL performance is greatly increased. This mode of working is called "logical Cancels".

As far as your programme is concerned, the behavior of logical and real CANCELs is identical. If the dynamically allocated memory requirements exceed the size you set for dynamic_memory_limit, then all the memory that should have been freed by any CANCELs is freed. If you set this limit to zero, logical CANCELs are disabled.

This run-time tunable is equivalent to the -l run-time switch. The value of -l is used if the values are different.

Default:

Logical cancels are used.

file_io_buffer_mode

Syntax:

```
set file_io_buffer_mode={0|1|2}
```

Value:

Specifies how file I/O buffering should be handled:

2	Enables buffering for all sequential, line sequential and relative files. This setting turns off the COBEXTBUF environment variable.
1	Equivalent to turning on the COBEXTBUF environment variable.
0	All buffering is turned off.

File_io_buffer_mode is automatically set to zero (no buffering) if two instances of the same file are open, or if the file was opened without usingLOCK MODE IS EXCLUSIVE.

Note: If file buffering is set, WRITE statements write data to the buffers, not directly to the file. Data is written to the file only when the buffers are flushed (this happens periodically at no set interval, or when you close the file). You can write buffered information to disk immediately by calling EXTFH with an opcode of 0C.

HP-UX: If this tunable is specified, its setting overrides that of the HP-UX tunable file_io_buffering.

Default:

1

HP-UX: *If the HP-UX tunable file_io_buffering is set to:*

- TRUE (the default), the default for file_io_buffer_mode is 2
- FALSE, the default for file_io_buffer_mode is 0

As file_io_buffering is by default set to TRUE, then if file_io_buffering is not set, file_io_buffer_mode is set to 2.

Isam_block_size

Syntax:

```
set isam_block_size={512|1024|2048|4096}
```

Value:

Specifies the size, in bytes, of the block to use when creating indexed files. For example:

```
set isam_block_size=1024
```

specifies a block size of 1024 bytes (or 1K)

This tunable replaces the cobcf utility that was available on some earlier products.

Default:

1024.

Isam_open_key_check

Syntax:

```
set isam_open_key_check={TRUE|FALSE}
```

Value: TRUE or FALSE

Specifies whether or not the key descriptions specified in the programme should be verified with those in an existing file during open processing.

Default: TRUE.

lock_mode

Syntax:

```
set lock_mode={0|1|2|3}
```

Value: 0, 1, 2, or 3

Selects the locking implementation to be used, as follows:

Lock Mode	Description
0	Uses the locking mechanism provided by v3.1 and earlier versions.
1	Provides compatibility with DOS and OS/2 locking mechanisms.
2	Provides interlanguage locking. This method causes record locks to lock the physical record.
3	Provides compatibility with C-ISAM version 5 and above.

Default:
2

Long_filenames

Syntax:

```
set long_filenames={TRUE|FALSE}
```

Value: TRUE or FALSE

Specifies whether file-names longer than 14 characters are to be allowed. If you create a file on a device that does not support long file-names you must set long_filenames to FALSE when accessing that file on a device that does support long file-names.

Default:
TRUE

noretry_on_decl

Syntax:
set noretry_on_decl={TRUE|FALSE}
Value:
TRUE or FALSE

Specifies whether or not locked records are retried when declaratives exist for the file, and the programme has been compiled with RETRYLOCK NORM.

Note: This must be set to provide compatibility with COBOL v1.3.

Default:
FALSE

pc_mono_palette

Syntax:

```
set pc_mono_palette=integer
```

Value:

Integer selects the style of monochrome attribute palette that will be used by the run-time system when a call to the call-by-name routine CBL_SCR_SET_PC_ATTRIBUTES is made and a terminfo for which there is no colour information is being used.

Integer can be:

0	Selects a CGA-emulation palette. This is the default, and is the recommended setting.
1	Selects a backwards-compatible palette that works in the same manner as previous products. This palette should not be used as it is incorrect (it does not conform to any actual PC monochrome palette), but is provided in case certain programmes or files rely upon it (for instance, character screen sets saved using Dialog System when running under this incorrect palette). Wherever possible, you should attempt to convert such programmes/files to use the correct palette.

Default:

0

posix_lock_prob

Syntax:

```
set posix_lock_prob={TRUE|FALSE}
```

Value:

TRUE or FALSE

The implementation in Object COBOL of compatibility with DOS and OS/2 files has created a problem in how UNIX handles file locks.

On UNIX, if a file is opened twice within a programme, and that file is subsequently closed using a file descriptor received from one of the open operations, any locks obtained by the other open operation are lost. This is the expected behavior of a file-close operation, as described in the POSIX standard X/Open guidelines.

This tunable provides compatibility with the behavior exhibited in V3.0. To obtain the old behavior, set the tuneable to TRUE.

Default:
FALSE
program_search_order
Syntax:

```
set program_search_order=integer
```

Value:

Integer selects the programme search order to be used, and can be a value from 1 to 4 as shown as shown in the following table:

Search Order	Description
1	Uses the following search sequence: a. The run-time system is checked to see if the programme is statically linked. b. If the COBPATH environment variable is set, the paths specified are searched in order. Otherwise, the current directory is searched. c. The path in which the calling programme was loaded is searched. d. If COBDIR is set, the path specified is searched. Otherwise,/opt/lib/cobol/ (on SVR4) or/usr/lib/cobol (UNIX SVR3) is searched.
2	Uses the following search sequence: a. The run-time system is checked to see if the programme is statically linked. b. The path in which the calling programme was loaded is searched. c. If the COBPATH environment variable is set, the paths specified are searched in order. Otherwise, the current directory is searched. d. If COBDIR is set, the path specified is searched. Otherwise,/opt/lib/cobol/ (on SVR4) or/usr/lib/cobol (UNIX SVR3) is searched.
3	Uses the following search sequence:

a. The run-time system is checked to see if the programme is statically linked.
b. The current directory is searched.
c. If the COBPATH environment variable is set, the paths specified are searched in order.
d. If COBDIR is set, the path specified is searched. Otherwise,/opt/lib/cobol/ (on SVR4) or/usr/lib/cobol (UNIX SVR3) is searched.

4 Uses the following search sequence:

a. The run-time system is checked to see if the programme is statically linked.
b. If the COBPATH environment variable is set, the paths specified are searched in order. Otherwise, the current directory is searched.
c. The path in which the calling programme was loaded is searched.
d. If COBDIR is set, the path specified is searched. Otherwise,/opt/lib/cobol/ (on SVR4) or/usr/lib/cobol (UNIX SVR3) is searched.
e. The current directory is searched.

Note: When using cobrun COBPATH is set to $COBDIR/dialog:$COBPATH

Set program_search_order to 2 for compatibility with previous UNIX versions of Micro Focus COBOL, or to 3 for compatibility with previous DOS versions.

Note: If a programme is called with a specific path the search sequence is not affected by the value of program_search_order and instead:

- The run-time system is checked to see if the programme is statically linked.
- The path specified in the call is searched.

Default:

1

routine_table_size

Syntax:

```
set routine_table_size=integer
```

Value:

integer

Integer is a value in the range 10-65535 specifying the maximum number of simultaneously loaded COBOL programmes. Note that some system support programmes (such as Adis) require slots in the routine table, so the maximum number of user programmes may be smaller *than the specified value. The default value of 255 means that only 128 programmes can be animated. To animate more than 128 programmes, increase the value of* integer.

Default:

255.

same_proc_excl_detection

Syntax:

```
set same_proc_excl_detection={TRUE|FALSE}
```

Value:

TRUE or FALSE.

Detects if you have tried to open a file multiple times in one run unit. If TRUE, any OPEN request has conditions applied to determine whether or not it is already open, and if so, if it was opened exclusively, in which case a file error is generated. Currently, if the same file is opened twice by the same run unit, no file error is generated. This flag should be set to TRUE for RMCOBOL compatibility.

Default:

FALSE.

se_compat_locking

Syntax:

```
set se_compat_locking={TRUE|FALSE}
```

Value:

TRUE or FALSE.

Specifies file locking compatibility. If set to TRUE, file locking is compatible with Server Express; otherwise file locking is compitable with Object COBOL for UNIX.

Default:

FALSE

shared_memory_segment_size

Syntax:

```
set shared_memory_segment_size=integer
```

Value:

integer

where *integer* specifies, in bytes, the initial size of the shared memory block allocated by the run-time system. The minimum value you can specify for *integer* is 8192 (8K).

Default:

65536 (64 K)

signal_interface

Syntax:

```
set signal_interface={TRUE|FALSE}
```

Value:

TRUE or FALSE.

TRUE causes the run-time system to use the signal() signal handling interface as used in Micro Focus COBOL version 3.1 and before. FALSE causes the run-time system to use the more robust sigaction() signal handling interface, if it is available on your system. If it is not available the signal() interface is used.

The default value should not need to be changed unless you are using signal handlers in non-COBOL programmes. See the chapter Mixed-Language Programming in your Programmer's Guide to Writing Programmes for more information on using signal handling in the COBOL environment. See your operating system documentation for more information on signal() and sigaction().

Default:

FALSE

signal_regime

Syntax:

```
set signal_regime(sig)=integer
```

or:

```
set signal_regime=1
```

Value:

integer

Selects the action the run-time system takes for the signal

sig. The value of sig must be between 1 and the maximum signal number on your operating system. See your operating system documentation for details on signal values.

You should only use this tunable when Micro Focus Object COBOL is being used with third party software that uses signals.

If you are using signal handling in you own applications, you should use the cobpostsighandler() interface, and not the operating system signal handling interfaces, with this tunable. Also see the chapter Interfacing and Mixed Language Programming *in your* Programmer's Guide to Writing Programmes.

Integer can have the following values:

Value	Action
0	The run-time system uses the signal *sig* if it needs to. By default, the run-time system sets-up signal handlers for all signals whose operating system default action would cause termination. The run-time system can thus catch these signals and tidy-up (for example, close any open files to prevent file corruption) before exiting.
1	The run-time system uses the signal *sig* if, and only if, a handler was not already posted for this signal. This is useful if the third-party software is invoked before Micro Focus Object COBOL and sets up a handler for signal *sig*. If this tunable is not set for this signal, the run-time system overwrites the third-party software's handler with its own; this will lead to unpredictable behavior, such as run-time system error 115 ("Unexpected signal") being produced. If a handler was posted, the run-time system will not post any handlers for this signal and so any run-time system functionality which relies on this signal will not work.
2	The run-time system never uses the signal *sig*. This is only of use if the third-party software is invoked after Micro Focus COBOL and sets-up a

handler for signal *sig*. Use of this setting is strongly discouraged for any signal whose operating system default action is to cause termination; if this signal is received between the run-time system being invoked and the third-party software setting up its handler, the default action of the operating system occurs, and the process exits without the run-time system being able to tidy-up. This could lead to problems such as file corruption.

Any run-time system functionality which relies on this signal will not work.

Default:

0 for all signals

Comments:

If you use the alternative syntax (set signal_regime=1), then the signal regime for all signals is set to 1. Note that, for this syntax, the only value you can set is 1.

skip_on_lock

Syntax:

```
set skip_on_lock={TRUE|FALSE}
```

Value:

TRUE or FALSE

Specifies whether or not a READ WITH LOCK of a locked record in a programme compiled with the directive NODETECTLOCK causes a subsequent READ NEXT/ PREVIOUS to reread the logical NEXT/PREVIOUS record or the currently locked record.

Default:

FALSE

ENVIRONMENT VARIABLES

The environment variables available to you are described fully in the main body of this manual. They are summarized in the appendix *Micro Focus Environment Variables*.

DESCRIPTIONS OF RUN-TIME SWITCHES

Describes the available programmable and run-time switches. Each entry first describes the effect of the switch when it is set on; unless otherwise specified, the opposite effect can be assumed if the switch is set to off. The default setting that applies if you do not explicitly set any of these switches is also given. Switches can be set either on the command line or in the COBSW environment variable unless otherwise indicated. For further information on setting and testing switches, see the chapter *Running*. Key

The function of each switch is given, followed by these headings:

Properties:

Default	The default setting of the switch.
Environment	Indicates the run-time systems and the operating system that this switch works with. If no operating system is specified, it works on all operating systems supporting the specified run-time system. 16-bit run-time systems means both the shared and static-linked run-time systems.
Comments	Additional information about the switch.

See Also:

Pointers to further information

LIST OF SWITCHES

0, 1, 2... 8	Programmable switches
A	Choose ANSI file handling and status codes (16-bit only)
A	Invoke Animator for intermediate code (32-bit and 64-bit systems only)
A1	Display trailing spaces (DOS, Windows and OS/2 only)
A1	Invoke Base Animator for intermediate code (UNIX only)
B, B1	Skip locked record
B2	Choose the sorting algorithm
C	Enable screens longer than 25 lines
C1	Nonstandard size screens
C2	Disable COBOL Text Window
C4	Sets screen into 43-line mode
C5	Sets screen into 50-line mode

D	Invoke the ANSI COBOL Debug module
d	Set memory size for dynamic paging buffer
D1	Control search method for.dll files
D2	Disable DLL-cancel error reporting
E	Execute code containing S-level errors
e	Search for C as well as COBOL programmes
/E	Signal-handling stack size
F	Validate numeric data in intermediate code
/F	Change file open limit
G	Reduce the size of I/O buffers
i	Enable keyboard interrupts
I1	Change programme search order
I2	Redirect RTS errors to STDERR
K	Enable sequence checking on indexed write
K1	Use old IBM PC keyboard handling
K2	Use extended IBM PC keyboard handling
K3	Enable Shift+Ctrl+Break behavior
K4	Pause on RTS error
L	Make I/O errors return to programme
l	Specify memory available for application
L1	Enable the exception popup on OS/2
L2	Determine record terminator for line sequential files
L5	Handle LEVEL II COBOL files
L6	Specify subprogram search order
/L	Specify number of record locks
M	Free up memory on DOS
M2	Disable paging of active programmes
/M	Change default number of heaps on OS/2
N	Insert nulls in line sequential files
O	Enable divide-by-zero error
P	Use high-level printer I/O
p	Fix up all linkage item addresses on entry
P1	Sound system bell using the BIOS
P2	Enable logical cancels
P3	Increase number of programmes loadable
/P	Specify address of port for security key
Q	Map extended file status codes
R	Retry locked record until available

S	Order duplicates in sort/merge operations
s	Specify memory available for sort
S2	Disable video "snow" protection
S3	Enable video "snow" protection
S5	Use ansi.sys-compatible console I/O
S6	Change DISPLAY UPON CRT attribute behavior
/S	Change default stack size
T	Insert tabs in line sequential files
Z	Control conversion of DBCS spaces
/Z	Dummy parameter switch

DESCRIPTIONS OF SWITCHES

Programmable Switches

Sets the corresponding COBOL switch when the programme is entered.

Properties:

Default:	All off
Environment:	All

Comments: These switches enable the COBOL switches 0-8 that you defined in the Special-Names paragraph of your programme (see your Language Reference for details). You can specify these switches in any order, but each individual switch must be preceded by a sign.

A - ANSI File Status Switch

Implements file handling and status codes according to the particular ANSI standard for which your programme was compiled.

Properties:

Default:	On
Environment:	16-bit run-time systems

If your programme was compiled with the ANS85 directive, ANSI'85 file status values are returned. If switch A is off, ANSI'74 status values are returned.

A – Animator

Invokes Animator to animate intermediate code which is

either invoked using the cobrun command or dynamically loaded by a statically linked module.

Properties:

Default:	Off
Environment:	32-bit and 64-bit run-time systems

Comments: If you want to animate intermediate code created by the cob command, you can use the animcommand which automatically sets this switch on. This switch overrides the A1 switch.

A1 - Display Trailing Spaces

Disables the display of trailing spaces by causing DISPLAY... UPON CONSOLE statements to strip off any trailing spaces in the data item being displayed before outputting the data to the screen.

Properties:

Default:	On (16-bit)Off (32-bit)
Environment:	16-bit run-time systems and 32-bit on Windows NT and OS/2 V2

Comments: This switch provides compatibility with earlier COBOL systems from Micro Focus.

When this switch is off, the trailing spaces are included in the display, as required by the ANSI COBOL Standard.

A1 - Base Animator

Invokes Base Animator to animate intermediate code which is either created using the cobrun command or dynamically lóaded by a statically linked module.

Properties:

Default:	Off
Environment:	UNIX

Comments:

If you want to animate intermediate code created by the cob command, you can use the animbase command which automatically sets this switch on.

This switch overrides the A switch.

B, B1 - Skip Locked Record

Causes the record pointer to be updated past any locked record encountered when using the READ NEXT statement.

Properties:

Default:	Off
Environment:	All

Comments: Set the B switch for indexed sequential files open INPUT or I-O. Set the B1 switch for indexed sequential files open INPUT. Setting either of these switches permits a file to be sequentially read, even if another process has records locked in that file.

A file status of "locked record" is returned when a locked record is read when the B switch is set; a file status of "00" is returned when a locked record is read when the B1 switch is set.

Note: This switch also affects relative and record sequential files when your programme is compiled with the CALLFH directive set.

See also:

CALLFH Compiler directive

B2 - Alternative Sorting Mechanism

Changes the sort algorithm used by the run-time system to one which is more suitable for dealing with huge sorts.

Properties:

Default:	Off
Environment:	16-bit run-time systems

Comments: Normally sorts are optimized to make use of all free memory. This is faster for small sorts. However, when performing a sort on data which is many times the size of free memory, this optimization requires that you have free disk space which is at least twice the size of the data records being sorted.

Setting the B2 switch on optimizes disk usage during a sort so that you only require free disk space which is roughly equal to the size of the data being sorted. Moreover, because less paging to disk occurs, it speeds up large sorts.

C - Large Screen

Enables the use of screens longer than the traditional 25 lines.

Properties:

Default:	Off
Environment:	16-bit run-time systems

Comments:

This switch is available for use only with the shared run-time system, which by default treats all screens as 25 lines long. The static linked system always handles screens of any length.The screen width cannot be altered; only screens 80 columns wide are supported.

C1 - Nonstandard Screens

Enables the run-time system to execute with any screen mode or size.

Properties:

Default:	Off
Environment:	16-bit run-time systems

Comments: Most system software (for example Animator) does not function correctly using screens of more or less than 80 columns. Enhanced accept/display operations function with any screen size.

C2 - COBOL Text Window

Disables the creation of a COBOL Text Window for Presentation Manager applications.

Properties:

Default:	Off
Environment:	16-bit run-time systems

Comments: Specifying +C2 disables the creation of a COBOL Text Window for Presentation Manager applications. However.

If a run-time system error occurs with this switch set, a Text Window displaying the error message text is created. This provides compatibility with previous releases of this COBOL system.This switch does not have any effect running under Windows.

C4 - 43-line Mode

Forces the screen in 43-line mode on an EGA or VGA monitor, or with the COBOL Text Window under Windows.

Properties:

Default:	Off
Environment:	16-bit shared run-time system and 32-bit for Windows NT and OS/2 V2

Comments: The original screen mode is restored upon return to the operating system.

If you have set up programme items for COBOL components under Windows, setting this switch causes the components to start in 43-line mode.You must set the +C switch with the +C4 switch.

See also:

C RTS switch

C5 - 50-line Mode

Forces the screen in 50-line mode on an EGA or VGA monitor, or with the COBOL Text Window under Windows.

Properties:

Default:	Off
Environment:	16-bit shared run-time system and 32-bit for Windows NT and OS/2 V2

Comments: The original screen mode is restored upon return to the operating system.

If you have set up programme items for COBOL components under Windows, setting this switch causes the components to start in 50-line mode.You must set the +C switch with the +C5 switch.

See also:

C RTS switch

D - Standard ANSI COBOL Debug

Invokes the standard ANSI COBOL Debug module.

Properties:

Default:	Off
Environment:	All

Comments: See your Language Reference - Additional Topics for a description of the Debug facilities. This switch must be set on the command line.

Example:

The Command:

```
DOS, Windows and OS2:
myprog (+D)
UNIX:
cobrun +D myprog
```

Loads the programme myprog with the standard ANSI COBOL Debug module invoked.

d - Dynamic Paging Buffer

Specifies the amount of memory in bytes to be used for the run-time system dynamic paging buffers.

Properties:

Default:	-d245760 (240 K)
Environment:	UNIX

Comments: Dynamic paging is used by programmes such as the Compiler. By increasing the amount of memory you might be able to improve the performance of such programmes. Once the amount of memory allocated for dynamic paging is exceeded, the run-time system pages any further requirements onto disk.

For example, when compiling a large COBOL programme, the amount of memory for dynamic paging buffers might be exceeded due to the Compiler requiring a large amount of dictionary to store the symbol table it creates.

When the dynamic paging buffer space is exhausted, the run-time system starts to page dynamic accesses to disk, which might have a performance overhead.

By raising the amount of memory for dynamic buffering, paging to disk can be avoided (or at least reduced) and therefore better Compiler performance achieved.

Example

To double the amount of memory (to 500k) the run-time system could use before paging to disk, you would set the COBSW environment variable as follows:

```
COBSW=-d500000
```

See Also:

dynamic_dictionary_limit run-time tunable

D1 - DLL Search Compatibility

Provides compatibility with the method of searching for.dll files on OS/2 as used by Micro Focus COBOL systems before V3.1.

Properties:

Default:	Off
Environment:	16-bit run-time systems on OS/2

Comments: When an application causes the run-time system to try to load a.dll programme and the file is not specified with a fully qualified pathname, OS/2 tries to locate the programme from the given base-name by searching directories specified in LIBPATH. Before COBOL V3.1, the RTS also searched for the file in the directories specified in the COBDIR environment variable.

Specifying +D1 causes the RTS to search for.dll files in the directories specified in the COBDIR environment variable in addition to OS/2 searching in the directories specified in LIBPATH. The effect is exactly the same as in earlier products.

D2 - DLL-Cancel Error Reporting

Disables run-time system error 177 ("Attempt to cancel programme failed") when a cancel of a COBOL DLL fails.

Properties:

Default:	Off
Environment:	16-bit shared run-time system on OS/2

Comments:

If the run-time system encounters an error when it tries to cancel a COBOL Dynamic Link library (DLL) on OS/2, it issues error 177. Setting this switch causes the RTS to ignore the error and logically cancel the DLL.

E – Error

Executes intermediate code which contains S-level syntax-check errors.

Properties:

Default:	Off
Environment:	16-bit shared run-time system, and 32-bit and 64-bit run-time systems

Comments: If you try to run intermediate code programmes which contain S-level Compiler errors when this switch is set to off, you receive a run-time system error. See yourError Messages for full details of these errors.

e - COBOL Symbol

Causes the run-time system to search for COBOL or C programmes or symbols to satisfy call operations or external data items.

Properties:

Default:	On
Environment:	UNIX

Comments: The run-time system does not search for any C programmes or symbols if you set this switch off.

E - Signal-handling Stack Size

Specifies in bytes the size of the stack to be used to handle signals.

Properties:

Default:	/E2560
Environment:	16-bit shared run-time system on OS/2

Comments: Under normal circumstances you do not need to change the size of the stack used to handle signals. However, if your application does require more stack space than the default for handling signals you can increase its size using this switch.

See also:
/S RTS switch

F - Numeric Field Check

Checks all numeric items for valid numeric data.
Properties:

Default:	On
Environment:	All

Comments: If the data is not valid, run-time system error 163 ("Illegal character in numeric field") is produced. Setting this switch to off suppresses this checking.

This checking is only done on generated code created with the CHECKNUM Compiler directive, and on intermediate code. The run-time system and generated code try to optimize many types of numeric operations.

These operations can cause invalid results if the numeric operands do not contain valid numeric data. By default, the run-time system gives the run-time system error 163 when a numeric operation is tried with invalid numeric data.

Invalid data is handled differently by intermediate and native code, by this COBOL system on other environments and different versions of this COBOL system. We recommend that you enable numeric field checking while you are developing your programme.

If you receive run-time error 163, we recommend that you adjust your code so that no invalid data is used. You can locate the invalid numeric data in your code by setting the +F switch on and then animating your programme until run-time system error 163 is detected.

If you are not able to correct your code, you might want to use one or more of the following Compiler directives to resolve invalid data in numeric fields:

- BADSIGNS (on the 16-bit COBOL system) and HOSTSIGNS (on 32-bit and 64-bit COBOL systems) - enables arithmetic with COMP-3 items that have illegal sign nibbles to produce the desired result.
- HOST-NUMCOMPARE - controls the operation of

comparisons between integer numeric data items of USAGE DISPLAY and alphanumeric literals or figurative constants. You can set the ZWB Compiler directive with HOST-NUMCOMPARE to affect comparisons involving signed and unsigned data items. These directives emulate mainframe behavior, so you do not need to change your data.

- *HOST-NUMMOVE*: Causes the Compiler to switch off checking for illegal characters in numeric fields during the execution of certain MOVE statements. (Use with care.)
- *SIGNCOMPARE (16-bit only)*: Affects the way some numeric comparisons are performed in a programme using the EBCDIC character set.
- *SPZERO*: causes space characters in numeric data items of USAGE DISPLAY to be treated as zeros.

Example

One of the checks enabled or disabled by this switch is the numeric field check. When the switch is set on, if the run-time system loads an item into one of its numeric registers it firswt checks whether the loaded value contains a non-numeric character. If it does, run-time error 163 is output.

For example:

```
working-storage section.
     01 item-a     pic 9.
procedure division.

 If item-a = 0.
           Display "zero"
     else
           display "nonzero"
     end-if.
```

The variable item-a is not initialiszed by a VALUE clause, and so contains a space character x"20". Running this programme with the F switch set on causes the run-time system to check whether the numeric field contains a non-numeric value resulting in run-time error 163.

F - Files-open Limit

Specifies the maximum number of files allowed to be open at a time.

Properties:

Default:	100 on DOS and Windows. 255 on OS/2.
Environment:	16-bit shared run-time system

Comments: You cannot specify a limit lower than 20.

On OS/2, the maximum value you can specify is 65535. If you specify a larger number, a run-time error message is returned.

On DOS and Windows, the maximum value you can specify is 255. If you specify a larger number, 255 is used instead. The value specified by the FILES parameter in your config.sys file is also used to determine the maximum number of open files. The COBOL run-time system uses whichever is the smaller value of FILES or/F. For example, if FILES = 20 and/F is set to 255, then the maximum number of open files allowed is 20. Similarly, if FILES = 255 and/F is set to 20, the maximum number of open files allowed is 20. To be able to open 255 files you would would need to set both FILES and/F to 255.

G - File Buffer Size

Forces all buffers to be 512 bytes.

Properties:

Default:	Off
Environment:	16-bit run-time systems

Comments:

Normally, files opened for random access use 512 byte buffers; however, those opened for sequential access use 4K buffers. Setting this switch to on is useful if memory is at a premium, for example during animation; however, this can impact performance.

i - Keyboard Interrupt

Enables keyboard interrupts. If your system supports Job

Control, this switch also enables the Suspend Interrupt key (usually Ctrl+Z).

Properties:

Default:	On
Environment:	UNIX

Comments: If you want to disable keyboard interrupts, including the suspend key, for your application, use the -i switch.

I1 - Programme-file Search Order

Changes the order in which the run-time system searches for programme files.

Properties:

Default:	Off
Environment:	All

Comments:

Normally, the run-time system searches for programme files in the order:

.gnt
.int
.lbr

Setting this switch to on changes the search order to:

.int
.gnt
.lbr

See Also:

program_search_order run-time tunable

I2 - Run-time System Error Redirection

Redirects run-time system errors to STDERR

Properties:

Default:	Off
Environment:	16-bit shared run-time system on DOS and OS/2

Comments: The I2 switch is only enabled when used in conjunction with the +S5 switch. If set off run-time system error messages are sent to STDOUT (standard output). If set on the error messages are sent to STDERR (standard error). On OS/2 messages sent to STDERR can be redirected using the "2>" operator on the command line.

This switch has no effect when running on Windows.

See also: S5 RTS switch

K - Indexed Files Sequence Check

Enables sequence-checking of keys in indexed files.

Properties:

Default:	Off
Environment:	UNIX

Comments: Setting the K switch to on enables records to be written in any order to indexed files opened in sequential mode. Otherwise records must be written in key sequence.

K1 - Old Keyboard Handling

Enables the use of old keyboard BIOS calls.

Properties:

Default:	Off
Environment:	16-bit run-time systems

Comments: Setting the K1 switch to on enables the COBOL system to be used on a new IBM PC keyboard in conjunction with a keyboard resident programme which knows only about the old IBM PC keyboard BIOS routines.

K2 - Extended Keybord Handling

Enables the use of extended keyboard BIOS calls.

Properties:

Default:	Off
Environment:	16-bit run-time systems

Comments: Setting the K2 switch to on enables the COBOL system to be used on a new extended IBM PC keyboard in conjunction with a keyboard resident programme which knows only about the old IBM PC keyboard BIOS routines.

K3 - Shift+Ctrl+Break Behavior

Enables you to bring up and switch to an operating system

command prompt by pressing the Shift, Ctrl and Break keys simultaneously.

Warning! If you use this switch and enter the new command shell you should be very careful about which commands you use.

Properties:

Default:	Off
Environment:	16-bit shared run-time system

Comments: The K3 switch is turned on automatically in the COBOL development environments such as Workbench and Professional COBOL.To leave the command prompt and return to your COBOL application, use the exit command.

The K3 switch should be used with caution; if a disk clean-up facility (for example, CHKDSK/F) is used while in the new command shell and the application had any open files when the new command processor was loaded, the file system can become corrupted.

K4 - RTS Error Behavior

Causes run-time system error messages to stay on the screen until a key is pressed.

Properties:

Default:	Off
Environment:	16-bit shared run-time system and 32-bit on Windows NT and OS/2 V2

Comments: This is useful in batch runs where you want to know if any programme terminates with a run-time system error message, or in a system that displays menus, where RTS error messages can sometimes be quickly overwritten.

L - Auto-fail Critical Errors

Causes any critical I/O errors (for example "Disk drive door not closed") to return control immediately to the user programme with an appropriate file status or error.

Properties:

Default:	Off
Environment:	16-bit run-time systems

Comments: Usually, these conditions make the programme pause with a message enabling the user to abort, retry, fail or ignore the error. Setting the L switch on suppresses this message so that all error handling can be controlled by the application.

l – Memory

Enables you to set the maximum amount of memory to be made available to the run-time system, or to cause the run-time system to perform physical cancels instead of logical cancels.

Properties:

Default:	The maximum number of bytes available to the run-time system.
Environment:	UNIX

Comments: This switch is lower-case "L", not upper-case "I".

The format of this switch is lnnnnnn, where nnnnnn is the amount of memory in bytes to be made available to the run-time system.

You can use this switch to limit the amount of memory the run-time system will use. This might be useful to enable you to tune your system.

By default the run-time system performs logical cancels unless all available memory has been used up. As far as your programmes are concerned, the behavior of logical and physical cancels is identical, but logical cancels are faster. A logical cancel flushes all file buffers but does not release any memory. To force all cancels to be physical, you must specify this switch with parameter zero; for example:

```
+l0
```

By default, when the run-time system requires memory space it checks that the new request does not exceed the available memory. If it does, the memory that should have been freed by any cancels is freed and the run-time system repeats its request for memory. The run-time system loads programmes that have been logically canceled in preference to reloading from disk. Statically linked COBOL programmes cannot be physically canceled because they cannot be removed from memory.

Duplicate entry point names are not allowed in statically linked programmes; you must ensure that all such programmes have unique entry point names.

Logical cancels behave in the same way as these physical cancels under statically linked programmes. Therefore, an application developed using.int and.gnt files with logical cancels should exhibit the same behavior when generated as object code files and statically linked. However, if you used physical cancels and duplicated entry point names while developing the application, the application might fail to static link.

See Also:

dynamic_memory_limit run-time tunable

L1 - Exception Popup Window

Disables the interactive popup window that appears when an exception error occurs while running on OS/2 or Windows.

Properties:

Default:	Off
Environment:	16-bit run-time systems

Comments:

Instead of the interactive popup window, a general OS/2 or Microsoft Windows error message is displayed and control is returned to the operating system prompt without any user intervention.

L2 - Record Terminator

Determines the character(s) to be used as the record terminator when reading a line sequential file.

Properties:

Default:	Off
Environment:	All

DOS, OS/2 and Windows

On DOS, OS/2 and Windows, when off (-L2), x"0A" is

taken as the record terminator. This provides compatibility with COBOL for UNIX.

Unix

On UNIX, when off (-L2), x"0A" or "0D0A" is taken as the record terminator. This provides compatibility with COBOL for DOS, Windows and OS/2.

DOS, OS/2, and Windows

On DOS, OS/2, and Windows, when on (+L2), x"0D0A" is taken as the record terminator. This provides compatibility with earlier versions of this system, correctly reading files written using a WRITE... AFTER ADVANCING statement.

Unix

On UNIX, when on (+L2), x"0A" is taken as the record terminator. This provides compatibility with earlier versions of this system, correctly reading files written using a WRITE...AFTER ADVANCING statement.This switch only affects read operations and not write operations.

L5 - LEVEL II COBOL File Compatibility

Enables the COBOL system to determine the size of sequential or relative files created by Micro Focus LEVEL II COBOL, which are padded out to a 128-byte boundary with x"1A" characters.

Properties:

Default:	Off
Environment:	16-bit run-time systems

Comments: You must set this switch to handle sequential or relative files created using Micro Focus LEVEL II COBOL.

This switch can only be used for non-shared files.

L6 - Subprogram Directory Search Order

Changes the way the run-time system searches for subprograms.

Properties:

Default:	On
Environment:	16-bit shared run-time system

Comments: When this switch is on, the RTS searches for subprograms, first in the directory from which the calling programme was loaded, and then in the directories specified in the environment variable COBDIR. When this switch is off, subprograms are searched for first in the current directory and then in the directories specified in COBDIR.

L - Number of Record Locks

Specifies the number of record locks that can exist at any one time.

Properties:

Default:	/L200
Environment:	16-bit shared run-time system

Comments: The maximum number you can specify is 600.

The number applies to all locks held by the system and not for each file.

M - command.com Transient Area

Makes the command.com transient area available for use by the application. Warning! Setting this switch prevents the last command entered from being saved in the buffer; therefore, you are unable to use the standard DOS command line editing facility.

Properties:

Default:	Off
Environment:	16-bit shared run-time system on DOS

Comments: Using this switch increases memory by 21K on DOS 3.3 and by 28K on DOS 4.x and above. We recommend that you do not set this switch if you are running your application from a batch file.

M2 - Active Programme Discard

Prevents the run-time system from paging out procedure code of an active programme.

Properties:

Default:	Off
Environment:	16-bit shared run-time system

Comments: When this switch is off, the RTS memory manager, when short of free memory, discards procedure code of currently active programmes. Discarded code is reloaded when it next needs to be executed. This can cause "out of memory" errors if there is no room to reload a programme when a subprogram it has called returns to it. If this switch is on, procedure code of currently active programmes is not discarded; thus you never get a "memory full" error when a subprogram returns. Applications using this switch should use the ON EXCEPTION/OVERFLOW syntax to check for memory being full when a subprogram is called.

M - Number of Heaps

Specifies, in multiples of 128, the number of heaps available for each application.

Properties:

Default:	/M3 (That is, 3 x 128 heaps.)
Environment:	16-bit shared run-time system

Comments: The default number of heaps made available for each application is 384. System software uses some of the heaps made available to an application, so the number of heaps usable is slightly less than the number specified.

You might need to increase the number of heaps when animating large applications.

The only possible settings of this switch are:/M1,/M2,/M3 and/M4.

N – Null

Enables null insertion for all line sequential files in your programme.

Properties:

Default:	On
Environment:	All

Comments: This switch is especially useful if the format of your files is incompatible with this version of COBOL.

Setting this switch to on means that when a programme writes records to a line sequential file with a record containing control characters (that is, all characters with ASCII codes less than or equal to x"1F"), the system adds a null character (x"00") before each control character. Similarly, on reading a record from a line sequential file, these null characters are stripped from the control characters. Setting this switch affects only the physical storage of data in a line sequential file. Records written with one setting and read back with the same setting are returned in exactly the same way. However, if you try to read a file with one setting which was written with the other setting, the results are unpredictable.

Setting this switch off enables control characters to be written and read in the same way as other characters.

When the N switch is on:

- Any character is allowed in the data record of a line sequential file.
- Each record is examined before it is written. All characters whose value is less than or equal to x"1F" are written with a preceding null (x"00") to form two-byte pairs. On output to disk, trailing spaces are removed, and a record terminator of x"0D0A" is appended to terminate the record.
- The file is read as records, some of which might contain two-byte pairs where the first byte is null. The records are terminated by a record terminator. The leading null of each two-byte pair is removed to give the final data record. Tabs (x"09") that do not form part of a two-byte pair are expanded.

Note: Control characters depend on the operating system. Their hexadecimal values are always less than x"1F". CR (x"0D"), LF (x"0A"), TAB (x"09"), NUL (x"00"), and EOF (x"1A") are all recognized control characters on DOS, Windows and OS/2.

When the N switch is off:

- Data records in a line sequential file must contain only ASCII text characters (those with a value greater than x"1F").

- Trailing spaces are removed on output to disk, and a record terminator of x"0D0A" is appended to terminate the record. Printer control characters might also be written to disk.
- The file is read as data records with each record terminated by a record terminator. If the data contains either x"0D" or x"0A", results can be unpredictable. Tab characters (x"09") are expanded to spaces; otherwise the data record is returned intact.

Example

The command:

DOS, OS/2 and Windows:

```
myprog (-N)
```

UNIX:

```
cobrun -N myprog
```

Loads the programme myprog and specifies that, in line sequential files, all characters less than or equal to x"1F", except for Tab and the file control characters, are treated as data. Null is not inserted before data characters less than x"1F" on output.

O - Divide-by-zero

Enables run-time system error 48 ("Attempt to divide by zero").

Properties:

Default:	On
Environment:	All

Comments: A programme compiled with CHECKDIV" OSVS", CHECKDIV"VSC2" or CHECKDIV"COBOL370" set produces run-time system error 48 upon an attempt to divide by zero. Setting this switch off (-O) disables this error, causing the programme to continue with undefined results. This switch has no effect on programmes that were not compiled using one of the above directive settings.

See also: CHECKDIV Compiler directive

P - High-level Printer I/O

Causes the DOS shared run-time system to perform its

printer I/O by calling a standard DOS routine instead of by invoking standard BIOS routines.

Properties:

Default:	Off
Environment:	16-bit shared run-time system on DOS

Comments: This switch is particularly useful when accessing a printer attached to a local area network or when accessing slow local printers which keep timing out because their buffers are full.

With the P switch set, the system cannot detect whether the printer is available when it is opened; only when an attempt is made to write to it.

p - Dynamic Linkage Fixup

Causes the run-time system to set the addressability for all Linkage Section items in a programme when it is called.

Properties:

Default:	On
Environment:	UNIX

Comments: This switch is lower-case "p".

Setting this switch to off causes the run-time system to set up COBOL parameters (that is, Linkage Section items) on demand. By default, the run-time system sets up the addressability for all the Linkage Section items in a programme when it is called.

Setting this switch to off can improve the run-time performance of subprograms with large linkage areas. This is because the linkage fixup is performed the first time an item is accessed, so if an item is not accessed no fixup is performed for it.

P1 - Bell Enhancer

Sounds the system bell by using a call to the BIOS.

Properties:

Default:	On
Environment:	16-bit run-time systems

Comments: Normally, the system sounds the bell by accessing the hardware directly. On some clone machines this does not work, and the bell can only be sounded via the BIOS. Setting this switch makes the system sound the bell via the BIOS.

P2 - Logical Cancel

Enables support for logical cancels in the run-time system.

Properties:

Default:	Off
Environment:	16-bit shared run-time system

Comments: By default the CANCEL statement physically cancels a prog.amme from memory. A subsequent call to that programme requires the programme to be physically reloaded from disk.

If you specify +P2, the memory for a programme is not released when it is canceled, though the run-time system marks it as logically canceled. So, a subsequent call to that programme does not need it to be reloaded from disk; the RTS simply reinitializes the copy of the programme already in memory.

See Also: For the equivalent function on UNIX, see the -l (lower case "L") switch.

P3 - Programmes Loadable

Increases the number of programmes that can be loaded at a time from approximately 200 to approximately 400.

Properties:

Default:	Off
Environment:	16-bit shared run-time system on DOS with XM, on Windows and on OS/2

Comments: Changing the setting of the/S switch to give a larger stack reduces the number of programmes that can be loaded at a time. If you have a large application or need to increase the size of the stack, we recommend you set this switch.

See also: /S RTS Switch

P - Security Key Port Address

Specifies the address of the parallel port to which the security key is attached.

Properties:

Default:	/P956
Environment:	16-bit run-time systems

Comments: The system first looks for a security key in the port specified by this switch, the default being the standard IBM port address. If a security key is not found at this address, addresses 632 and 888 are checked.You might need this switch if you are using a clone machine that has nonstandard parallel port addresses.

Q - File Status Error

Maps extended file status codes (9/nnn) to a status that conform to the statuses returned in the COBOL dialect of your choice.

Properties:

Default:	Off
Environment:	UNIX

Comments: Setting this switch on causes all extended file status codes to be mapped, using an internal run-time system table, to a status that conforms to the statuses returned in the COBOL dialect of your choice.*See the chapter* File Status in your Programmer's Guide to File Handling *for details of how to configure the COBOL dialect you want to use. See your*Language Reference *for full details on file status errors.*

R - Retry Locked Record

Repeats the read operation on a record that is found to be locked until the record becomes available.This switch is maintained for compatibility with older COBOL systems. Use the RETRYLOCK Compiler directive instead. The RETRYLOCK directive gives the same functionality, and creates a programme that is portable to other environments. The R switch will be removed in a future version of this

COBOL system. Warning! This feature makes possible a deadly embrace. One programme might have locked record A and be trying to read record B, while another programme has locked record B and is trying to read record A. Should this happen you will probably have to reboot your system.

Properties:

Default:	Off unless the programme is compiled with the RM directive.
Environment:	16-bit run-time systems

Comments: This affects files of any organization which are open for input or I-O and which have no file status item declared.If this switch is set to off and a read is tried on a record which is locked, the read is not tried again.This switch is overridden by the RETRYLOCK Compiler directive.

S – Sort

Causes duplicates in all SORT operations to be ordered. This switch has the same effect on MERGE operations, although the WITH DUPLICATES IN ORDER phrase is valid syntax only for SORT statements.

Properties:

Default:	Off
Environment:	32-bit and 64-bit run-time systems

Comments: Setting this switch is the only available method of ensuring that all duplicates in a SORT operation are in order. Although you can explicitly specify the WITH DUPLICATES IN ORDER phrase in your source code it has no effect at run time.

The SORT puts temporary work files in the directory specified by the system defined environment variable, TMPDIR on UNIX, TMP on Windows NT and OS/2 V2. If this environment variable is not set, the system default temporary directory is used instead.

s - Sort Memory

Specifies the amount of memory used as an internal workspace when performing a SORT operation.

Properties:

Default:	-s3145728 (3 Mbytes)
Environment:	UNIX

Comments: Setting this switch specifies the amount of memory used in bytes. This switch can make your application run more slowly.

S2 - Video Snow

When set, indicates that the system need not wait for the vertical retrace signal to be active before accessing the video RAM.

Properties:

Default:	Off
Environment:	16-bit run-time systems

Comments: This is a specialist switch for use only on IBM compatible PC's where the need for protection of the video RAM is different to that on a standard IBM PC, AT or PS/2. If S2 and S3 are both off, the system determines the setting automatically. On some machines it might choose the wrong setting.

S3 - Video Snow

When set, indicates that the system must wait for the vertical retrace signal to be active before accessing the video RAM.

Properties:

Default:	Off
Environment:	16-bit run-time systems

Comments: This is a specialist switch for use only on IBM compatible PC's where the need for protection of the video RAM is different to that on a standard IBM PC, AT or PS/2. If S2 and S3 are both off, the system determines the setting automatically. On some machines it might choose the wrong setting.

S5 - Ansi.sys-Compatible Console I/O

Enables ansi.sys-compatible console I/O.

Properties:

Default:	Off
Environment:	16-bit shared run-time system on DOS and OS/2, and 32-bit for Windows NT and OS/2 V2

Comments: This function is achieved by the run-time system forcing all ACCEPT FROM/DISPLAY UPON CONSOLE statements to be executed such that I/O to and from the screen and keyboard can be redirected by using the ">" and "<" operators on the DOS or OS/2 command line.

This switch has no effect when running under the 16-bit run-time system on Windows.

S6 - DISPLAY Attributes Behavior

Changes default behavior of attributes for DISPLAY... UPON CRT of non-Screen Section items.

Properties:

Default:	Off
Environment:	16-bit run-time systems

Comments: When attributes have been written to a screen area with a DISPLAY statement using a data item that is not in a Screen Section, a DISPLAY statement with no attribute specification uses, by default, the attributes already existing in that area. If the +S6 switch is specified at run time, normal attributes are used instead. When attributes have been written to an area on the screen with a DISPLAY of a Screen Section item, a subsequent DISPLAY in that area with no attribute specified inherits those attributes regardless of the setting of the +S6 switch.

This switch also affects screen displays done using Panels.

S - Stack Size

Specifies, in bytes, the default size of the PERFORM/CALL stack.

Properties:

Default:	/S8192
Environment:	16-bit shared run-time system.

Comments: The number of bytes follows the/S immediately, without a gap.We recommend that you do not set a stack size larger than 32K (/S32768).You should always ensure that the stack size you set is the minimum required by your application.

Setting the/S switch affects the number of programmes that may be loaded at any time. The default stack size of 8K allows for around 200 programmes to be loaded; any increase in stack size reduces that number.

A stack of 32K allows only 80 programmes to be loaded. If you need to increase the setting of the/S switch, consider setting the +P3 switch as well. Assuming a stack of 32K, this increases the number of programmes from 80 to approximately 200 again.

Example:/S8192 sets a stack size of 8192 bytes.

T – Tab

Enables insertion of tab characters in all line sequential files.

Properties:

Default:	Off
Environment:	All

Comments: This switch is especially useful if the format of your files is incompatible with this version of the COBOL system.On output to disk, multiple spaces before a tab stop position are written as one tab character.

The T switch does not affect any trailing spaces as these are not part of the line sequential record, and they are removed on output. Tab positions are every 8 character positions (for example, 9, 17, 25) and cannot be changed.

On input, tab characters are always expanded to spaces to the next position, regardless of the setting of the T switch.

With this switch set to off, all spaces in a line sequential file are written to disk as space characters.

Z - DBCS Space Conversion

Enables conversion of double-byte character set (DBCS)

spaces to ASCII spaces when reading a line sequential file or input from the console.

Properties:

Default:	Off
Environment:	UNIX

Comments: DBCS spaces such as x"8140" for Shift-JIS and x"A1A1" for EUC in Japanese environments are converted to ASCII spaces x"2020".

See Also:

DBSPACE Compiler directive

Z - Dummy Parameters

Dummy parameters switch.

Properties:

Default:	/Z0 (no dummy parameters)
Environment:	16-bit shared run-time system

THE COBOL PROFILER

The COBOL Profiler is a facility that enables you to obtain detailed statistics on the run-time performance of a COBOL programme.When you submit a COBOL source programme to the cob command (see the chapter *COBOL System Interface (cob)* for details on the cob command), you can specify the PROFILE Compiler directive.

This causes the Compiler to include code in your programme to produce performance statistics about each paragraph of the programme each time you run the compiled programme. If your programme contains no paragraphs, this report is not produced.

The performance statistics produced using the PROFILE Compiler directive for that run of the programme are contained in a file called:

`programme-name.ipf`

Where *programme-name* is the name of the programme that was run. If an executable file is produced, then *programme-name* is the first entry point name in the executable file.These performance statistics are in compact form and first must be converted to a readable format. This is done by running Profiler, provided as part of your Micro Focus COBOL system.

INVOKING THE PROFILER PROGRAMME

To run Profiler, enter a command line of the form:
cobprof *filenames directives*
Where the parameters are:

Filenames	One or more files containing compact Profiler output. Profiler always searches for a file with the extension.ipf; if you specify any other extension, it is ignored. If you profile more than one programme at one time, Profiler output for all programmes is appended to the output file for the first programme,that is filename1.prf.
Directives	One or more of the directives that control the operation of Profiler. To specify a directive to Profiler, you must precede it with a plus sign (+). Each directive can be preceded by a plus sign, but only one is required at the start of a list of directives. Directives must be separated by one or more spaces. Where a Profiler directive takes a parameter, you can enclose the parameter either in quotation marks or in parentheses. If you use either of these, however, you must escape them using the backslash character (\). Descriptions of the available Profiler directives are contained in the section Directives for Profiler.

Profiler Output

When you run Profiler, the following banner is displayed:

```
* Micro Focus COBOL for UNIX Profiler Vv.r
* Copyright (c) 19nn Micro Focus Ltd.
* name-1
.
.
.
```

```
* name-n
```

where *name* is one of the names in file list in the command line.

For example, if you submit a programme prog1 to the cob command with the PROFILE directive, run the programme, and then enter:

```
cobprof prog1 +LIST
```

the following output is produced on the console:

```
* Micro Focus COBOL for UNIX Profiler Vv.r
* Copyright (c) 19nn Micro Focus Ltd.
* prog1
Total time: 172 milliseconds. Module called once.
```

%Time	Time	Entries	Ms/Entry	Paragraph
64.53	111	21	5	TEST-ROUTINE
17.44	30	1	30	PARA1
16.28	28	15	2	NAME-ENTRY
1.74	3	1	3	END-SECTION
0.00	0	1	0	INITIAL(UNNAMED)
PARAGRAPH				

The Profiler output gives the total execution time (in milliseconds) for the programme run and then breaks this down for each section and paragraph in the programme as follows:

Output	Description
%Time	Total percentage of execution time spent in the named section or paragraph
Time	Total time (in milliseconds) spent in the named section or paragraph
Entries	Number of times the named section or paragraph was entered
Ms/Entry	Average time (in milliseconds) per entry to the section or paragraph
Paragraph	Section or paragraph to which performance statistics apply. The initial (unnamed) paragraph listed is the initialization code executed before the user part of the programme is entered.

The product of the ms/entry and the number of entries should equal the total time spent in the section or paragraph; however, because all three values are truncated, there can be a slight discrepancy.

DIRECTIVES FOR PROFILER

This section lists and describes the Profiler directives you can use to control the behavior of the COBOL Profiler. To specify a directive to the Profiler, you must precede it with a plus sign (+). Each directive can be preceded by a plus sign, but only one is required at the start of a list of directives. Directives must be separated by one or more spaces. Where a Profiler directive takes a parameter, you can enclose the parameter either in quotation marks or in parentheses. If you use either of these, however, you must escape them using the backslash character (\).

Descriptions of Directives

Descriptions of the Profiler directives appear alphabetically.

All

Outputs a full performance profile. If you do not set the ALL directive, no statistics are produced for sections or paragraphs that are not entered or PERFORMed.

Alpha

Outputs performance statistics in alphabetical order by paragraph name. If you do not specify ALPHA, statistics are output in descending order of the total percentage time spent in each paragraph.

Form"Integer"

Specifies the default page size in lines for the listing file. The minimum value you should specify is 6. The default size is 60 lines.

List["Destination"]

Specifies where the listing is to be produced. The possible values of destination are:

- The console
- A specified file
- A default file

If destination is not specified, then the output is sent to the console, with page headings and page throws omitted. The VERBOSE Profiler directive also is set automatically.

If destination is specified with a filename, then the output is written to that file. If you do not set the LIST Profiler directive, then by default the output is produced in a file called filename.prf, where filename is the first name in file list in the command line.

[No]Verbose

Displays on the screen messages output by Profiler. The default setting is NOVERBOSE, unless the LIST directive is set without a specified parameter, in which case VERBOSE is set automatically.

Wide

Allows lines in the Profiler output to be up to 131 characters wide. If the WIDE directive is not set, lines are truncated to 79 characters.

7

Terminfo Database and Terminal Devices

OVERVIEW

Interactive COBOL applications rely heavily on sophisticated use of the terminal device for full-screen input and output, using the ACCEPT and DISPLAY statements. UNIX allows virtually any type of terminal device to be connected and provides the terminfo database as a means for handling the diversity of terminals. This chapter describes how the terminfo database is used by your COBOL system and what details need to be included in the database to enable COBOL to use particular terminal features. The chapter also describes the Micro Focus terminfo utilities mftic, mfinfocmp and termconv.

The Device Handling in your Programmer's Guide to Writing Programmes discusses devices in general including terminal devices. This chapter describes the detailed use and configuration of terminal devices for UNIX.

TERMINALS AND THE TERMINFO DATABASE

The terminal is perhaps the most important and complex device that a typical COBOL programme uses. It can be used in two ways:

- For simple unformatted line input and output
- For formatted, full screen, field input and output

For unformatted screen I/O, the COBOL system takes no special action. It simply uses the logical UNIX devices stdin, stdout and stderr (see the chapter Device Handling in your

Programmer's Guide to Writing Programmes) assuming that these are redirected by the operating system from or to the terminal.

For formatted screen I/O, the COBOL system has to take action at two levels: the logical level and the physical level. The Adis module (see the chapter Adis in yourProgrammer's Guide to Creating User Interfaces) translates the high-level COBOL requirements into logical, low-level, terminal-independent operations. The libscreen module translates these logical operations into the terminal-dependent physical character strings and escape sequences required by the attached terminal. The libscreen module also translates any response from the terminal into logical form and returns it to the Adis module.

To carry out the mapping between logical and physical form, the libscreen module needs to know the type of terminal that is attached, the capabilities of that terminal type and the physical format of any I/O activity. UNIX provides a standard method for providing this information; the environment variable TERM contains the name of the terminal type, and the details for that terminal type are held in a UNIX system database, known as terminfo.

SYSTEM TERMINFO

Your COBOL system can understand and use the standard UNIX System V terminfo format and structure, although it ignores any non-standard UNIX vendor-specific extensions. Some UNIX systems do not use the standard terminfo format and structure and in this case your COBOL system uses the alternative portable UNIX terminfo database described below.

The system terminfo database is located in/usr/lib/terminfo and is available for general use by any system application, a typical example being the system editor vi. If a particular process requires use of an alternative general terminfo database, then this can be selected by specifying its location in the environment variable TERMINFO.

The terminal details are held in a terminfo database for general use by non-COBOL applications. They can be made suitable for use by COBOL applications but frequently there is a conflict. COBOL terminal I/O is generally more sophisticated than that of most UNIX applications and has more stringent minimal requirements of the terminfo database. The precise meaning of some the terminal information can be ambiguous and sometimes the terminfo database reflects an interpretation that differs from that made by the COBOL system. In addition, the terminfo database is sometimes modified to configure a non-COBOL application and so becomes unsuitable for use with a COBOL application.

PORTABLE TERMINFO FOR COBOL

This COBOL system supports the use of a portable UNIX terminfo database and provides one that includes details for a selection of terminals. The format follows the UNIX specification but omits the UNIX vendor-specific portions. The database can be used by COBOL applications as an adjunct or alternative to the system databases. The system COBOL terminfo database is held in the directory terminfo in the COBOL system directory $COBDIR. The default value for $COBDIR is/usr/lib/cobol or/opt/lib/cobol depending on the operating system.

If a particular COBOL process requires use of an alternative COBOL terminfo database, then this can be selected by specifying its location in the environment variable COBTERMINFO The portable UNIX terminfo database can be maintained using the utilities mftic and mfinfocmp that are described later in this chapter. It can be generated from IBM AIX format using the utility termconv.

COBOL SCREEN HANDLING REQUIREMENTS

When COBOL provides formatted field input and output on the terminal, it carries out some sophisticated screen handling compared to many UNIX applications. Certain terminal capabilities must be available and described in the terminfo entry referenced by TERM otherwise the Run-time system gives a run-time error. Your COBOL system tries to optimize the use of the terminal and uses some optional terminal capabilities if they are described in terminfo. Required and optional terminal terminfo details are described later in this chapter.

SPECIAL TERMINAL FACILITIES

Some terminal facilities, such as Ctrl and Alt key support, are not automatically specified via the terminfo database. Other facilities such as controlling a terminal printer or wide terminal mode are specified via the terminfo database but are not part of the standard COBOL screen I/O. These special facilities are described later in this chapter.

OPERATION

SEARCHING PORTABLE AND SYSTEM TERMINFO DATABASES

The COBOL system recognizes two types of terminfo database: the portable terminfo for COBOL and the system terminfo. When it requires details for a terminal it searches each database that is specified by the environment until it finds details for that terminal.The COBOL system searches first for a COBOL-specific terminfo file and if that is not found it searches for a system terminfo file (see steps below). Non-COBOL utilities such as vi only search for a system terminfo file.

For a particular terminal, COBOL applications and non-COBOL applications such as vi can have different requirements for a terminfo file. Not only can different entries be required but also they can require different binary formats. COBOL might require a portable format and non-COBOL requires a system-specific format.

It is important to distinguish between general terminfo files and COBOL-specific terminfo files (examples provided with this system), to place them in separate locations and at run time to set up the environment variables COBTERMINFO (see the appendix Micro Focus Environment Variables) for the COBOL-specific files and TERMINFO for the system or general terminfo files as appropriate.

The COBOL system then searches for a terminfo file using the following steps:

- If the COBTERMINFO environment variable is not set, it is considered set to $COBDIR/terminfo. On SVR4-based systems, COBDIR is set to/opt/lib/cobol by default, while on most other UNIX systems, the default is/usr/lib/cobol.
- If COBTERMINFO is set, it is read as a set of colon-separated paths to the terminfo database. If the required file is found on any of the paths (parsed from left to right), then it is used.
- If the TERMINFO environment variable is set, it is used as a path to the terminfo database. If the file is found, it is used.
- Use/usr/lib/terminfo as the path to the terminfo database. If the file is found here, it is used.
- If the file is not found, an error is returned.

TERMINAL DEVICES

UNIX environments support virtually any terminal type, terminal definitions being held in a system database. This database must contain enough details for the terminal being used in order that Adis can function.Adis uses the standard input and output device interfaces for terminal I/O and so such terminal I/O can be redirected but with the restriction that you must not redirect standard input from a file unless it is a terminal device.

So, for example, the following is legal:

```
cobrun prog 'tty' >'tty'
```

(Use the appropriate (') character) whereas redirecting the input from an ordinary file or/dev/null is not legal and could result in a run time error.

SCREEN HANDLING REQUIREMENTS

The COBOL run-time system depends on a terminfo database being available and providing various terminal details to support the Adis module. The run time system regards some details as essential, and returns a run time error if they are not available. It regards all others as optional (making use of many of them and ignoring the rest). The following tables list entries in a terminfo terminal description that are recognized by the COBOL system. See your UNIX system documentation for details on the system terminfo database and how to specify terminal capabilities.

ESSENTIAL ENTRIES

The following entries must be present for the Micro Focus COBOL system to operate correctly. Entries marked with an asterisk (*) should be set appropriately for the type of terminal.

Entry	Mnemonic
Auto right margin. *	Am
Clear to end of line.	El
Clear screen.	Clear
Clear to end of screen.	Ed
Cursor address (row, column).	Cup
Cursor down.	Cud1
Cursor home.	Home
Cursor left.	Cub1
Cursor right.	Cuf1
Cursor up.	Cuu1
Eat newline glitch. *	Xen1
Entries for cursor keys	Kcud1, kcub1, kcuf1, kcuu1
Entries for function keys f1 to f63. *	Kf1 to kf63
Entries for home, next page, previous page, end, backtab, insert, delete and clear-to-end-of-field keys. *	Khome, knp, kpp, kend, kcbt, Kich1, Kdch1, kel
Exit attribute mode.	Sgr0
Number of columns. **	Cols
Number of lines. **	Lines
Xon/xoff. *	Xon

** The number of lines and columns can be overridden using the environment variables LINES and COLUMNS. See the appendix *Micro Focus Environment Variables* for details.

OPTIONAL ENTRIES

The following entries should be used if they are required for the particular type of terminal. However, the Micro Focus COBOL system does not insist that they are present.

Entry	Mnemonic
Bell.	Bel
Carriage return.	Cr
Enter ca mode.	Smcup
Exit ca mode.	Rmcup
Keypad local.	Rmkx
Keypad transmit.	Smkx
Move safely in standout mode (if appropriate)	Msgr

Some terminals must have smcup and rmcup in order to work correctly.

Highlighting

For terminals that have additive attributes the following are used. Entries marked with an asterisk (*) should be set appropriately for the type of terminal:

Entry	Mnemonic
Enter blink mode. *	Blink
Enter bold mode. *	Bold
Enter dim mode. *	Dim
Enter reverse mode. *	Rev
Enter underline mode. *	Smul

For terminals that do not have additive attributes, the following is needed:

Entry	Mnemonic
Set attributes.	Sgr

Highlighting is also affected by the COBATTR environment variable. See the appendix Micro Focus Environment Variables for details.

Performance Consi Derations

The following optional entries can be included and can

improve the performance of screen displays in some situations:

Entry	Mnemonic
Parameterized cursor down.	Cud
Parameterized cursor left.	Cub
Parameterized cursor right.	Cuf
Parameterized cursor up.	Cuu

If the following entries are present, scroll region s can be used to scroll areas of the screen that greatly speeds up such operations:

Entry	Mnemonic
Change scroll region.	Csr
Insert line.	Il1
Delete line.	Dl1

Wide Terminal Mode

If you want to use wide terminal mode, you must ensure that the sequence to set the number of columns appears in one of the following entries:

Entry	Mnemonic
Initialize string 1.	is1
Initialize string 2.	is2
Initialize string 3.	is3
Reset string 1.	rs1
Reset string 2.	rs2
Reset string 3.	rs3

Printer Support

The following entries are required for printer support:

Entry	Mnemonic
Turn on printer.	mc5
Turn off printer.	mc4
Print screen.	mc0
Parameterized print string.	mc5p

Line Drawing

For terminals that have additive attributes the following are used:

Entry	Mnemonic
Enable alternate character set.	Enacs
Alternate character set characters.	Acsc
Enter alternate character set.	Smacs
End alternate character set.	Rmacs

For terminals that do not have additive attributes, the following is needed:

Entry	Mnemonic
Set attributes.	Sgr

If you do not specify the appropriate alternate character set characters for your terminal, or your terminal does not provide a complete set, normal ASCII characters are substituted for the missing line drawing characters.

Colour

Only the Tektronics method can be used, for example, ANSI colour terminal s.

The following entries are required:

Entry	Mnemonic
Number of colours.	Colours
Set foreground.	Setf
Set background.	Setb
Original colours.	Oc
Original pairs.	Op

Only one of oc or op needs to be specified, but it must reset to the default colours.

Check that these entries are included in your terminfo database by running the mfinfocmp utility. See the section Terminfo Lister (mfinfocmp) in this chapter for details.

.Should you require, you can add entries to your terminfo database by running the operating system utility tic See your operating system manuals for details of how to do this.

Alternatively, you can create a new set of COBOL-specific terminal details in a COBOL-specific terminfo database using the mftic utility. See the sectionTerminfo Compiler (mftic) in this chapter for details.

Notes: If you use an attribute that is defined in your terminfo, but your terminal does not recognize, the attribute is not displayed and no error message is given.

Any attributes in ACCEPT or DISPLAY statements are automatically disabled by the run-time system if your terminal uses character positions to store attributes. This is the case for terminals that support the magic cookie glitch; that is, terminals that have "xmc" defined in their terminfo file.

SPECIAL TERMINAL FACILITIES

The following sections cover special terminal considerations.

WYSE TERMINAL SUPPORT

Your Micro Focus COBOL system supports terminals, such as Wyse terminals, whose escape sequences are prefixed with a character other than escape (0x1b). The cursor and function keys are fully operable.

CONTROL AND ALT KEY SUPPORT

Most UNIX terminals are not capable of detecting the Alt, Ctrl and a number of other keys (such as Shift) when they are pressed alone. Therefore, an alternative is provided. Enter/a to simulate the depression or release of the Alt key. Enter/c to simulate the depression or release of the Ctrl key

To use the forward slash character, enter it twice://. To get help on these and other keyboard mappings, enter/m. See the appendix UNIX Key Usage Chart for a list of keystroke mappings.

If your UNIX system supports the use of Alt and Ctrl keys (for example, SCO Open Desktop from Version 2.0 onwards) you should use the detect_alt_ctrlrun-time configurable option. See the chapter Run-time Configuration for information on detect_alt_ctrl.

WIDE TERMINAL MODE

This facility is for use with COBOL only, and enables you to use a wide mode if it is supported on your terminal; for example vt100 style terminals have a 132 column mode. All normal methods of screen output are allowed including ANSI DISPLAY, Adis DISPLAY and the cobprintf() call. See the chapter *Adis* in yourProgrammer's Guide to Creating User Interfaces for details. Cursor addressing must be consistent with the current terminal mode. For example, if you ask Adis to position the cursor at column 100 while in 80 column mode, this is not successful, neither does it cause an automatic switch from normal to wide mode. Wide mode must be set explicitly as shown below.

To use this facility you must include a record in the Working-Storage Section of your programme as follows:

```
01 mode-number pic x comp-x.
```

Then at run time you use the following call:

```
call "cobtermmode" using mode-number
```

where *mode-number* can have one of the following values:

Value	Meaning
0	Standard terminal mode. The standard terminal terminfo file is used.
1	Wide terminal mode. The standard terminal name suffixed by -w is the name of the terminfo file used.

The value of RETURN-CODE is set to zero if the call completes successfully. It is set to non-zero if the call fails, for example if the required terminfo file cannot be found. The method of searching for terminfo is described in the earlier section Searching Portable and System Terminfo Databases.

If the call is successful, the screen handling system is initialized (if it was not already) and:

- A RETURN-CODE of zero is returned.
- Adis restarts in the new mode.
- All character and attribute maps are cleared.
- The screen is cleared and the cursor positioned in the home position.

As the screen handling system is now initialized, all DISPLAY statements now use it, including ANSI DISPLAY statements. If the call fails, the RETURN-CODE is nonzero and the screen does not change. The RETURN-CODE is set as follows:

Value	Meaning
0	Operation successful.
1	The terminfo file has not been found, is not readable, is corrupt or there is not enough memory.
2	The terminfo file does not contain one or more of the required capabilities.
3	The environment does not support the requested code.

When using the cobtermmode call, you must be aware of the following:

- The number of columns in wide mode must not exceed 255.
- As this call causes Adis to be reinitialized, Adis support must be present in those run-time systems that support this call. If you try to exclude Adis from these run-time systems, you receive a run-time error.
- When running under Animator, this call causes the terminal to be initialized to the new mode, that can produce some flicker of the display. Switching between Animator and user screens causes mode changes as the wide terminal mode is not supported for Animator's screen.
- When the run-time system exits, the terminal is restored to normal mode. This applies only to mode changes made under the control of this call.
- Since the usual path-searching rules are used, if the directory pointed to by COBTERMINFO contains an entry for the terminal in normal mode, but not wide mode, but the system terminfo directory does contain an entry for that terminal in wide mode, the normal mode uses the COBTERMINFO version and wide mode uses the system version. This can cause unexpected results where the two files differ in capabilities other than column size changes.

- The COBCTRLCHAR environment variable must not be set. See the chapter *Portability Issues* in your *Programmer's Guide to Writing Programmes* for more information.
- If you have already set the TERM environment variable to indicate that a wide mode is required (that is the TERM value already has a -w suffix), issuing the call to use wide mode results in a suffix of "-w-w". This almost certainly fails, unless the terminal has a double wide mode and a terminfo file for this mode is available.

To cause the terminal to switch states, six terminfo facilities are used:

Full Name	Abbreviated Name
Init_1string	is1
Init_2string	is2
Init_3string	is3
Reset_1string	rs1
Reset_2string	rs2
Reset_3string	rs3

These are fully documented in the AT&T UNIX System V Interface Definition (SVID) and are used as follows:

- When the screen libraries start up normally, is1, is2 and is3 are output in that order. When the terminal mode is changed, rs1, rs2, rs3 are output, then is1, is2, is3 of the new terminfo are output in that order.
- Standard terminfos can contain the column switching sequences in either the rs*x* family or the is*x* family, hence both need to be used. Terminfos that do not provide it in either need to be modified, or a new terminfo file needs to be supplied.

Ensure that the terminal mode and terminfo specified by the terminal name in TERM match when you run an application.

CONTROLLING TERMINAL PRINTERS

Your Micro Focus COBOL system supports a number of

calls that enable you to control a printer attached to your terminal. Using these calls, you can switch the printer on-line or off-line, print the current screen, and print a string of characters.Using these calls can affect the portability of your application.These calls cause the screen handling system to be initialized, if it is not already.

Putting the Printer On-line

To switch the attached printer on-line or off-line, you need to add the following record to the Working-Storage Section of your programme:

```
01 state pic x comp-x.
```

Then at run time you use the following call:

```
call "cobprt" using state
```

where the parameter is:

State	Set to 0 to put the printer off-line or 1 to put the printer on-line.

When the printer is on-line, all screen output goes to the printer; it can also show on your screen, but this is terminal dependent. You must be aware that the behavior of your terminal and printer, once you have set the printer on-line, is entirely hardware dependent.

The screen handling library sends various control codes to the terminal (for example, to position the cursor) that some terminals might pass to the printer, though this is undefined, as is the action the printer takes if these codes are passed to it.

Once the printer is placed off-line, the run-time system redraws the screen to ensure it is up to date, as the terminal might not have updated it during printer output.

If the printer is placed on-line by this call and the run-time system terminates, the run-time system automatically places the printer off-line. Results of animating programmes that make this call are undefined.

Printing a Screen

To print the contents of the current screen on the printer, you use the following call at run time:

```
call "cobprtscrn"
```

Although this call causes the screen handling system to be initialized, this call is pointless if the screen handling system has not already been initialized as it simply causes a blank screen to be printed.

Printing a String of Characters

To print a string of characters on the printer you need to add these records to the Working-Storage Section of your programme:

```
01 strng pic x(100).
01 strng-length pic x comp-x value 100.
```

Then at run time you use the following call:

```
call "cobprtstring" using strng
 strng-length
```

where the parameters are:

Strng	A string that can contain only printable characters: control characters are not allowed.
Strng-length	The number of characters to be output.

This causes the string to be output to the printer, and possibly to the screen as well depending on the terminal.After the completion of this call, the run-time system redraws the screen.

Points to Note

When using the above three calls, you must be aware of the following:

- If the printer is switched off, not available or otherwise off-line, the results are undefined. Some terminals can wait forever for the printer to be available, some give up.
- Some terminals hold back all screen output while a print-screen is occurring, some allow screen output to continue. For those that allow screen output to continue, it is not defined if the new output appears on the printer while it is working its way down the screen.
- If highlighting appears on the screen and the screen

is printed, the highlighting can be preserved by some terminal/printer combinations, thrown away by some, or cause unexpected results in others. Again, the actual behavior is entirely hardware dependent.

- RETURN-CODE is set to zero if the required capability for the call was found and no errors were encountered. It is set to nonzero if the capability was missing or some other error was encountered.
- The COBCTRLCHAR environment variable must not be set. See the chapter *Portability Issues* in your *Programmer's Guide to Writing Programmes* for more information.

Terminfo Requirements

The calls described in the sections above require additional terminfo capabilities as shown below. The last column shows the behavior if the named capability is not present:

Call	Capabilities Required	Action if Not Present
cobprt 1	prtr_on	The printer cannot be placed on-line.
cobprt 0	prtr_off	The printer cannot be placed off-line.
cobprtscrn	print_screen	Trying to print the screen has no effect.
cobprtstring	prtr_non	Trying to print a string has no effect.

THE PORTABLE TERMINFO UTILITIES MFTIC AND MFINFOCMP

The UNIX operating system enables applications to handle terminal I/O from any terminal attached to the system, though each terminal can be of a different type with different capabilities. It does this using a database of terminal types, the terminfo database, that includes a file for each type of terminal. Each terminfo file holds details of the capabilities of the terminal-type identified by the filename. The details are stored in a machine-readable, compiled format that is specified in your operating system documentation, such as the AT&T,

UNIX System V Release 4, "System Administrator's Reference Manual" in the entry for term(4). The specification includes an initial generic portion and allows for a subsequent vendor-specific portion.Each vendor's UNIX generally provides a utility, tic, that creates a terminfo file from human-readable parameters given in a terminfo "source" file and a utility, infocmp, that creates a terminfo source file from a compiled terminfo file. Both utilities assume the vendor-specific format for the terminfo file.

This COBOL system uses the terminfo database to handle any terminal I/O that your applications require. It uses the generic portion of the terminfo file and ignores any vendor-specific portion. It uses only some of the terminal capabilities that can be specified, some are mandatory and some are optional.

Two machines running UNIX from two different vendors and having identical terminal types attached can run the same COBOL application. This COBOL system can use an identical terminfo file on each machine. However, it can be difficult to exploit this capability if a UNIX vendor does not conform to the standard for the generic portion of the terminfo file or if a UNIX vendor adds a vendor-specific portion to the terminfo file that is inconsistent with that from other vendors.

You can solve this problem by using the COBOL system utilities mftic and mfinfocmp in place of the system utilities tic and infocmp.

Both COBOL utilities can operate in the following two modes:

1. Micro Focus format mode
2. UNIX vendor-specific format mode

Micro Focus mode assumes that the terminfo file format comprises only the standard generic portion of the specification and that only the capabilities recognized by this COBOL system are present. This format is fully portable between different versions of UNIX; however, it might not include all the capabilities required by non-COBOL applications.

UNIX vendor-specific mode assumes that the terminfo format is fully compatible with the system tic and infocmp utilities. This format is generally not portable between different versions of UNIX, but it does enable you to define all the capabilities available to non-COBOL applications.

For a detailed description of the terminfo source and binary formats, including the list of capabilities your environment supports, see your operating system documentation. For a list of essential terminal capabilities required by the Micro Focus COBOL system, see the section *Screen Handling Requirements* earlier in this chapter.

TERMINFO COMPILER (MFTIC)

The terminfo compiler, mftic, translates a terminfo source file from the source format to the compiled format, that is placed in a terminfo database. See the section*Search Sequence* for details of how this database is located.

By default, mftic produces terminfo binaries in a Micro Focus generic format. It can also produce terminfo binaries in the same format as the system format. supports the concept of use= links, as tic does. When it encounters a use=*name* entry in a source file, mftic tries to augment the current terminal description with the description of the terminal *name*. mftic first searches for *name* in the current source file and if not found it searches the compiled terminfo database. If *name*is still not found then mftic reports an error and stops. mftic recursively follows use= links if necessary.

INVOKING MFTIC

The command line to invoke mftic is:

```
mftic [-vn] [-c] [-m] [-S] filename
```

Where the parameters are:

-v*n*	Specifies whether or not the compiler gives verbose messages. The value of *n* is one of: 0 - suppress all messages 1 - give verbose messages
-c	Prevents the creation of terminfo binaries. When this option is used, mftic only checks the input source file for errors (it does not check use= links for errors).

-m	Produces terminfo binaries in Micro Focus format rather than in the UNIX vendor-specific format. These formats are described in the section *The Portable Terminfo Utilities mftic and mfinfocmp* earlier in this chapter. This is the default.
-S	Treats the input binary as UNIX vendor-specific format rather than in the Micro Focus format.
Filename	The name of the terminfo source file to be compiled.

TERMINFO LISTER (MFINFOCMP)

The mfinfocmp utility performs either of the following functions:

- Lists a terminfo source description from the specified binary file
- Compares two or more terminfo binary files.

The binary, compiled, files must be held in a terminfo database. See the section *Search Sequence* for details of how this database is located if the -A or -B options are not set.

INVOKING MFINFOCMP

The command line for invoking mfinfocmp is:

```
mfinfocmp [-1] [-m] [-w n] [-A dir] [-B dir] [-
S]
```

[*filename* [...]]

Where the parameters are:

-1	(Numeric one, not a lower case "L") Outputs the results in single-column format.
-w *n*	Limits the width of the output to *n* characters. The default value of *n* is 60.
-m	Treats the input binary file as Micro Focus format, that is, a file produced by mftic with the -m option set. Results are undefined if this option is used to list a terminfo file in system format. This is the default.
-A *dir* -B *dir*	Changes the location of the terminfo database when comparing two or more files. The -A option changes the database location for the first file to the directory specified. The *-B* option changes the database location for the second and subsequent files to the directory

specified. (Note that the binary files do not usually reside in the same directory as the database. For example, the file containing details for the vt100 terminal typically resides in a subdirectory v in the database.)

-S Treats the input binary as UNIX vendor-specific format rather than Micro Focus format.

filename Either the name of the terminfo binary file to be listed or the names of the terminfo binary files to be compared. The function performed depends on the number of filenames specified on the command line as follows:

If no file is specified, mfinfocmp takes the name held in the TERM environment variable and lists that file's terminfo source description

If one file is specified, mfinfocmp lists the given file's terminfo source description

If two or more files are specified, mfinfocmp compares the first file with the second and subsequent given files.

SEARCH SEQUENCE

Mftic produces, and mfinfocmp lists, compiled format terminfo files for a terminfo database. Unless an option is specified to override it, by default, the directory containing the database is located using the following search sequence:

- If the COBTERMINFO environment variable is set, its contents are taken to be the directory name.
- If the TERMINFO environment variable is set, its contents are taken to be the directory name.
- If neither environment variable is set, the default directory used depends on whether or not the -m option is specified. If -m is specified then the directory$COBDIR/terminfo is used; if it is not specified then/usr/lib/terminfo is used. See the sections Invoking mftic and Invoking mfinfocmp earlier in this chapter for details on the -m option.

Note: If Micro Focus format terminfo files are placed in a database located in a directory other than $COBDIR/terminfo, then at COBOL application run time you must use the COBTERMINFO environment variable (rather than the TERMINFO environment variable) to locate this directory. If you do not do this, either COBOL or non-COBOL applications can fail to run correctly.

CONVERTING TERMINFO USING TERMCONV

Aixm

The operating system AIX does not support the UNIX System V definition of terminfo. This COBOL system only supports the UNIX System V terminfo definition and so does not directly support the AIX system terminfo. On AIX, the COBOL system can only use the portable terminfo, that by default is located at$COBDIR/terminfo.

Terminfo entries that are held in the AIX system terminfo database can be converted to the portable terminfo format using the utility termconv that is included with this system for your convenience.

Invoking Termconv

The command line for invoking termconv is:

```
termconv -i format -o format filename
```

-i *format*	This option specifies the input terminfo file format where *format* can be one of the following: Aix Input file is an IBM AIX terminfo file Unix Input file is a UNIX SVR3/SVR4 terminfo file
-o *format*	This option specifies the output terminfo file format where *format* can be one of the following: Aix Output file is an IBM AIX terminfo file Unix Output file is a UNIX SVR3/SVR4 terminfo file
filename	This is the name of the file to be converted. This original input terminfo file is saved as *filename*.bak during the conversion.

Example of Using termconv

This section describes how you can use termconv to convert AIX terminfo format to UNIX terminfo format.

The example shows how to convert a wy60 entry for a Wyse60 terminal.

You need to be logged in as root to do this.

- Using the first letter of the terminfo entry name for the terminal (wy60 in this case), create a terminfo directory under $COBDIR/terminfo if one does not exist already:

  mkdir $COBDIR/terminfo/w

- Create a temporary directory and make it the current directory:

  mkdir/tmp/terminfo

  cd/tmp/terminfo

- Copy the existing wy60 AIX terminfo file to your temporary directory:

  cp/usr/lib/terminfo/w/wy60/tmp/terminfo/wy60

- Run the Micro Focus conversion utility to convert the AIX specific terminfo file format, to generic UNIX System V format:

  termconv -i aix -o unix wy60

- Copy the new file into the COBOL terminfo directory:

  cp/tmp/terminfo/wy60 $COBDIR/terminfo/w/wy60

8

Learning Model

MODEL

Although various mathematical models have been suggested as descriptive of the phenomenon, only one—the constant-percentage or log-linear model—is widely used and discussed in the managerial accounting literature. The log-linear model basically states that the improvement in productivity is fairly constant as output increases. A basic knowledge of the working of these models is important for an efficient implementation in actual managerial situations.

GENERAL MODEL

The learning phenomenon based on the constant-percentage model is generally expressed by the mathematical function

$(Y, I_* \text{ or } M) = ax$

where the right side of the function is defined as

- a = the number of direct-labour hours required to produce the first unit of output,

where:

- r = the rate of learning or improvement represented by the constant percentage decrease in hours,
- f = the factor increase in output (usually discussed in terms of 2).

As can be seen from the formulae, the dependent variable is represented by either Y, I_* or M. This is due to the existence of three types of learning curve models which differ in their definition of the dependent variable. They are the average time model, the marginal time model, and the individual unit-time model. They may be defined as follows: The average time model specifies that the new cumulative average time per unit (Y) will decrease by a constant percentage (r) as the cumulative production doubles.

The marginal time model specifies that the new marginal time per unit (M) will decrease by a constant percentage (r) as cumulative production doubles. The individual unit-time model specifies that the new individual time per unit (I_*) will decrease by a constant percentage (r) as cumulative production doubles. In what follows I will explain each of these models, present a synthesis of the three models, provide guidance for the choice of one of these models, and elaborate on the relationships between the percentage of learning and the b parameter (the learning exponent).

Average Time Model

As stated earlier the average time model specifies the relationship between the cumulative average time per unit (Y) and the cumulative production (X). More precisely, the basic formulae for the average time or average curve specifies that the new cumulative time per unit (Y) will decrease by a constant percentage (r) as the cumulative production doubles. Besides the average time, the model provides formulae for the total time or total curve, the individual time or individual curve, and the marginal time or marginal curve. Formula 1 computes the average curve Y (that is, the average cumulative labour hours, labour dollars, or material cost for all units produced up to any particular point):

$Y = aXb$

where

Y = Average cumulative labour hours, labour dollars, or material costs for X number of units,

a = Theoretical value or actual value (if known) of the first unit,

X = Cumulative number of units produced,

b = Slope coefficient, exponent, or learning index. It is always negative, since the cost or number of hours is decreasing.

A much more used logarithmic version of formula 1 is

$$\log Y = (\log a) + (b \log X).$$

Formula 2 computes the total curve T (that is, the total labour hours required to produce a predetermined number of units):

$$T = YX = XaXb = aXb\text{-}1$$

where T = total labour hours required to produce a predetermined number of units. Formula 3 computes the individual unit time I (that is, the change in successive times):

$$I = aXb{+}1 - a(X - J)b + 1$$

Formula 4 computes the marginal curve M (that is, the relative change in total time to produce the xth unit, or slope of total time):

$$M = dt/dn = (b + 1)aXb$$

where M = marginal time to produce the xth unit.

To apply any of the four formulae, the value of the exponent b is first computed as follows:

$$b = \log r/\log 2 \text{ or } \log r = b \log 2.$$

To illustrate the average time model, let us assume that

- It takes 800 hours to produce the first unit of a product, and
- An 80 per cent learning rate is found to exist in the average assembly time when cumulative production doubles. Determine the value of b and the cumulative average labour hours for 4 units of output by first determining the value of *b*:

  $b = \log (0.80)/\log 2$

Common Logarithms of Numbers

No.	0	1	2	3	4	5	6	7	8	9	Avg. diff.
1.0	0.0000	0043	0086	0128	0170	0212	0253	0294	0334	0374	
1.1	0414	0453	0492	0532	0569	0607	0645	0632	0719	0755	
1.2	0792	0828	0864	0899	0934	0969	1004	1038	1072	1106	
1.3	1139	1173	1206	1239	1271	1303	1335	1367	1399	1430	
1.4	1461	1462	1523	1553	1584	1614	1644	1673	1703	1732	
1.5	1761	1790	1818	1847	1875	1903	1931	1959	1987	2014	

No.	0	1	2	3	4	5	6	7	8	9	Avg. diff.
1.6	2041	2068	2095	2122	2148	2175	2201	2227	2253	2279	
1.7	2304	2230	2355	2380	2405	2430	2455	2480	2504	2529	
1.8	2553	2577	2601	2625	2648	2672	2665	2718	2742	2765	
1.9	2788	2810	2833	2856	2878	2900	2923	2945	2967	2989	
2.0	0.3010	3032	3054	3075	3096	3118	3139	3160	3181	3201	21
2.1	3222	3243	3263	3284	3304	3324	3345	3365	3385	3404	20
2.2	3424	3444	3464	3483	3502	3522	3541	3560	3579	3598	19
2.3	3617	3636	3655	3674	3692	3711	3729	3747	3766	3784	18
2.4	3802	3820	3838	3856	3874	3892	3909	3927	3945	3962	17
2.5	3979	3997	4014	4031	4048	4065	4082	4099	4116	4133	17
2.6	4150	4166	4183	4200	4216	4232	4249	4265	4281	4298	16
2.7	4314	4330	4346	4362	4378	4393	4409	4425	4440	4456	16
2.8	4472	4487	4502	4518	4533	4548	4564	4579	4594	4609	15
2.9	4624	4639	4654	4669	4683	4698	4713	4728	4742	4757	15
3.0	0.4771	4786	4800	4814	4829	4843	4857	4871	4886	4900	14
3.1	4914	4928	4942	4955	4969	4983	4997	5011	5024	5038	14
3.2	5051	5065	5079	5092	5105	5119	5132	5145	5159	5172	13
3.3	5185	5198	5211	5224	5237	5250	5263	5276	5289	5302	13
3.4	53151	5328	5340	5353	5366	5378	5391	5403	5416	5428	13
3.5	5441	5453	5465	5478	5490	5502	5514	5527	5539	5551	12
3.6	5563	5575	5587	5599	5611	5623	5635	5647	5658	5670	12
3.7	5682	5694	5705	5717	5729	5740	5752	5763	5775	5786	12
3.8	5798	5809	5821	5832	5843	5855	5866	5877	5888	5899	11
3.9	5911	5922	5933	5944	5955	5966	5977	5938	5999	6010	11
4.0	0.6021	6031	6042	6053	6064	6075	6085	6096	6107	6117	11
4.1	6128	6138	6149	6160	6170	6180	6191	6201	6212	6222	10
4.2	6232	6243	6253	6263	6274	6284	6294	6304	6314	6325	10
4.3	6335	6343	6355	6365	6375	6385	6395	6405	6415	6425	10
4.4	6435	6444	6454	6464	6474	6484	6493	6503	6513	6522	10
4.5	6532	6542	6551	6561	6571	6580	6590	6599	6609	6618	10
4.6	6628	6637	6646	6665	6665	6675	6684	6693	6702	6712	10
4.7	6721	6730	6739	6749	6758	6767	6776	6785	6794	6803	9
4.8	6812	6821	683	6839	6848	6857	6866	6875	6884	6893	9
4.9	6902	6911	6920	6928	6937	6946	6955	6964	6972	6981	9
5.0	0.6990	6998	7007	7016	7024	7033	7042	7050	7059	7067	9

No.	0	1	2	3	4	5	6	7	8	9	Avg. diff.
5.1	7076	7084	7093	7101	7110	7118	7126	7135	7143	7152	8
5.2	7160	7168	7177	7185	7193	7202	7210	7218	7226	7235	8
5.3	7243	7251	7259	7267	7275	7284	7292	7300	7308	7316	8
5.4	7324	7332	7340	7348	7356	7364	7372	7380	7388	7396	8
5.5	7404	7412	7419	7427	7435	7443	7451	7459	7466	7474	8
5.6	7482	7490	7497	7505	7513	7520	7528	7536	7543	7551	8
5.7	7559	7566	7574	7582	7589	7597	7604	7612	7619	7627	8
5.8	7634	7642	7649	7657	7664	7672	7679	7686	7684	7701	7
5.9	7709	7716	7723	7731	7738	7745	7752	7760	7767	7774	7
6.0	0.7782	7789	7796	7803	7810	7818	7825	7832	7839	7846	7
6.1	7853	7860	7868	7875	7882	7889	7896	7903	7910	7917	7
6.2	7924	7931	7938	7945	7952	7959	7966	7973	7980	7987	7
6.3	7993	8000	8007	8014	8021	8028	8235	8041	8048	8055	7
6.4	8052	8069	8075	8082	8089	8096	8102	8109	8116	8122	7
6.5	8129	8136	8142	8149	8156	8162	8169	8176	8182	8189	7
6.6	8195	8202	8209	8215	8222	8228	8235	8241	8248	8254	7
6.7	8261	8267	8274	8280	8287	8293	8299	8305	8312	8319	6
6.8	8325	8331	8338	8344	8351	8357	8363	8370	8376	8382	6
6.9	8388	8395	8401	8407	8414	8420	8426	8432	8439	8445	6
7.0	0.8451	8457	8463	8470	8476	8482	8488	8394	8500	8506	6
7.1	8513	8519	8525	8531	8537	8543	8549	8555	8561	8567	6
7.2	8575	8579	8585	8591	8597	8603	8609	8615	8621	8627	6
7.3	8633	8639	8645	8651	8657	8663	8669	8675	8681	8686	6
7.4	8692	8698	8704	8710	8716	8722	8727	8733	8739	8745	6
7.5	8751	8756	8762	8768	8774	8779	8791	8791	8797	8802	6
7.6	8808	8814	8820	8825	8831	8838	8842	8848	8854	8859	6
7.7	8865	8871	8876	8882	8887	8893	8899	8904	8910	8915	6
7.8	8921	8927	8932	8938	8943	8949	8954	8960	8965	8971	6
7.9	8976	8982	8987	8993	8998	9004	9009	9015	9020	9025	5
8.0	0.9031	9036	9042	9047	9053	9058	9063	9069	9074	9079	5
8.1	9085	9090	9096	9101	9106	9112	9117	9122	9128	9133	5
8.2	9138	9143	9149	9154	9159	9165	9170	9175	9180	9186	5
8.3	9191	9196	9201	9206	9212	9217	9222	9227	9232	9238	5
8.4	9243	9248	9253	9258	9263	9269	9274	9279	9284	9289	5
8.5	9294	9299	9304	9309	9315	9320	9325	9330	9335	9340	5

No.	0	1	2	3	4	5	6	7	8	9	Avg. diff.
8.6	9345	9350	9355	9360	9365	9370	9375	9380	9385	9890	5
8.7	9395	9400	9405	9410	9415	9420	9425	9430	9435	9440	5
8.8	9445	9450	9455	9460	9465	9469	9474	9479	9484	9439	5
8.9	9494	9499	9504	9509	9513	9510	9523	9528	9533	9538	5
9.0	0.9543	9547	9552	9557	9562	9566	9571	9576	9581	9586	5
9.1	9590	9595	9600	9605	9609	9614	9619	9624	9628	9633	5
9.2	9638	9643	9647	9652	9657	9661	9666	9671	9675	9680	5
9.3	9685	9689	9694	9699	9703	9708	9713	9717	9722	9727	5
9.4	9731	97.6	9741	9745	9750	9754	9759	9763	9768	9773	5
9.5	9777	9782	9786	9791	9795	9800	9805	9809	9814	9818	5
9.6	9823	9827	9832	9836	9841	9845	9850	9854	9859	9863	4
9.7	9868	9872	9877	9881	9886	9390	9894	9899	9903	9908	4
9.8	9912	9917	9921	9926	9930	9934	9939	9943	9948	9952	4
9.9	9956	9961	9965	9969	9974	9978	9983	9987	9991	9996	4

$\log \pi = 0.4071$ $\log \pi/2 = 0.1961$

$\log \pi 2 = 0.9943$

$\log \theta = 0.4343$ $\log (0.4343) = 0.6378 - 1$

These pages give the common logarithms of numbers between 1 and 100, correct to four places. Moving the decimal point n places to the right [or left] in the number is equivalent to adding *n* [or - *n*] to the logarithm. Thus, log 0.017453 - 0.2419 - 222, which may also be written 2.2419 - 10.

$\log (ab) = \log a + \log b$ $\log (a) = \log a$

Next, the four formulae—the average time, the total time, the individual unit-time, and the marginal time—may be used to determine the average labour hours, the total labour hours, the individual unit labour hours, and the marginal labour hours required for different numbers of units.

The Marginal Time Model

As stated earlier, the marginal time model specifies the relationship between the marginal time per unit (*M*) and the cumulative production (*X*).

More precisely the basic formulae for the marginal time or marginal curve specifies that the new marginal time per unit (M) will decrease by a constant percentages (r) as cumulative production doubles.

Besides the marginal time, the model provides formulae for the total time or total curve, the individual time or individual curve, and the average time or average curve. Formula 1 computes the marginal curve M (that is, the marginal labour hours, labour dollars, or material cost for all units produced up to any particular point):

$$M = aX$$

where

M = marginal time per unit for X *** numbers of units produced, a = number of hours to build the first unit, X = number of units completed, b = learning factor.

To apply these formulae, assume that:

- It takes 700 hours to complete the first unit of output,
- An 80 per cent learning curve exists in the marginal time when production doubles. As in the earlier example (in the average time model), b may be found to be equal to -0.3200. Inserting the proper values in the form formulae will yield the marginal time, total time, and average time for different levels of production.

The Individual Unit-Time Model

As stated earlier, the individual unit model specifies that the new individual time per unit (I_*) will decrease by a constant percentage (r) as cumulative production doubles. More precisely, the basic formulae for the individual unit-time or unit-time curve specifies that the new individual time per unit (I_*) will decrease by a constant percentage (r) as cumulative production doubles.

Besides the individual time, the models provide formulae for the total time or total curve, the average time or average curve, and the marginal time or marginal curve.

Distinguishing among the Three Forms of the Constant Percentage Learning Curve Model

The three models differ in their definition of the

dependent variable (the left side of the equation) which is subject to the learning phenomena.

- In the average time model, the dependent variable is the new cumulative average time per unit Y.
- In the unit time model, the dependent variable is the individual time per unit, I_*.
- In the marginal time model, the dependent variable is the marginal time per unit, M_{**}.

It is important to determine which is the correct dependent variable which is subject to the learning phenomena because it dictates the types of formulae to be used. The formulae for the three types of models

Which Model to Use

The process being studied determines whether the average time, the marginal time, or the individual unit time should be used.

The procedure consists of the following steps:

- Collecting average time, marginal time, and individual unit-time information and cumulative output information.
- Plotting the information on a log-log graph and the line providing the best visual fit between, on one hand, the average time, the managerial time, or the individual time information and, on the other hand, the cumulative output defines the model to be used.
- To be more exact in determining whether the average time, marginal time, or individual unit time applies, perform a logarithmic linear regression of either one of the possible dependent variables with the output, that is, log (time, average, total, or individual unit) = log a + b log (cumulative units).

The model which provides the best statistical fit in terms of the highest coefficient of determination, R, should be used as the right model for the observed learning phenomenon.

Relationships between Percentage of Learning and Parameter b

To simplify the computations necessary in the applications

of the learning curve, the relationships between the percentage of learning (r) and the exponent (b) can be established for all possible values of r. In general, the relationship is computed as b = log 2/log 2. For example, for 2 = 70 per cent, b = -0.51457. This relationship for all values of r ranging from 51 through 97, and it can be used as an expedient way to find the appropriate value of b.

FORMULAE FOR DETERMINING THE SLOPE

The average time model of the log-linear model is represented by the formula $Y = ax$. If production doubles, then the formula becomes $Y = a(2x)$.

Given that learning (r%) takes place when production doubles, then. If we take the logarithm of both sides and solve for b, then we obtain For example, the slope b for a 50 per cent curve is

COST ESTIMATION

The learning curve can be used in cost estimation. Cost estimation when cumulative costs are known and when the learning phenomenon is in effect consists of estimating the coefficients of the learning curve from past data using the logarithmic linear equation log Y = log a - b log x.

In one method, the regression analysis of the logarithmic data on y and x using the least-squares method will provide a regression line. Its slope coefficient, exponent, or learning constant can be determined using the least-squares method as follows: where N = number of observations for which cost and hours are available, XY = product of log y and log x, X = log of the cumulative production, Y = log of the cumulative labour hours.

For a first example, suppose you were provided the data disclosing only the first three columns: column

- For the weeks, column.
- For total production, column.
- For direct-labour hours. On the basis of these data two new columns are added: column.
- For cumulative units completed and column.

- For cumulative direct-labour hours. The data for columns and
- Are then plotted on a log-log graph. If the scatter diagram indicates the presence of a learning phenomenon, then we need to determine the following information to insert in the formula for the slope coefficient:

Inserting the correct values in the formula yields

Next the learning rate

- Can be determined as follows: $b = \log 2/\log 2$ or $\log r = b \log 2 = -0.267(0.3010) = -0.080367$ $r = 83.3\%$

The other method of finding the learning rate is the doubling approach. Basically, it reads the gain time over any doubled quantity. The learning factor can be expressed as the ratio between the time taken to produce Z units and the cumulative time to produce 2Z units.

If double quantities are not available, use instead the following formula:Using the, the learning rate may be computed as follows. If the time to produce 10 units is 174 hours and the cumulative time for 20 units is 290 hours, the learning factor is equal to,

$$(290/20 \div (174/10) \times 100\% = 83.3\%.$$

After determining the learning rate using either the regression approach or the doubling approach, any of the computational formulae can be used to compute the average cumulative labour hours, unit labour hours, total labour hours, or marginal hours required to produce a specific number of units. The results of these computations. Finally, assuming the rate of learning will continue beyond total estimated production of 80 units, the learning curve can be used to make cost estimates.

WARRANTY MAINTENANCE AND MAINTENANCE FORCE

The learning phenomenon has been used in both the areas of warranty maintenance and estimating the size of a maintenance force. In the area of warranty maintenance, Kneip suggested that a progress function exists in the relationship of a product's maintenance requirement to cumulative production. Whereas in the conventional application of the learning phenomenon, the dependent variable (cost *r* labour time) is a production efficiency variable, in the maintenance progress function, the dependent variable is a quality, reliability, and serviceability characteristic. The results of regression analysis on two products showed that the maintenance progress function exists, that it relates warranty period maintenance to cumulative production, and that the relationship is logarithmic. Kneip also made the following interesting note:

Progress in a product's maintenance requirement is thus a characteristic of the organization, dependent upon both its structure and personnel, as well as the nature of the product. It cannot be overemphasized that progress is neither automatic nor self-perpetuating, but is the result of continual effort towards improvement.

Furthermore, its use as a management control device involves the possibility of actually impeding progress that might otherwise have been attained through the selection of a progress rate too slow to provide challenging objectives. The selection of the progress rate is a critical decision in the application of the function. In the area of maintenance force, Clarke used the learning phenomenon to predict the required size of a plant's maintenance force.

MAKE OR BUY DECISIONS

Learning curves are very helpful in make or buy decisions, which involve a choice between the cost of producing an item and the cost of purchasing it. The learning curve can provide the data for determining the necessary labour hours and the cost of producing the item. There are other costs involved, of course, but the labour costs are usually considered more illustrative. Once they have been determined, the make or buy decision is reduced to simpler terms.

Andress gives the following illustration of the usefulness of the learning curve in make or buy decisions. An aircraft company is faced with an economic slowdown and the necessity of reconsidering some existing subcontracts. It produces a landing flap assembly in its own plant as well as subcontracting it to another company. An existing subcontract to be considered for cancelling was for 372 landing flap assemblies.

In examining its learning curve, the aircraft company noticed that it produced 165 assemblies with a unit time of 445 hours for the 165th unit and that it would take a total labour cost of 111,000 hours if it decides to make the 372 additional units.

On the other side, the subcontractor relying also on the learning curve has produced the 165th unit with a unit time of 42 hours—43 hours less than the aircraft company. However, he found that the additional 372 units would require 164,000 hours, or 53,000 more than the aircraft company.

Obviously the short-run analysis using the learning curve argued in this case for making rather than subcontracting. Using the same example as the one used by Andress, Katz cautions that the decision may very well hinge on the nature of the future demand. He states:

In the short run (for the first 372 units) it would be more economical to cancel the subcontract. In the long run, however, it would be less expensive to leave the work with the subcontractor, as he could produce the product for 10% less labour once it fabricated as many units as the company. Therefore, this decision would hinge largely on the profitability of future demand for these products.

Since, in the particular case under consideration, the future demand was considered very difficult to measure, the decision was to make the units in the house and cancel the subcontract. To use another illustration of the use of the learning curve in make or buy decisions, let's assume that the XYZ Company purchases 800 pumps from the ABC Company.

The price was set last year at $70 per unit. Given the higher price, the XYZ Company decided to make some cost estimates to consider the feasibility of making rather than buying the pumps. The following estimates were made for an assembly run of 100 units:

Purchased components	$ 1,300	
Assembly labour	4,000	
Variable factory overhead	4,000	(100% of assembly
labour)		
Fixed factory overhead	5,000	
General and administrative		
overhead	3,200	
	$17,500	

A conventional make or buy analysis would compare the incremental costs with the supplier's price. In this case the incremental price will include only the relevant costs, that is, purchased components, assembly labour, and variable factory overhead. The incremental price is computed as follows:

	Cost of 100 pumps assembly run	Per unit
Purchased component	$1,300	$13
Assembly labour	4,000	40
Variable factory overhead	4,000	40
	$9,300	$93

In this case the XYZ Company must elect to buy the pumps rather than make them given that the supplier's price of $70 per unit is lower than the company's cost of $93.

If, however, the XYZ Company was experiencing an 80 per cent learning factor, the analysis used would be different. With an 80 per cent learning phenomenon the XYZ's assembly labour and variable overhead costs should decrease by 20 per cent every time there is a doubling of cumulative production.

The following labour cost and variable overhead cost behaviour by lots would occur:

Quantity Per lot	Cumulative average labour Cumulative	Cost per unit	100
100	$40		
100	200	32	(40 x.8)
200	400	25.6	(32 x.8)
400	800	20.48	(25.6 x.8)

This means that the average cumulative cost of the assembly labour for the first 800 pumps is $20.48 per pump. A revised analysis which considers an 80 per cent learning cost per unit factor is shown below:

Incremental Costs to Manufacture 800 Pumps

Purchased components	$13
Assembly labour	20.48
Variable factory overhead	20.48
Total incremental cost	$53.96
Cost to purchase	$70.00
Savings if pumps are manufactured	$16.04

Therefore, if XYZ Company is experiencing an 80 per cent learning curve, it should manufacture the pumps rather than purchase them.

WORK-ACCIDENT EXPERIENCE

Work-accident is an unfortunate but recurring event in all types of human endeavors. Public data on the subject are available in most industries. Among those industries which collect, tabulate, and publish the work-accident experience of its member firms is the American Petroleum Industry. In that industry "disabling injury" and the computation of injury experience are accomplished on the basis of USASI Standard Z16.1. One of the statistics defined by that standard is this:

The assumption taken in the foundation of the standard is that in every unit of time some constant number of exposures occurs and is some multiple of the duration. Greenberg argued that the method was misleading and that the denomination of the standard should be in units of production rather than in units of time, especially in light of evidence that the incidence of accidents was highly negatively correlated with productivity. He also found that accident experience follows a learning curve pattern, showing a decreasing trend in accident sequence as productivity increases. In fact, using mining industry data, Greenberg showed again in another study that mining accidents also conformed to a learning model. Such accident-experience learning curves may be used to evaluate the effectiveness of a safety programme and to open new possibilities in the analysis and prevention of accident occurrence.

STANDARD COSTS AND EFFICIENCY VARIANCE ANALYSIS

A standard cost is a forecast of what costs should be used as a basis of cost control and as a measure of productive efficiency when ultimately compared with actual costs. In a traditional labour variance analysis, where standard costs are compared to actual costs, the standard cost is assumed to be a constant amount per unit of output.

The analysis proceeds generally by dichotomizing the difference between the actual cost and the flexible budget into wage rate and efficiency variances as follows: $WRV = H\ (r - r)$ $EV = r\ (H - H)$ where WRV = wage rate variance, EV = efficiency variance, H = actual labour hours, r = actual wage rate per hour, r = standard wage rate per hour, H = standard labour hours.This traditional labour variance analysis rests in the assumption that no learning phenomenon is affecting labour usage and that it is realistic to assume that standard labour is constant over the total production of the period.If learning was present, then the assumption of constant standard cost is unrealistic and the traditional labour variance analysis inapplicable. In such a case, it would be preferable to consider one of two possible approaches:

1. One approach would be to use "moving standard costs" rather than "constant standard costs." The moving standard costs would be computed on the basis of the relevant learning curve formulae.
2. A second approach would be to dichotomize the traditional labour efficiency variance into (a) labour efficiency variance due to learning, and (b) a labour efficiency variance due to factors other than the learning factors.

To illustrate the three possible approaches, the traditional and the two approaches incorporating the learning effect, let's use this example: The XYZ Company makes personal computers. Its engineering department has determined that 800 direct-labour hours are necessary to assemble the first unit of a new model and that an 80 per cent learning phenomenon is present in the assembling process. The standard direct-labour rate per hour is $20. During the month of January, 10 personal computers were assembled in 800 hours. The actual direct-labour rate per hour is $75. Discussion of the three approaches to labour variance analysis follows:

FIRST APPROACH: NO LEARNING EFFECT INCLUDED IN THE ANALYSIS

Under this approach the traditional labour variance analysis consists of computing a labour rate variance and a labour efficiency variance based on a standard labour hours per unit of 100. It will be computed as follows:

SECOND APPROACH: LEARNING EFFECT CONSIDERED WITH MOVING STANDARD COSTS

The standard labour hours per unit is adjusted to take into account the learning effect resulting in the use of a moving standard cost. In such case, the standard direct-labour hours allowed for actual production of 20 personal computers is derived using the learning curve formulae as follows:

Therefore, the analysis can now proceed as follows: As can be seen by the analysis, the labour efficiency variance is $79,800 unfavorable taking the learning effect into account rather than $4,000 favourable effect in the traditional approach.

THIRD APPROACH: TOTAL CONSIDERATION OF THE LEARNING EFFECT

In this case the traditional labour efficiency variance is dichotomized into both a labour efficiency variance due to the learning effect and a labour efficiency variance due to factors other than the learning factors.

This approach shows the whole picture by disclosing the pure efficiency variance due to the nonlearning factors and the learning efficiency variance due to the learning effect. This approach should allow for a better analysis and effective control of labour cost.

External Reporting

External reporting may be affected by the learning phenomenon. It may be suggested that the cost savings due to the learning effect should be abstracted from the profit so actual increased productivity can be examined rather than productivity due to a repetition of tasks.

A more important problem is the distortion of profit that can occur when production costs follow the learning curve phenomenon if two conditions exist:

1. The contract(s) cover two or more periods, and
2. The unit price is based on a cumulative average cost permit.

To correct for the possible misstatement of profit, that a cost allocation model based on the learning phenomenon will disclose the relationships between efforts and accomplishments better than the conventional method.

To illustrate the problem of profit misstatement and how to correct it with the learning curve allocation model, let us use the data shown in

Let us also assume that 40 units are sold in 19 × 1, and 120 units are sold in 19 × 2; the unit selling price is $50 per unit in both years; the factory overhead and the direct-labour cost are each incurred at the rate of $5 per direct-labour hour; and the material cost is $1 per unit.

The income statements for both years under the conventional method of matching actual costs with revenues and the learning curve allocation model. Under the conventional method the company shows a loss of $608 the first year followed by a profit (net income) of $1,168 in the second year; the learning curve cost allocation model shows a profit of $140 in the first year and a profit of $420 the second year. Notice that the total profit for the two years is $560 under both methods. To avoid such reporting differences which may adversely affect the market image of the firm, Morse proposed the following reporting system:

As production takes place, any excess of the projected cost of each unit over the expected average cost of all anticipated production is charged to a deferred production expense account, and inventory is charged with an amount equal to the expected average unit cost of all anticipated production. When the projected unit cost is less than the expected average unit cost of all anticipated production, this difference is deducted from the deferred production expense account, and inventory is charged with an amount equal to the expected average unit cost of all anticipated production. As production takes place, any differences between actual and projected costs are written off as a period variance unless a change in a parameter of the model occurs.

Applying this reporting system to the previous problem yields the following journal entries:

Year 1	
Deferred Production Expenses	$748
Work in Process	748

To defer the differences between the actual costs of $2,408 and average cumu- lative costs of $1,660

Year 2	
Finished Goods	$748
Deferred Production Expenses	748

To change the differences between the actual costs of $4,232 and average cumulative costs of $4,980

Cost Reduction

Finding ways to reduce costs sometimes may be crucial to firms and is a necessity most of the time. The learning phenomenon and the learning curve offer opportunities for cost reduction programmes in general and in the preproduction planning and the product redesign areas in particular.In the preproduction planning stage, the type of learning curve to be used subsequently may be affected by the level and content of organizational planning. More precisely, the more preplanning that is done in all aspects associated with the launching of a new product, the lower the cost of the initial unit. With the cost of the initial unit being the starting point of the learning phenomenon, the lower it is through effective preproduction planning, the greater the savings generated by the resulting learning curve. Various studies, including an empirical one, have pinpointed the impact of preproduction planning on the time taken to produce the first unit and the dynamic rate resulting during the course of production.

Other authors have emphasized the importance of proper preproduction planning undertaken at the initial stages to lessen the scope of improvement during the course of production, which results in a flatter function, lying considerably below one which depicts a smaller amount of preproduction planning. Bhada identifies the following factors which influence initial cost and production time, indirectly affecting the dynamic rate:

- Anticipated duration of the production run.
- Estimated rate of output.
- The type of tooling utilized.

The degree of detail presented by engineering specifications. Effort expanded on settling problems regarding manufacturing design and inspection procedures. The degree of coordination achieved between different functions within the organization. The importance given to proper working methods, planning and shop organization. The influence of experience gained on similar product and processes

The impact of preproduction planning was even demonstrated in an experiment investigating the impact of types of organization structures on complex problem solving. Note: "Groups with higher initial performance (a values) demonstrated relatively smaller indices of performance improvement than groups that began with relatively lower initial performance."

In the same vein, Abernathy and Baloff examined the supply-demand imbalances during the preproduction stage and suggested that effective and proper planning at the production marketing phase would help prevent costly imbalances because the rate of increase in productivity was different from the rate of increase in sales.

In the redesigning state of a product, the learning curve may also be used to reduce the cost and help estimate the engineering effort required to do the job. More explicitly, it can be applied to the engineering effort in repeated design passes directed towards the reduction of total cost of the first unit.

Bruns presented a two-dimensional model relating the curve of the manufacturing learning improvement to the engineering learning improvement curve. Bruns shows that the unit cost depends on the engineering design as well as a manufacturing cost factor and uses the model to determine how many engineering design passes are needed to drive the product cost down to some predetermined target. The model allows reconciliation of the various approaches to new-product development where, on one side, researchers and scientists are attempting to build the first unit of some useful object at any cost, and, on the other side, engineers are trying to reduce cost while meeting given requirements. Bruns concludes:

In any event, whether engineering learning improvement is applied objectively or intuitively, this procedure warns the manager that the engineering effort to achieve a goal can vary widely, and may be beyond the range of interest or capability. New materials, processes, or designs and new personnel suggest possible reduction of costs through redesign. Conversely, experienced people and a steady technology suggest that great cost progress at small expense should not be expected.

Price Estimation

The learning curve is a study tool that can help managers understand and predict trends in cost. As such it can also be used to develop price strategies aimed at controlling market share and profitability. During phase A of, the dominant producer creates a price umbrella by keeping the price constant (or showing little decline), which may attract more producers. During phase B the price declines as a result of a price war where aggressive competitors strive for dominance. Finally, during phase C the price war is over, and a more stable and competitive situation is established among the price war survivors. The weak producers may have been eliminated or have differentiated their product.

Given that the cost function (Y) follows the pattern Y = KXb, the dominant producer may adopt a parallel stable pattern for the price function: Y1 = K1Xb, where Y1 is the average price and K1 the price of the first unit. This may discourage the entry of competitors. Although initial margins are small, final margins are usually greater.

Basically prices are set using the learning curve as an anchor. They are set at low levels with slim margins but which will generate higher sales volume and profits. The preemptive pricing strategy was successfully used by the so-called trusts of the late nineteenth century. The strategy consists of deferring the rewards and using the low prices generated on the basis of the learning curve to create a shakeout in the industry. Preemptive pricing is not successful in those situations where there is a constant need for product model changes or new-product introductions.

The following features were found to be important for an effective use of preemptive pricing:

- The expected product life is long.
- The product is standardized, like a commodity, with little risk that consumer tastes will suddenly turn against it.
- The expected growth of the market is rapid.
- The apparent slope of the learning curve is steeper, since the learning curve in that instance can constitute a substantial barrier to the entry of other firms into-the industry.
- The product is not patent protected.
- The company is not particularly strapped for cash.

A price umbrella at a high price followed by a sudden price shakeout. It is an aggressive strategy aimed at eventual industry shakeout and "brutal" elimination of competitors.

Although other price patterns may exist, the predictive ability of the learning curve can be generally used as a determinant in estimating the number of labour hours required for production. This facilitates the seller's pricing of the output, of course. Thus, given a knowledge of prime costs, the labour hours determined from the learning curve can be used as an allocation base for other indirect costs. Furthermore, the buyer, aware of the learning characteristics of the seller's costs, may be willing initially to pay a higher price that is to be reduced as the supplier's production increases and its costs begin declining.

Capital Budgeting

For most companies capital budgeting is a very serious and precarious proposition, and any reduction in the uncertainty of the potential cash flow is desirable. First, in a capital budgeting situation the company is likely to be at the top of its learning curve; hence, it can derive significant labour and time savings estimates from the curve. Second, the greater the proposition of labour assembly time, the more likely the curve will explain cost behaviour. Third, the more planning the company does, the more useful will be the predictive aspects of learning curves.

As an example of the application of the learning curve, let's assume the following fictional example of the XYZ Company which is considering the investment of $50,000 in equipment having a five-year expected life and no salvage value. The investment is expected to generate a cumulative expected demand of 200 units composed of 25, 40, 60, 40, and 35 units per year for the respective five years. The required minimum rate of return is 20 per cent.

The engineering estimation led to the following costs for 200 units of production: direct material, $500; direct labour ($5 per hour for an average per unit of 100 hours), $500; variable factory overhead (50% of direct labour), $250; variable selling and administration (10% of the sales price of $2,500 per unit), $250.

The total fixed costs are estimated to be $5,000 per year. Based on these data the capital budgeting analysis will proceed. It shows that a net present value in favour of production equals $6,739. The XYZ Company has, however, determined that an 80 per cent learning rate is applicable to both labour and variable overhead. It concluded that the capital budgeting analysis should instead include the correct time required as determined by the learning curve. Using the information that the first four prototypes required 1761.2 hours, it proceeded to compute the parameters of the learning curve b and a from the average model$y$ = $ax$where

y = Cumulative average time,

a = Time required for the first unit,

b = Learning exponent,

x = Cumulative production.

For an 80 per cent learning curve, b was rapidly determined to be equal to -.3219. Given that it took 1761.2 hours for the first four prototypes, the cumulative average hours per unit is y = 1761.2 hours/4 = 440.3 hours. Using the logarithmic form of the equation $y = ax$, we can solve for a as follows:

$\log y = \log a + b \log X$

$\log 440.3 = \log a + (-.3219) \log 2$

$a = 55.04$

Using the information obtained $a = 55.04$, $b = -.3219$, the marginal formula $y = (b + 1)ax$ and the demand distribution (25, 40, 60, 40, and 35), we can obtain the respective marginal time required (4,882 hours, 4,452 hours, 5,204 hours, 3,108 hours, and 2,444 hours). All this information may then be used in the capital budgeting analysis with learning-based costs. It shows a negative present value of $161.14. Using the improved cost projections of the learning curve, the capital budgeting analysis argues against the proposed investment.

Break-Even Analysis

Break-even analysis or cost-volume-profit (CVP) analysis is an established managerial tool that attempts to formulate a firm's cost and revenue functions and the relationships between the two. Basically, it involves an examination of cost and revenue behavioural patterns and their relationships with profit.

The analysis separates costs into fixed and variable components and determines the level of activity where costs and revenues are in equilibrium. The cost-volume-profit analysis is a normative model for understanding the relationships between the cost, revenue, and profit structures of a firm. It is a key factor in all decisions based on selling prices, variable costs, and fixed costs. The conventional approach to break-even analysis is used to compute the break-even volume or level of activity for which the profit generated is zero and beyond which any increase in production will lead to positive results on profit. The break-even point corresponds to the volume of activity at which total revenues equal total costs. In other words:

$r = P_q - (F + V_q)$

where

r = Profit before income taxes,

P = Unit selling price,

q = Sales volume in units,

F = Total fixed costs,

V = Unit variable cost.

The break-even point at which sales equal total costs and profits equal zero may be found as follows:

$P_q^* - (F + V_q^*) = 0$

where q^* = break-even volume. Consequently, we may write where $P - V$ = contribution margin permit. Therefore, the break-even point equals the ratio of total fixed costs (F) divided by the contribution margin per unit ($P - V$). To illustrate consider the following example. Susan Pineda plans to open a frozen yogurt business. She determined the following revenue and expense relationships:

	Dollars	Per cent
Sales price per cup of yogurt	50	100
Variable expense per cup	30	60
Monthly Fixed Expenses		
Rent	$1,000	
Wages	1,500	
Payroll fringe costs	550	
Other fixed costs	6,450	
Electricity	500	
	$10,000	

The break-even analysis proceeds as follows:

- The unit contribution margin or excess of unit sales price over unit variable cost is $P - V = \$.50 - \$.30 = \$.20$.
- The break-even point in terms of units sold is

The above "conventional" break-even analysis assumes linearity for both the costs and the reverse functions. With regard to costs, the linearity assumption means that the unit variable cost is a constant. In other words, no learning is taking place to reduce the unit variable cost. Needless to say, this is a very limiting assumption. The unit variable cost, in general, and the unit labour cost in particular may be subject to the learning phenomenon. A declining labour cost due to the learning phenomenon would substantially change break-even analysis and improve its use as a tool for planning and control of operations. In fact, various authors have attempted to present models for cost-volume-profit analysis which incorporate a nonlinear cost function to express the effects of employee learning. Their contributions are examined next.

Brenneck was one of the first to integrate conventional break-even analysis with the learning curve theory. He argued that as the cycle time per unit decreases because of learning, both the unit direct-labour cost and variable cost will drop. He concludes that such a decrease in cost should be incorporated in the conventional break-even analysis to improve its reliability.

McIntyre examined also the effects of the break-even equation and solution. This analysis follows.

The profit equation without learning is $r = px - cyx - f$ where r = profit that is, x units would be produced by n labour teams of one or more employees each, with each team producing x/n units. To determine the break-even point, the last equation must be set equal to zero and solved for x. Due to the exponential form of the equation and the presence of fixed cost, it is not possible to present a general solution for this breakeven quantity. The cumulative break-even volume may be determined for specific values of the parameters, however, by using the method of successive approximation to solve the equation for M = 0. Pegels used start-up curves to determine the break-even point. Using the marginal time model, he suppresses total costs as where *cx* is a variable cost that is not affected by learning. He also sequences the revenue function as $R(x) = px$.The break-even point is where $TC(x) = R(x)$ which after solving for n gives the following break-even point *xB*: If the cost of the first unit is *AC*(1), then the break-even formula becomes p = selling price per unit less all variable costs other than labour costs,

c = labour costs per unit of time,

f = fixed costs per period,

y = cumulative average production time per unit after x units have been produced.

The average time model, which states that cumulative average time per unit will be reduced by 1 - R every time production doubles is $Y = ax$

where

Y = the cumulative average production time per unit after x units have been produced,

a = the time required to produce the first unit,

x = cumulative production,

b = index of learning = log R/log 2,

R = learning rate.

The profit equation which incorporates the learning phenomenon will be as follows:

$r = px - cax+1 - f$.

If there were n production processes operating simultaneously, the profit equation will be

$r = px - nca\ (x/n) - f$

As an example, suppose that $AC(1)$ = \$400, p = \$300, and c = \$200. For a = 80, b = 0.32193, and a = 0.67807, one finds that, In other words, the break-even volume is approximately 75 units.

POSSIBLE LIMITATIONS

INFLUENCE OF CAUSAL FACTORS

Common to all the learning curve models is the need to estimate these two basic parameters:

1. Input resources associated with the production of the first unit, and
2. The learning curve characteristic or some measure of the rate reduction.

The exact determination of these two parameters is essential to the validity of the use of the learning curve. There are, however, factors which may affect the exact determination of these parameters. Hammer, for example, alluded to the fact that the incurring of more effort in the preproduction stage would lower the initial cost while the incurring of more resources during the production stage would increase the learning rate and cost reduction as production accumulates. Conway and Schultz attempted to categorize the factors which influence cost initially and during production. The preproduction factors which will have a bearing on initial cost and influence the number of opportunities for cost reduction subsequently include the following:

- *Tooling*: Type of tooling used and degree of completion or development prior to production.
- *Equipment and Tool Selection*: Volume for which production was planned.
- *Product Design*: Extent to which manufacturability was considered and the degree of change required subsequently. Degree to which product design and manufacturing engineering were coordinated prior to initiation of production.
- *Methods*: The degree to which work methods in detail are predesigned and the effort devoted to associated jig fixture design, flow analysis, etc.
- *State of the Art*: Relationship between the difficulty of the task and the ability of the organization to perform it.
- *Magnitude of the Design Effort*: Time and effort devoted to the problem of preproduction manufacturing design, specification, test, inspection, etc.
- *Shop Organization*: Including branding methods, preproduction training, skill, planning organization, etc.

All these factors suggest that to be useful the determination of the first piece cost of any item should be made far in advance of production.The production factors which will influence learning subsequently include the following:

- *Tooling*: Changes during production, method of increasing capacity for increasing demand (replication or redesign of production method).
- *Methods*: Changes during production, work simplification and similar programmes, operator originated changes, method of capacity increase.
- *Design Changes*: Degree to which manufacturing and product designs are changed to allow minor economies, specification and inspection changes as experience is gained.
- *Management*: Improved planning, scheduling and supervision to encourage progress, increase effectiveness, diminish delays and idle time.
- *Volume Changes*: Changes in rate or anticipated duration of production which affect other factors and decisions.
- *Quality Improvements*: The gradual reduction of re-work and repair operations, the reduction of scrap losses.
- *Incentive Pay Plans*: Manner in which administered, when installed.
- *Operator Learning*: Degree to which operations decrease time utilized in execution of a specific task.

All these factors affect the determination of the basic parameters of the learning curve and may cause the learning relationship computed to differ under various circumstances. The last factor, operator learning, has been considered by some writers to be the most important causal factor in those cases where the operator can contribute improvements in task method., Others maintain that in most cases the tooling, flow, and methods changes are the most significant causal factors of the learning phenomenon. They result more from management effort than operator learning. A more reasoned position is that the learning curve depends equally on both factors. More precisely, this position is supported by McCampbell and McQueen, who maintain that the function is based on the following:

- The human element (man's ability to learn and improve and the elimination of direct thought-process activities through repetition).
- The natural process of methods improvements and his foreman.
- More efficient material handling, transportation, pallet moving, and so forth.
- Less percentage owed to scrap, rejection, and re-works.

MEASUREMENT AND AGGREGATION PROBLEMS

In trying to determine the parameters of the learning curves in industrial situations, the cost analyst should beware of various measurement problems reported in the literature and in practice.

Some of these problems follow:

- The accuracy of the industrial data may be in doubt in most firms which use individual incentives such as piece rates for wage payment and control purposes. In effect such situations may create an environment in which output is restricted, actual times are seldom accurately recorded, and considerable doubt exists as to the validity of operator times charged to direct versus indirect labour accounts.
- The determination of the production count may be difficult because such factors as varying lot sizes, varying lead times, and varying schedules distort the association between costs and production quantities.
- The learning curve is generally determined for an aggregation rather than individual operations. What items to aggregate to determine the learning curve is a difficult and serious question. The aggregation may be determined following the organization of the facility and the method of production or following

the inherent characteristics of operations performed and the components of the product or operation. The problems of what to aggregate may be exacerbated by the mechanics of aggregation when product is produced at different times in different lots.

Some writers have preferred to work from disaggregated data before determining the learning curve for a product or assembly. For example McCampbell and McQueen maintained that the learning curve model for a product would depend on each type of operation and its corresponding percentage of total unit labour:

$$C = (X_1)(Y_1) + (X_2)(Y_2) + \ldots + (X_n)(Y_n)$$

where

C = the learning curve for an assembly, X_i =% of the labour for each operation, Yi=% curve of each operation, n = operation number.

For example, suppose:

Machining: 30% of the labour with a curve of 100%

Punch Press: 20% with 80% curve

Burring, Sanding, Hand Forming: 10% with 90% curve

Assembly: 40% with 70% curve

then, the curve for this product is 83%.

A fourth problem can be added:

- Whatever learning rate is found, it is important not to think of it as universal. Overwhelming evidence shows that the rate of learning differs between products, manufacturing facilities, and industries. To think otherwise is illogical and hard to verify empirically. Progress does exist for some operations but not necessarily at the same rate. No give slope is universal. Even if a given slope seems to be recurring, the learning functions are generally deter mined with tolerable amounts of error. "There is no such thing as a fundamental law of progress such as the '80% learning curve' used in the aircraft industry."

One interesting finding reported is that it is common to find different learning curve ratios for similiar products within a given production facility, and identical products produced in different production facilities. Another extensive study of data gathered in machine shops found, however, that while each basic manufacturing operation has an individual learning function for a product, it is based on a time-proportion weighted combination of individual progress functions.

NARROW UNDERSTANDING

One of the deficiencies in the learning curve literature is the narrow understanding of the causes and existence of the learning curve. The causes and existence of the learning phenomenon have been typically associated with clearing, or adaptation on the part of direct-labour workers, especially those involved in assembly. In general the contribution of engineers and indirect labour to the learning curve phenomenon has been ignored. In short, the learning phenomenon has been limited to direct labour, manual adaptation to repetitive tasks and has eliminated the machine-paced or machine-intensive manufacture.

Some authors have considered the generality of the learning phenomenon and criticized the narrow understanding of the causes and existence of the learning curve. For example Baloff states: "However, the emphasis on direct-labour learning as the primary cause of the learning phenomenon and the implications for machine-intensive manufacture that have been drawn from it appear to have very limited applicability."

What Baloff was alluding to is the generally accepted thesis in a variety of machine-intensive industries that a distinct learning phenomenon occurs during the start-up or debugging of new products and new production processes. An example of the learning phenomenon in the debugging of automated processes was provided by Bright. This learning or debugging is not necessarily the result of an improvement in direct labour but more likely in direct labour, indirect labour, and technical personnel. In these cases, it is more the effort of engineers and other indirect labour employees that generated the learning in the start-up or debugging. According to Baloff, this learning includes "such cognitive activities as redesigning the product or process, altering raw-material and end-product quality specifications, evolving more effective maintenance procedures and finding the proper operating (balance) of a manufacturing process."

NATURE OF THE LEARNING CURVE MODEL

Another deficiency in the learning curve literature is the uncertainty as to the actual form or statement of the learning curve model. There is not one single model of the learning curve.

The following seven models are possible:

- The log-linear model
- Pegels's exponential function
- Levy's adaptation function
- The Stanford-B model
- DeJong's learning formula with an incompressibility factor
- The S-curve
- Glover's learning formula with a work commencement factor

Some of these models have also been described by Carlson. Given that relative superiority is attributed to each of these models and specific industrial applications have been presented, it is recommended that new users of learning curves should make some test runs in their choice of the learning curve model most appropriate to their case.

PRACTICES IN ESTIMATION OF PARAMETERS

One of the major deficiencies in the learning curve literature is the dubious practice in the estimation of the *b* parameter in the learning curve model. As one may see by a cursory review of major cost account textbooks, it is the practice to simplify the parameter estimation problem by assuming that the *b* parameter retain the same constant value from start-up to start-up, *i.e.*, "empirical parameter value." Baloff calling for more empirical investigation to shake the tenacity of this unfortunate assumption states: This is not meant to eschew the role of empirical investigation, however, for it is clear that the generalization of the learning curve techniques will ultimately depend on empirical demonstration of the phenomenon in a variety of contents. Empiricism can make a further contribution in scrutinizing such dubious practices as the constant *b* parameter value and "interminable progress" assumptions that have plagued past applications of the learning curve.

In fact, evidence of the instability of the b parameter has been reported by Alchian in different airframe start-ups during World War II, Asher for a number of other postwar airframe start-ups, Conway and Schultz in the electronics industry, and Hirsh in the start-ups of machine tools.

SEPARATING THE WHEAT FROM THE CHAFF

The learning curve may be used by management as an artificial device to secure contracts and justify their cost estimates. In other words management may estimate their labour requirements with a false learning curve presumably based on empirical performance. If the contract is accepted, the learning curve-based estimates are used to prove its own existence. In other words the reduced labour became cursed by budgetary action more than by improved productivity through learning.

This artificial technique may be produced by:

- Increasing the labour content of the first unit or setting it at a very high point,
- Fluctuating labour classifications by frequently shifting the designation of workers between "direct" or "support/indirect" and hence reducing the labour content on a specific unit,
- Using manufacturing methods and tooling changes to create a reduction in the labour content, and
- Using at the start of the process small manufacturing lot sizes resulting in a high labour content for the first unit. These are some of the factors which obscure the true significance of the learning curve by causing it to reflect budgetary- and management-directed influence more than the increased productivity

resulting from skill acquired in reflective operations. These factors which obscure the true significance of the learning phenomenon have been mostly noted to last in the aerospace industry. That industry is conducive to the use of the learning curve as an artificial device because of specific conditions in that industry that are outlined as follows:

Profit is a negotiated element, dependent on cost.

There is little direct incentive to reduce cost, and there is incentive to maintain a high cost level. The basic product starts the production cycle with relatively little definition, thus requiring much rework, modification and delays and an abundance of manpower to cope with those problems. The customer may direct changes to be made that are outside of the contractor's original contract scope, and the contractor anticipates this by carrying additional personnel.

Objective manufacturing criteria generally are not used to achieve the most efficient production. Variable-type time allowances that are often the basis for staffing tend to create the appearance of a "cost reduction curve."

There is customer emphasis on reduction curves which stimulates contractors to "sell" and emphasize reduction curves. Given these conditions which may also exist in other industries, the challenge to management and to other parties is to separate the wheat from the chaff and to identify the real learning curve if there is one.

ILLUSORY SAVINGS AND VERIFICATION

Illusory savings may be the result of errors in the selection of labour hour data to be used in plotting the curve. First, automation may lead to a reduction in labour input per unit. Second, a direct-labour savings may disguise a greater use of indirect labour. Third, a change in the "labour mix" through hiring more qualified workers may lead to savings in direct-labour hours and an increase in direct-labour cost. Finally, the savings in labour may be due to a change in volume rather than to learning. All this creates a problem of verification. The problem of verification pertains mainly to the possibility of obtaining inaccurate data for direct labour, and to the potential inability to isolate accurately the learning factor that led to the reduction in direct labour. As a result, the learning curve in its present state has been criticized as failing to be a "scientific tool."

NEGATIVE OR DEFEATIST ATTITUDES OF EMPLOYEES

The negative or defeatist attitudes of employees may act as a barrier to the implementation or acceptance of the learning curve. Attitudes which ignore, belittle, or negate the presence of learning threaten the applicability of the learning phenomenon. For the learning phenomenon to be used effectively, positive attitudes have to be generated from the employee. Faith in the phenomenon is important. If progress is believed possible, then the learning phenomenon has a chance to occur. Open ended expectations and the absence of "ceiling psychology" are two factors most conducive to a learning effect. Some companies have been reported to have obtained more progress when the workers are not informed of the target rate. This is possible because the target set does not become a self-fulfilling prophecy. Finally, credibility in the phenomenon and its possibilities act as a major drive for its use. As Hirschmann states:

If the premise is valid that learning performance can be an underlying natural characteristic, then such performance should be found not only for more types of activities already recognized as responsive, but also for operations not previously reported or believed possible. Petroleum refining is considered to have such operations. It is characterized by large investments in heavy equipment, and is so highly automated that learning is thought to be nonexistent or too small to be of value. What Hirschmann is alluding to is progress by serendipity whereby the assumption that continual progress can occur may also create an atmosphere conducive to a learning phenomenon. He states again: Nevertheless, discovering such performance for operations previously considered unresponsive does provide additional tangible evidence that learning can be an underlying natural characteristic of organized activity. It does not merely extend the catalog of learning curves. Instead, it can help to breed the correction that such performance should be found elsewhere, and thereby lead not only to scrutinizing all operations to see which additional ones are susceptible, but to assuming that all operations have learning curve potential and to devising ways of making this potential a reality. Thus, it is prudent to reflect learning potential in plans and forecasts. White goes further by suggesting the use of learning curve theory to predict expected improvement in advance and sets these goals as an incentive to accomplishment.

ANOMALIES IN THE LEARNING CURVE SHAPE

It is common practice to assume that improvement in direct-labour activity associated with a start-up will continue throughout the production history of the product. These assumptions are at best tenuous. For example, Asher found evidence of plateaus developing in the start-up histories of several postwar airframes produced in the United States. Similarly, Conway and Schultz found distinct steady-state conditions occurring at the end of several new product start-ups. It is generally more accepted that there are several variations to the smooth learning curve forms, mainly with respect to the start-up point. The steepness of some curves may be due to an assumed high labour requirement. For example, if the proportion of assembly work was supposed to be lower, the downward slope of the curve would not be as steep. In addition to the steepness, there may be anomalies to the learning curve shape.

Hirschmann listed the following possible anomalies to the learning curve shape:

- A leveling off or a toe up may occur due to such factors as the closing of operations at the end of a contract. The costs may increase, which is a condition known in the industry as reverse learning.
- An aberration may also occur in the middle of the curve.

Hence, if the production process is interrupted for a significant length of time, resumption of the work will reflect a sharp increase in the learning curve. The aberration may be due to inefficiencies resulting from the employees' loss of skill and from the reorganization costs. Such a situation is called a scallop.

It may also result from the change in the design of a product followed by two costs:

1. The cost of added design less the quoted cost of the design removed, and
2. A loss of learning resulting in not being able to produce an assembly at the full quantity contracted. Hirschmann listed a third anomaly: A leveling down or a toe down may result from major innovations or sudden improvements in the learning process. The possible anomalies in the learning curve. The leveling-off phenomenon has been observed by others and labeled as the phenomenon of plateauing. The results of the empirical analysis of different start-ups showed that the learning phenomenon occurs regularly, is generally pronounced, but is ultimately followed by plateauing or steady-state conditions.

Baloff states the findings as follows:

- There is clear indication that a definite learning phenomenon occurs regularly in the several forms of manufacture investigated, and that this phenomenon is common to both new process and new product start-ups.
- The productivity consequences of the phenomenon are generally pronounced; all of the start-ups were marked by large regular increases in productivity for some months following the inception of manufacture.
- These productivity increases do not continue interminably; they are typically interrupted by the eventual development of a distinct steady-state operating condition.

In fact, Baloff observed plateauing in both machine-intensive manufacturing as well as labour-intensive manufacturing, with more likelihood of it happening in the machine-intensive cases where management is not willing to invest in capital to sustain learning. The two phases of plateauing in the learning curve. Another interruption in the learning phenomenon can be caused by production breaks. The production break is the time lapse between the completion of a contract for the manufacture of certain units of equipment and the commencement of a follow-on order for identical units. Anderlohr focused on production breaks between manufacturer lots and the resulting loss of learning which takes place. The following five factors associated with loss of learning are identified: production personnel learning, supervisory learning, continuity of production, improvement of special tooling, and improvement of methods. In fact, all the interruptions identified in this section lead to some form of learning loss.

For example, Hall suggested that design changes lead to two costs:

1. The cost of added design less the quoted cost of the design removed.
2. Loss of learning resulting in not being able to produce an assembly at the full quantity contracted.

9

Applications

ACOUNTING

Prevailing political and social attitudes point to further expansion of this segment of economic activities. Society-at-large demands that certain public and nonproprietary services be provided for the benefit of all of its citizens regardless of their ability to pay. Profit-motivated enterprises are not able to make such services available to everyone within socially acceptable norms. Moreover, upon investigation it appears that the free-enterprise system (like any other known economic system) is incapable of alleviating all perceived inequities within our society.

NATURE AND SIZE

Economists generally divide the production activities of our economy into a private and a public sector. The simplest way to define the public sector is to include within it all organizations not privately owned and operated, that is, nonproprietary organizations, as well as all not-for-profit organizations. This public sector can be subdivided by placing all governmental units (local, state, and federal) into one category and all nongovernmental not-for-profit organizations into another. However, the foregoing delineations are not clear-cut.

Despite the hybrid nature of some nonproprietary and some not-for-profit organizations, the public sector is treated. Accounting and reporting problems are quite similar between units of governments and privately organized associations having no deliberate or avowed profit motive. Hence, the general frame of reference for not-for-profit organization or agency, generally without specific regard for the public versus private ownership question.

GROWTH OF PUBLIC SECTOR ACTIVITIES

Not-for-profit activities have experienced substantial growth in our society over the last forty years when measured in terms of the resources committed to them. One interesting comparison is that all government expenditures prior to 1940 do not equal the amount presently spent in one year by the federal government alone. Of our total Gross National Product, which currently exceeds 1 trillion a year, approximately one-fifth comes from federal government sources.

Federal Outlays for Social Programmes

Category	Actual			Estimates		
	1960	1965	1970	1971	1972	1973
Community Development and Housing	1.0	0.3	3.0	3.4	4.0	4.8
Education and Manpower	1.1	2.3	7.3	8.7	10.1	11.3
Health	0.8	1.7	13.0	14.5	17.0	18.1
Income Security	18.2	25.7	43.8	55.7	65.2	69.7
Total Social Programmes	21.1	30.0	67.1	82.3	96.3	103.9
Total Federal Outlays for All Programmes	92.2	118.4	196.6	211.4	236.6	246.3
Per cent Social Programmes to Total Programmes	23%	25%	34%	39%	41%	42%

State and local government expenditures over the past ten years have also increased. Their growth rate has been nearly double the rate of growth of the Gross National Product. Thus governmental units of all types spend about one-fourth of the economic resources of the total economy as represented by the

Gross National Product. Beyond government-related activities, there has been a significant growth in resources committed to the remainder of the not-for-profit sector of our economy. These nongovernment, not-for-profit activities include hospitals, private colleges and universities, religious institutions, private social agencies, the Red Cross, the March of Dimes, the Scout movements, and thousands of other similar organizations. In total, the size of not-for-profit economic endeavors is huge.

We should note here that comparable public interest resource commitments are relatively as large, and in some instances even larger, in countries outside the United States. While many other Western nations-like Canada and the Scandinavian countries-devote proportionately greater resources to federal level expenditures, the United States leads in efforts devoted to nongovernmental not-for-profit activities.

Profit and Non Profit Organizations

We must also recognize that we live in a social environment which imposes limitations on the use of available resources. Efficient use of limited resources once fell into the category of conventional political and individual judgment. Today it is clearly a social obligation and possibly even a moral obligation. It seems reasonable, then, that every effort should be made to maximize the benefits coming from the use of available resources.

Profit-motivated and not-for-profit organizations are alike in that both must strive in principle to marshall resources as best they can. Both must ultimately justify to society the commitment of resources to their respective operations. Both have the responsibility to operate as efficiently as possible in their resource conversion processes or in their outright consumption of resources. In this important aspect of social responsibility, no differences exist between the two types of organizations.

In another important respect, profit-motivated and nonprofit organizations are fundamentally different. In a market-oriented economy, a private enterprise that continuously consumes resources unwisely does not survive. If it is unable to produce market-acceptable goods or services efficiently and thereby provide adequate returns to its employees, creditors, and investors, it will go out of existence after a period of time. An unalterable process of elimination, perhaps a Darwinian "survival of the fittest," thus operates in the private sector of our enterprise system.

The potential elimination process operates quite differently in the public sector. Perceived social needs dictate the establishment and possible later termination of not-for-profit organizations without direct or singular reliance on a market system of economic checks and balances (though economic stress may be an overriding factor in the closing of a small private not-for-profit school or college). Some public sector organizations may even be forced to operate in an economically inefficient manner for a time because public interest considerations demand it.

In a financial control sense, profit-oriented organizations focus heavily on producing appropriate returns for creditors and investors. Hence they have accounting systems that emphasize the periodic measure-ment of results of operations. Public sector organizations are often concerned primarily with the size of their available cash resources, since the continued existence of public sector organizations or their programmes generally depends quite heavily on cash availabilities. Therefore measurements of financial position, including cash reserves and outstanding obligations, dominate public sector accounting.

Accounting Objectives

The objectives of accounting for not-for-profit organizations can be stated as follows:

- To provide the information necessary for efficient, effective, and economical management of a nonproprietary entity and of the resources entrusted to it. This is a management control objective analogous to its counterpart for private enterprises.
- To provide information that enables managers to

report to third parties and to the general public on the discharge of their responsibilities in administering the programmes of the entity and the use of the resources under their direction.

- To permit public officials to report generally on the results of organizational operations and the use of public funds.
- To confirm and report legal compliance with statutory or administrative rules and regulations that relate to the acquisition and expenditure of resources.

Accounting entities in the public sector can be categorized into five different levels of operation.

Each of these levels involves one or more of the following:

- A government-city, state, or national;
- An organizational unit within a government-a department, an agency, a bureau;
- A separately organized not-for-profit organization comparable to a governmental subunit-a college, a church, or a community health centre;
- A programme-usually a specified set of goal-oriented activities which, at times, cuts across organizational lines in large not-for-profit organizations; and
- A fund-usually a pool of resources subject to special restrictions or requirements.

Since the notion of a "fund" has a specific connotation in public sector accounting, we call attention to the definition provided by the National Committee on Governmental Accounting in its 1968 edition of *Governmental Accounting, Auditing and Financial Reporting:*

A fund is an independent fiscal and accounting entity with a self balancing set of accounts recording cash and/or other resources together with all related liabilities, obligations, reserves, and equities which are segregated for the purpose of carrying on specific activities or attaining certain objectives in accordance with special regulations, restrictions, or limitations.

The nature of these entities dictates an accounting orientation that seeks to substitute *effectiveness* in meeting specified objectives for the *periodic net income* measure of private enterprise performance. A second difference relates to *compliance* with laws, special limitations and restrictions, or organizational statutes. While legality is an ever-present ancillary goal of the private enterprise accounting process, it takes on the importance of ensuring specific statutory compliance in public sector accounting.

Compliance-efficiency-effectiveness are interlocking goals when it comes to public sector accountability. *Compliance* is a measurement of congruence with statutory or quasi-legal requirements.

Example

The Bel Ami Fellowship Fund requires that grants from its resources be made only to undergraduate students at accredited colleges and universities who can establish descendancy from French ancestors. Accountability for Bel Ami funds does not concern grade point averages, financial need, or subject area of study. Compliance is established so long as awards are made only to students with French forebears.

The notions of efficiency and effectiveness. *Efficiency* is related to economic performance. It is a measure of relationships for the entity between resource inputs and outputs. Different types of efficiency measures may be specified, for example, output efficiency or input efficiency.

Example

Output efficiency relates to specified levels of resource inputs. If the seating configuration of a commercial airliner is changed from five to six persons abreast in its coach passenger section, greater output efficiency (*i.e.*, more passenger miles per flight) is achieved.

Example

Input efficiency is measured against a desired level of output. The city of Bellevue requires 250 transit buses to run an average of fifteen hours per workday. Higher input efficiency is achieved if the average cost per mile of operating a bus can be reduced from thirty-one to twenty-nine cents. *Effectiveness* measures achievement against specified technological, social, or other performance goals. It is normally difficult to quantify effectiveness measures precisely.

TRADITIONAL ACCOUNTABILITY

The traditional mainstay of accountability in the public sector has rested with expenditure control. Expenditure control is largely a compliance-oriented activity.

Expenditure Control

Managers of not-for-profit organizations cannot spend funds comparatively as easily as managers of private enterprises. This is not surprising, since controlling expenditures is the important constraining factor in not-for-profit organizations.

Expenditure control is typically effected in four separate, sequential steps:

1. Preliminary approval by a legislative body or a board of trustees to appropriate funds to a given programme.
2. Actual appropriation of funds to an approved programme.
3. Obligations or encumbrances incurred against the funds appropriated.
4. Disbursement of funds.

This four-step expenditure control process is especially important for governmental units. Preliminary *approval* to appropriate funds to a given programme starts the programme by providing a blueprint on how programme expenditures are to be made eventually.

But approval represents *no more* than eventual permission to request funds. Many tentatively approved programmes falter every year in national, state, and local governments due to the failure of the respective legislative branches to appropriate funds for projects or programmes fully endorsed at an earlier stage.

An *appropriation* grants authority from a legislative body or a city council or a board of trustees to an agency of government or to a not-for-profit organization (for example, the local boys' club receiving an appropriation from the Central United Crusade) to either disburse funds as approved or obligate the respective government or not-for-profit organization for the future payment of money. The act of appropriation is significant for accounting because it is at this point that the accounting process in not-for-profit organizations begins.

Step 3 entails recognition of planned use of appropriated funds. If contracts are actually made but not yet fully completed, an *obligation* is recognized. Definite commitments to spend funds for specified purposes in the future result in so-called *encumbrances* (defined below) against appropriated funds. The formal recognition of an encumbrance illustrates an act of accounting in advance of a completed transaction. Recognition of obligations to expend funds provides a necessary control against incurrence of total obligations and expenditures exceeding available appropriations.Finally, *disbursements* are cash payments either liquidating public sector obligations or making direct payments for products and services as authorized.

The distinction between cash payments and obligations or encumbrances made on behalf of the not-for-profit unit is most important. New encumbrances must cease as soon as the appropriations level is reached—irrespective of actual cash payments to date. Moreover, since direct operating cash payments are usually needed to the very end of an individual programme, advance encumbrances must typically stop short of the appropriated funding level.In the public sector, then, accountants must provide continuing information to programme administrators on the following:

- Total appropriations available
- Total obligations and encumbrances to date
- Estimated funds needed to complete the programme
- Cash payments made to date
- Balances (for example, unused appropriations less

obligations and encumbrances needed to complete programme, and obligations and encumbrances to date less cash payments made)

Accounting Process

A highly simplified example of a small federal government agency is used to illustrate the accounting process just described. In accounting for profit-motivated enterprises, the financial position equation is usually stated as:

Assets = Liabilities + Owner's Equity, however, represents the following relationship:

Cash Fund = Obligations Payable + Agency Account

Agency (fund) Account

The agency account, or fund account, is the accounting quantity measuring the unencumbered or otherwise uncommitted amount of appropriated funds. As a book-keeping convenience, a nominal or subaccount for encumbrances is provided as an elaboration of the agency account.

Encumbrance

An encumbrance is an internal authorization to expend agency funds in the future for a specific purpose. An encumbrance is neither an actual expenditure nor an obligation already incurred.

The actual accounting process begins by formal recognition of appropriations becoming available to allow future expenditures. The typical process also recognizes commitments (encumbrances) as soon as they are made against available appropriations. The process does not await evidence of a completed transaction, as is usually the case for business enterprise accounting.

Control of Resources

Expenditure control, is the traditional mainstay of *compliance* accountability in the public sector. How does this traditional system of accounting achieve resource input control in not-for-profit activities?

Three major resource control techniques are used:

1. Precise specifications for appropriations of funds
2. Creation of special-purpose funds
3. Use of various cost concepts

Expenditure

Specification. One of the more effective cost control devices in not-for-profit organizations is the exact specification of the uses of funds at the time appropriations are authorized. Almost invariably the total amount of money is specified for a given appropriation. This places an upper limit on the cost that an agency or a programme can incur within the authorized appropriation. When cost overruns occur, the additional sums of money requested are separately identifiable and hence susceptible to management and public scrutiny and review. Public sector appropriations are typically also quite specific as to the time period for which a given appropriation is available.

This control technique ensures that unauthorized expenditures will not be made from carry-forward or carry-backward appropriations (our earlier illustration notwithstanding). When used in conjunction with other control efforts, the limitation on the length of time to complete an expenditure serves a good purpose. However, when used by itself, it may well induce expenditures not actually needed because "the appropriation will be lost if not expended by *x* date," and, moreover, "next year's budget will probably be cut because we didn't need all that was appropriated this year." Agency case histories are filled with instances when public monies were consumed almost solely to avoid *under*spending an established budget (appropriation).

Another possible appropriations specification concerns specific identification of the purposes for which designated funds are to be used (*i.e.,* so-called line item budgets). This technique circumscribes the ability of administrator-managers to use funds at their own discretion outside the specified purposes. Specification of purpose is an effective control too. It is particularly helpful in audit and review functions.

The auditors can match, after the fact, the purposes contemplated in the approval and appropriation processes with the purposes served by actual expenditures. If variations are identified, corrective actions can be recommended or required.

Fund Designation

Probably the oldest control technique utilized for not-for-profit organizations is the segregation of appropriations into separately established funds. For example, a small city government may have a fire department fund, a water department fund, a traffic court fund, a street and engineering fund, a planning commission fund, a public school fund, and so on. A local YMCA organization may have a capital project fund, a special programme fund, a scholarship fund, and an office and operations fund.

Since specification of nonproprietary resources into large batteries of individual funds is still used almost universally, accounting for not-for-profit organizations is often identified by accountants as "fund accounting." Under this concept, an individual fund becomes an *accounting entity* unto itself, and financial records and controls are established with a specific fund focus. Sometimes separate funds and separate accounts for them are required by law, especially in municipalities.

In fund accounting, it is common to distinguish between a general fund and special purpose funds. The general fund normally provides the resources needed to operate the unit or agency on a day-by-day basis. Salaries of employees, building maintenance, and general office expenses are items chargeable to a general fund. In contrast, special funds are established to yield accountability for separately identifiable activities which make individual control procedures necessary or desirable. The pervasiveness of fund accounting is illustrated by the fact that the semiannual Uniform Certified Public Accountants Examination usually contains at least one lengthy problem on this subject. Undergraduate accounting curricula of colleges and universities often devote at least one quarter or semester course to fund accounting.

Various Cost Concepts

Following the lead of private enterprise, accountants and administrators in the public sector have recently begun to utilize different concepts of cost behaviour for specified control purposes. The essence of cost behaviour distinctions is that different cost measurements are most useful for different managerial control decisions if specific and directly related cost measurements are established for individual circumstances. For example, the cost of acquiring an asset can be distinguished usefully from the cost of using that asset in a not-for-profit programme. Similarly, the cost of replacing an old asset with an equivalent new asset may be more important in certain decisions than original acquisition cost of the old assets.

MATCHING EFFORTS AND ACCOMPLISHMENTS

Compliance with expenditure authorizations is a key objective of the public sector accounting function. Measures of compliance are easier to establish than measures of efficiency or measures of effectiveness, since the output of not-for-profit organizations is by and large intangible and not market oriented. Our market-oriented economic system serves, among others, the crucially important roles of allocating resources and continually threatening the survival of weak or inefficient enterprises. Thus the profit motive ensures that the entire private sector runs relatively efficiently.

For private enterprises, periodic costs (efforts) and revenues (accomplishments) are accounted for systematically, and the difference between them is reported as period net income. For larger companies, this reporting must conform absolutely to the requirements of the federal SEC. Moreover, it must be reviewed and audited at least once a year by independent outside professionals. Determination of periodic net income is presumably the most critical performance measurement for a private enterprise.

Even though in the future we are likely to see greater emphasis upon measuring and reporting a company's social, legal, and environmental performance, the latter will not replace the basic measures of economic performance. So long as private capital finances enterprise investments, economic performance will retain its prominence in the overall system.

With the absence of the profit motive in the public sector and the compounding difficulty of producing intangible and quite often elusive products, periodic matching of efforts and accomplishments in terms of concise quantitative reports has proved difficult. Thus, for many years, the public sector did little more than measure and report its dollar performance.

Dollar Performance

Traditional financial accounting systems and reports of not-for-profit organizations are oriented to identifying and summarizing how money is expended and to what extent such expenditures are consistent with authorizations or budgets. This system provides dollar accountability, but it furnishes few clues about the results that may have been achieved. The degree of efficiency in operations cannot be determined from dollar performance reports. As we have seen, dollar performance is predominantly oriented to compliance. Dollar inflows are a measure of accomplishment for private enterprises if such inflows represent revenues. However, no implication of accomplishment can be attached to the donated or appropriated dollars flowing to a not-for-profit organization. Moreover, matching of costs and revenues in the private sector produces a measure of performance (however conventionally or arbitrarily defined) which, if consistently applied, is a useful economic indicator.

Neither money inflows alone nor calculations of *net* money inflows and outflows allow evaluation of the efficiency and effectiveness of a not-for-profit organization's activity. A system of accounts and reports primarily aimed at compliance is both necessary and desirable for the public sector. However, such a system does not adequately serve today's social needs and concerns.

PPBS System

During World War II, several federal government agencies and various units of the armed services began to distinguish between monetary expenditures and operational efficiency. Moreover, the stated objectives of an organization began to be distinguished from measured accomplishments of these objectives. These developments were the forerunners of an accounting process known as planning, programming, and budgeting system (PPBS), which is increasingly being used in not-for-profit organizations. PPBS came fully into its own when, in 1965, the late President Lyndon B. Johnson requested that all government agencies adopt this system.

PPBS is designed to create a framework within which each not-for-profit organization can consider its anticipated outputs (accomplishments) in relation to probably required inputs of resources (efforts) before it makes a commitment to the programme. Under PPBS, the supporters of an organization or programme begin their justification for financial support by identifying the goals (accomplishments) that the organization or the programme expects to achieve. Measurement is facilitated if goals can be stated in quantitative terms, though not necessarily dollar terms.

After programme goals are established, alternative courses of action are evaluated in terms of their probable achievement of the goals (*i.e.*, probable effectiveness) and their probable costs (*i.e.*, probable efficiency). Decision makers then choose the plan that allows optimal goal achievements in terms of required resource inputs (*i.e.*, optimal effectiveness-efficiency). With PPBS, some proposed programmes are never initiated because analysis shows excessive resource input requirements or low probabilities of achieving desired results. Also, PPBS allows periodic reporting just like most other formal accounting systems.

Goals in Relation to Accomplishments

The statement is made in the preceding section that identification of goals is the first significant step in a PPBS system. This statement needs elaboration. Goal-setting procedures in not-for-profit organizations technically involve

- Specification of objectives and
- Specification of measures of accomplishment.

Operationally, these two steps constitute the goal structuring needed in not-for-profit organizations.

Example: The stated objective of Unified School District 205 is to provide kindergarten, primary, and secondary education for all residents in its district through grade level 12. From this broad objective a hierarchy of sub objectives is established, like minimizing the number of high school dropouts per year, operating a special education programme for physically or mentally handicapped students, running summer school programmes for exceptionally able students, and providing various health care and counseling services for all students in the district.

The entire hierarchy of objectives is subsequently used to measure accomplishments. College admission percentages of high school seniors wishing to enter college may be one measure of accomplishment.

Lower in the hierarchy, performance on verbal and quantitative aptitude tests may measure math and language achievements of district sixth graders against national test scores. Not only do statements of objectives influence the selection of measures of accomplishment, but the selection of measures of accomplishment may influence statements of objectives.

Therefore the establishment of objectives and of criteria for the measurement of these objectives are interacting processes in the goal formation stage in PPBS.

PPBS Data Bases

As knowledge stands at present, most PPBS applications are plagued by inadequate data bases. Notwithstanding developmental efforts by the General Accounting Office (GAO), the American Accounting Association, and other concerned professional groups.

Relatively little is known about non-financial measures of efficiency and effectiveness, particularly where several different data bases have to be used. What information to seek and how to measure it are the two most significant barriers to making PPBS fully operational.

INDICATORS OF ACCOMPLISHMENT

Accounting for efforts expended in public sector programmes or organizations is similar to its counterpart in the private sector. Although there are certain operational differences, these are not extraordinary in nature. Accounting for costs of not-for-profit organizations can simply and directly be carried forward to any PPBS matching of efforts and accomplishments for not-for-profit activities.

The same cannot be said for the revenue or resource inflow side of the coin. Revenue measurements are not appropriate measures of accomplishment in the public sector.

Even if changes in revenue flows were one of the objectives of a programme or an organization, achievement of that particular objective would still not give any indication of overall efficiency or effectiveness. Consequently, we need something other than measures of revenue or cash flows before any effort and accomplishment relationships can be established. The missing link needed for activity evaluation in the public sector has been identified as "indicators of accomplishment."

These indicators are most conveniently classified as:

- Operations indicators and
- Programme impact indicators.

Operations Indicators

These measures relate to output activities and are often non-financial expressions of products or services produced by an agency or organization. Examples are miles of highways built in a given period, number of automobile licenses issued, number of tests administered, and number of families visited by a social worker. In many instances, these indicators are merely statistics that measure neither efficiency nor effectiveness. Operations indicators can be classified in many ways, including, for example, measures of volume, quality, and comparison.

Example: Street lighting in Ritzville is measured in three different ways. The number of street lights maintained is a volume indicator. An illumination index in terms of kilowatts made available is an indicator of the quality of service. Kilowatt hours of electricity used per street mile during December 197X is an example of a comparative indicator. None of these measures effectiveness of street lighting as a deterrent to crime or for the prevention of automobile accidents.

Of course, operations indicators may also be expressed in financial terms. For instance, federal assistance to minority business programmes during fiscal year 1971 produced these indicators, among others:

- Government grants, loans, and guarantees by programme agencies rose from approximately $200 million in 1969 to $434 million in fiscal 1971.
- SBA direct and guaranteed loans to minority enterprises increased from $105.4 million in 1969 to an estimated $254 million in 1971.
- The dollar value of government 8(a) procurement contracts for minority owned business enterprises rose from $8.8 million in 1969 to $66 million in 1971.
- Minority firms received $77.8 million in direct Federal procurement in fiscal 1971, almost 10 times the $8.2 million of the previous year.

Operations indicators generally provide little qualitative information. They are not very useful in measuring how well public needs are being met. Often these measures are selected on the basis of simplicity and ease of calculation and understanding rather than on the basis of relevant performance measurement.

Programme Impact Indicators

Indicators of this type are often directly expressed in, or at least implied by, programme objectives. They relate directly to public or social needs or policies. Here outputs of programmes are evaluated comprehensively vis-a-vis

- Other programmes,
- Actual planned accomplishments, or
- Public or social needs or policies.

Example: (Efficiency vis-à-vis another programme.) The primary objective of the Space Shuttle is to reduce substantially the cost of space operations and provide a capability designed to support a wide range of scientific, defence, and commercial uses. The National Aeronautics and Space Administration contracted with Mathematical, Inc., for an analysis of how economical the Shuttle would be compared with the present launch systems which are used only once. NASA and Mathematical officials stated that this study demonstrated the Shuttle to be economically justified.

Senator Walter F. Mondale asked the General Accounting Office (GAO) to review the cost-benefit analysis used by NASA. With the senator's agreement, GAO's report was released to the Congress in view of widespread interest in the Space Shuttle. GAO identified critical areas of uncertainty in the Mathematical study. GAO also identified the per cent of cost increase before an investment in the Space Shuttle programme would become uneconomical compared to the present launch systems.

Example: (Efficiency in meeting a social need.) The Detroit Management Information Systems Group of the international CPA firm

Touche Ross & Co. participated in a programme concerned with measurement of one aspect of the so-called war on poverty. Welfare recipients were analysed for certain personal characteristics, such as health, work experience, and educational background. On these indicators, deficiencies were scaled and multiplied by weights to develop an index of needs. Total needs were then aggregated to develop guides to the most effective areas for investment.

Problems with measuring programme impact indicators abound. Without technical elaboration, we can observe that some scale must be devised to measure each characteristic to be included in the analysis. This often proves most difficult, especially if some type of index has to be constructed and a number of indices aggregated to develop a single composite measure of programme accomplishment.

Despite these difficulties some public sector organizations, the Sierra Club Foundation for example, have begun public reporting of some of their programme performance in their annual reports. Other organizations, including private enterprises, seem certain to follow this lead.

SELECTED SPECIAL TOPICS

The scope of accounting for public sector organizations is as wide as the accounting scope in the private sector. Many special accounting problems arise along the line of this spectrum. Accounting for public revenues is singled out as a fairly comprehensive illustration of a special topic. As a second point of general interest, some recent standard-setting efforts are described.

Accounting for Public Revenues

Not-for-profit organizations, like all other units in our economic system, must generate resource inflows before continued resource outflows are possible. Quite naturally, the inflows and the outflows seldom match completely.

Example: If total revenue collections for the same period amounted to, let us say, $220 billion, a deficit of $26.3 billion would arise. This deficit is the difference, during 1973, between new monetary resources flowing to the federal government and its total monetary expenditures for the same period. To finance this deficit the federal government must borrow, and the national debt will increase by the difference.

Example: The Open Door Clinic is a university district medical and social aid facility. It was established with an initial grant from the federal government which was not renewed. United Crusade and state, county, and city governments were also unable to provide funds. The clinic's future revenue possibilities were not bright, and hence it could borrow very little money on its own account. Private contributions kept the clinic open, but on a much reduced scale of operations. As implied in these examples, nonproprietary organizations have two major sources of funds:

- Current revenues and
- Borrowing from the public or the private sector. Public borrowing occurs largely through the sale of bonds—U.S. savings and treasury bonds at the

national level and state, county, city, or school district bonds at the local level. Most governmental units have statutory power to tax citizens under their jurisdictions and consequently can offer their bonds as virtually risk-free investments. The low-risk feature accounts for the comparatively low interest rate on major government bond issues. Income tax exemption for interest from state and municipal bonds is also a factor, which is explored at greater length.

Public Revenue Origins

For not-for-profit accounting purposes, revenues are increases in expendable funds which have no corresponding liability increases and do not represent bookkeeping adjustments within the public sector.

Governmental revenues derive predominantly from tax collections. The right to levy taxes is among the most basic powers of our form of government. Other not-for-profit organizations rely heavily on voluntary contributions and transfer, payments. Both governments and other not-for-profit organizations collect revenues from both involuntary and voluntary sources. The largest single involuntary source of public revenues, namely, federal tax collections. Readers should note that, in turn, the largest single source of federal government revenue is the personal income tax.

Voluntary contributions are the major source of revenue for private nonprofit organizations. Again private individuals make the largest amounts of such contributions.

There is an impressive array of different types of sources (*e.g.*, taxes, gifts, investment earnings, collections, contributions, etc.) from which public sector organizations derive their revenues. This is in sharp contrast to the relatively small number of types of sources (*i.e.*, primarily consumer groups) from which revenues can be earned by private enterprises. Also it should be notèd that revenue collection control is often a problem. For example, private not-for-profit organizations depend heavily on volunteers for fund raising and for some administrative activities. The use of "nonaccountable" employees often leads to loose control over the collection processes. This is an ethical rather than an accounting question but one of which we should be aware.

Public Revenue Accounting Process

Accounting for public sector revenues is similar to accounting for business revenues. In both instances, care must be taken to separate revenues from funds inflows not representing revenues. Proceeds from borrowing no more represent revenue in the public sector than in the private sector.

In several ways, however, revenue accounting for not-for-profit organizations presents problems not found elsewhere. One issue relates to accrual (recognition) of public revenues. Conventional accounting in the private sector recognizes revenue as soon as a relatively certain claim to cash is established. To satisfy the realization principle, this occurs typically after goods have been manufactured and sold or after services have been performed. In the not-for-profit setting, revenue recognition is closely related to actual cash collection. There is no criterion of "earning" public sector revenue. Hence the notion of revenue accrual is also absent in most existing practices.

Example: Wiley Township is on a July 1 to June 30 fiscal year. Real estate tax bills for 1973-74 are prepared in March 1973 and are mailed late in April 1973, with one-half of the annual tax assessment due and payable October 31 and the other half April 30, 1974. Technically, these real estate taxes accrue proportionately month by month during the entire 1973-74 fiscal year. However, for traditional municipal accounting purposes, one-half is recognized October 31 and the other half April 30 of each year.

Example: The YWCA is planning a branch in South City. It needs a new building, furniture, and fixtures, plus a director and staff for the facility. A special fund-raising effort is undertaken which yields pledges promising payment of $XX each September 15 for the next five years. Does the total pledge constitute revenue in year one? Since it is easier to pledge than to contribute money, would it be best to wait until cash is actually received before any revenue is recognized in this case? Acceptable accounting practice would be to recognize each yearly pledge on the date it becomes due and payable. Past experience may be used to establish estimated uncollectible amounts in connection with each revenue accrual. However, the accrual method of revenue recognition could be useful in the public sector. For instance, month-by-month revenue recognition could yield better financial information.

A second issue in the not-for-profit revenue accounting area centers on reporting. Conventional reports of not-for-profit organizations relate revenues to cash collections and costs to cash disbursements. But are revenues really independent variables in the operations of not-for-profit units? Or should revenues be related to the expenditures they make possible? Or should revenues be compared to the benefits that result from the expenditures? These questions remain largely unresolved. Generally, the authors favour independent revenue and cash collection reports together with separate cost-benefit reports. This solution does, however, treat revenues and costs as separate variables.

Setting of Accounting Standards in the Public Sector

Efforts to set broad accounting standards for public sector accounting are widespread and intense. These efforts are relatively less unified than the comparable private sector efforts supporting the activities of the Financial Accounting Standards Board.The United States General Accounting Office (GAO) has statutory responsibility for all accounting systems and standards used by federal government units and agencies. Hence the GAO, with assistance from advisory councils and national commissions, is a key accounting standard setter in the public sector.State auditors usually have authority to set accounting standards at the state government level. Since state and local governments interact frequently on many public service activities, state auditors also have considerable indirect influence on accounting for local and municipal government operations.

A national association of municipal treasurers and financial officers has produced an authoritative set of recommended accounting standards for municipal governmental accounting. This group regularly updates its standards. The nongovernmental portion of public sector accounting is literally inundated with accounting standards suggestions. Each branch of private nonprofit organizations appears to have a national association eager to propose accounting standards for its members.

A list of such organizations includes, among many others:

- American Hospital Association
- American National Red Cross
- Club Managers Association of America
- Evangelical and Reformed Churches
- National Association of College and University Business Offices
- National Health Council
- United Cerebral Palsy Associations
- United Community Funds and Councils of America

ECONOMIC MANAGEMENT

Management problems exist whenever diverse resources have to be coordinated so that specified tasks can be achieved. This process often starts with the determination whether certain resources even exist (*e.g.*, uranium, oil, or skilled workers) or how much it would cost to acquire or possibly create them. One needs to think only of a space probe or the daily food and living requirements of the 11.5 million persons crowded into New York City to realise the enormity of certain management problems. As for economic and financial factors, accounting helps by providing decision-relevant information to the managerial decision makers.

Accounting at the enterprise or other individual organization level distinguishes between the needs of external users and the needs of internal users of accounting information. The accounting needs of private sector enterprises from those of public sector organizations. Even though the individual purposes to which accounting is put differ sometimes fundamentally one from the other, there are many commonalities within the accounting discipline. Managerial performance evaluation is a universal accounting objective, coupled in many cases with a form of wealth assessment. Capital investment analysis goals underlie much of what is done in accounting, as do organizational planning and control requirements. And the same data-gathering and data-processing techniques can often be used throughout the accounting field! In short, the different members of the accounting family are closely related.

The economy as a whole now becomes our focus of attention. If management and investment problems exist at the enterprise level, similar problems certainly exist at the economy (or macro) level. Relative size alone hints at the importance of the management problems for the total economy. As one wag observed, "Washington, D.C., is the only place in the world where 0.1 means $100 million" (since most economic measures of the national economy are stated in billions of dollars).

MANAGER TASK

Managerial tasks for the economy as a whole comprise a wide spectrum of activities. Very important is the collection of revenues so that the federal government can function and provide the many social, political, and national security services that the public demands. Public revenue is primarily collected through *taxation*. For ease (and economy) of administration, we have a self-assessment income tax system. Accordingly, each taxpayer must keep sufficient accounting records so that he or she can determine his or her tax liability in compliance with applicable laws and regulations.

Example: Huster Bowls is a taxi driver in New York City. He earns a monthly salary of $750 by driving a Purple Cab 50 hours per week. During the year he takes three weeks' vacation. On his personal income tax return he declared a gross income of $9,000 per year plus $500 in tips. He kept no records of tips received. Upon review, an Internal Revenue agent determined that taxi tips average $.50 per hour of taxi driving in New York. With forty-nine weeks worked at 50 hours per week, Mr. Bowls was driving his cab for 2,450 hours during the year. Therefore his income from tips should have been $1,225. He is assessed income taxes on additional gross income of $725.

A second major task facing national economy managers is the preparation of a federal budget which allocates available resources to authorized public activities. The key building blocks for federal budget proposals are the so-called national income accounts. These accounts show which industries and services produced the annual Gross National Product, how much of this total of available goods and services was consumed and how much was saved (*i.e.,* invested), and how the income of the nation was distributed between wage earners, interest and dividend recipients, social security payees, and others.

Example

Analysis of the national income accounts shows that output of goods and services is increasing at a slower rate than the demand for federal government services.

Now economy managers must decide whether to:

- Curtail federal government expenditures,
- Raise more revenue through taxation, or
- incur a budget deficit by raising the ceiling for the national debt. Each alternative can be evaluated, in part, through its probable effects on future national income.

Regulation of certain industries is a third essential component of economy wide management. The need for regulation comes about because it is in the public interest to grant business monopolies to certain segments of the economy. For instance, electric power and telephone companies are given exclusive rights to serve defined geographic areas, since it would be highly uneconomical to have several dozen power mains or telephone trunk lines buried in each street of a residential area. Public safety and convenience are additional considerations favouring the regulated monopoly approach.

Additional *regulated industries* include railways, trucking and moving companies, shipping companies, airlines, cable TV systems, warehouses, and many others. For all of them, specific accounting rules and procedures are prescribed so that the necessary regulation (mainly setting of fees and rates that may legally be charged to customers) can be put into effect on a uniform basis.

Example: Whidsee Island Telephone Company applies to the state's utility commission for a 12 per cent rate increase on its residential service. In studying the application, the commission's staff finds that certain assets of the company are not stated in accordance with prescribed uniform utility accounting rules. The ensuing adjustments reduce the company's "rate base" asset amount and thus the earnings needed to achieve the negotiated rate of return on allowable base assets. The consequence is that a rate boost of only 7.5 per cent is granted.

Our fourth area of concern relates to the management of *national policies* that affect private sector companies. For instance, it is the public will in the United States (but not in many foreign countries) that fair trade must be assured and restraint of trade through trusts and monopolies prevented. Price discrimination not supported by actual cost differences can be prosecuted in some circumstances. Other examples of management based on the public interest include uniform cost accounting standards being imposed on all parties or companies seeking contracts or actually working under contracts with the federal government where the contract sum exceeds $ $100,000. Price and wage controls have been in effect at various times. Direct foreign investment controls were instituted in the 1960s as a result of the "dollar glut" abroad. Specific licensing is required before radio or TV stations may be operated. And, of course, the Securities and Exchange Commission (SEC) oversees the nation's securities markets and imposes rather specific requirements on the issuers of securities sold to the public.

There are, of course, many other areas in which management of some part or aspect of the total economy takes place. At home, we might think of such huge management problems as those associated with the national debt, the United States international balance of payments, Social Security transfer payments from government to individuals, or agricultural subsidies. Abroad we have the challenges of foreign economic assistance, customs and tariffs, and U.S. personnel residing in other countries. In all of these areas decision-relevant accounting information is useful in management decision making.

Total economy management is a very specialized activity-size of amounts involved and ever-changing public policy directives being two of the factors that make it so. Since special objectives underlie each component of this total management activity, each component has its own accounting requirements and therefore a different structure for its accounting function. Yet the basic nature of accounting remains unchanged. This is demonstrated in the following rather abbreviated and very general descriptions of accounting applications in each of the four management domains introduced in the foregoing paragraphs.

Taxation

Accounting for federal income taxes must conform to extensive federal laws and regulations. As an introduction to this complex and highly technical accounting application, we observe that:

- Accounting rules defined by the Internal Revenue Code are similar but not necessarily identical to conventional accounting principles,
- Managements of business enterprises have an obligation to their shareholders to pay no more taxes than necessary and
- There are timing differences between tax accounting and conventional financial accounting for some revenue and expense items.

Before we acquaint ourselves with some selected specific tax accounting procedures, we must recognize fundamentally that the purpose of tax accounting is the assessment and collection of governmental revenues in a presumably fair and economical manner according to public policy. For policy reasons, tax laws may allow special benefits to certain persons or industries, for example, blind persons and agriculture. This is in marked contrast to the performance evaluation and wealth assessment objectives that characterize general financial accounting.

Income taxes collected from individuals, corporations, estates, and trusts constitute by far the most significant sources of tax revenues. " State and local taxes are also important because they provide the resources for the continually rising financial needs of local governments. At the state level there are corporate income and franchise taxes, personal income taxes, sales taxes, excise taxes, and property taxes. At the municipal level, one might find sales and use taxes, property taxes, business occupancy taxes, gross receipts taxes, and excise taxes.

Bibliography

Aberth, O.: *COBOL: from Micro to Mainframe : Preparing for the New Millennium*, London: Academic Press, 2005.

Alexandrescu: *COBOL Programming*, New York: Addison-Wesley Press, 2003.

Blanchette, J.: *Object-Oriented COBOL*, UK: Cambridge: Polity Press, 2008.

Bulka, D.: *Programming Techniques for Solving Problems*, New York: Addison-Wesley Press, 2003.

Carrano M.: *COBOL: A Self-Instructional Manual*, New York: Addison-Wesley Press, 2002.

Ford, W.H.: *Murach's Mainframe COBOL*, London: Prentice Hall, 2003.

Goodrich T.: *Programming: A Structured Approach*, NJ: Rutgers University Press, 2000.

Henning, M.: *Java for the COBOL Programmer*, New York: Application Development Advisor Company, 2001.

Kruse, R.: *Structured Programming with COBOL Examples*, London: Prentice-Hall, 2005.

Lakos J.: *COBOL: from Micro to Mainframe: Preparing for the New Millennium*, New York: Microsoft Press, 2003.

Lippman, B.: *COBOL Programmers Swing with Java*, London: Manning Publications, 2006.

Lischner, R.: *From COBOL to OOP*, New York: O'Reilly Media, 2003.

Mesick: *Structured Cobol Programming*, London: Manning Publications, 2004.

Meyers S.: *COBOL: A Systems and Structured Approach,* New York: Addison-Wesley Press, 2001.

Peters T.: *COBOL: Report to Conference on Data Systems Languages,* London: CRC Press, 2006.

Plauger P. J.: *COBOL: A Practical Approach,* London: Prentice-Hall, 2003.

Sedgewick R.: *COBOL for Students,* London: Cambridge University Press, 2001.

Sumner, P.: *The Management of Commercial Computing,* Dharwar: Karnataka University Press, 2007.

Index